"Richard Stivers is among the world's sharpest analysts and critics of the role of technology in society. In this book, he adds a fascinating exploration of how technologies—particularly those of advertising and television—have been able to penetrate the human psyche and to create an authority, believability, and power that border on the spiritual or magical. No one has made such a brilliant analysis of this tendency before, and Stivers is utterly convincing. He demonstrates along the way the profound social and political consequences of this psychic sleight of hand. For anyone interested in systematic analyses of technology or in the hidden techniques behind the powers of mass media and advertising, this book is absolutely a must."

—Jerry Mander, author of *In the Absence of the Sacred* and *Four Arguments for the Elimination of Television*

Technology as Magic

The Triumph of the Irrational

Richard Stivers

CONTINUUM • NEW YORK

2001

The Continuum Publishing Company
370 Lexington Avenue, New York, NY 10017

Printed in the United States of America

Library of Congress Cataloging in Publication Data
Stivers, Richard.
    Technology as magic : the triumph of the irrational / Richard
Stivers.
        p.   cm.
    Includes bibliographical references (p. 213) and index.
    ISBN 0-8264-1211-4 (hdb)   ISBN 0-8264-1367-6 (pbk)
    1. Technology—Social aspects.   2. Magic—Social aspects.
3. Civilization, Modern—1950–   I. Title.
HM846.S75   1999
306.4—dc21   99-27444
                                                          CIP

To
My Wife Janet

Contents

Acknowledgments

Once again I am indebted to the Earhart Foundation for a fellowship research grant that enabled me to write this book. Special thanks go to Moody Simms, friend and colleague, who read the entire manuscript, and to friend and colleague Wib Leonard, who read part of it. They made me rethink my arguments at times. Frank Oveis, publishing director of Continuum, has been a pleasure to work with. I have never had a better experience with a publisher. Conversations with Kim Goudreau, Jim Van der Laan, and Rachelle Stivers proved valuable. Others who helped include: Anne Wortham, Andrew Kimbrell, Richard Payne, Clay Morgan, Pat Walsh, Christine Gruber, Sharon Foiles, Jo Anne Geigner, Nancy Russell, Matt Weber, Michael Stivers, Mark Stivers, and Janet Stivers.

Introduction: The Paradox of Technology and Magic

And since man cannot live without miracles, he will provide himself with miracles of his own making. He will believe in witchcraft and sorcery, even though he may otherwise be a heretic, an atheist, and a rebel.

Fyodor Dostoyevsky
The Brothers Karamazov

The most widespread and pernicious form of modern superstition lies not with a too ready acceptance of mysterious relationships, nor with an appeal to quasi-science, but entirely within the sphere of purely rational thinking and confidence in true science and technology.

Johan Huizinga
In the Shadow of Tomorrow

Are there more seeming opposites than technology and magic? Technology works objectively and is usually efficacious, whereas magic, based on superstition, seems to be ineffective. The former is perceived to be rational and is associated with a scientific outlook; the latter is seen to be irrational and is associated with a religious sensibility. But, as I will argue, our expectations for technology have become magical and our use of it is increasingly irrational. Magic in turn has acquired a rational facade and is used like technology for purposes of efficiency. In short, technology and magic, while separate and distinct categories in some abstract sense, are now related to one another in such a way that each has acquired important characteristics of the other.

Magic begins historically in the attempt to influence nature, which was experienced as sacred. How can we harness the power of nature, to make it work for us? In prehistoric times humans participated with the rest of nature in the re-creation or renewal of nature. Magic represented an attempt to persuade nature to act in the best interest of humans. Today, however, technology is perceived to be a force greater than that of nature, for it is successfully used to exploit the resources of nature and to re-create nature. If the sacred is ultimately that which is experienced as absolutely powerful, then it was inevitable that technology would replace nature as the object of tacit veneration. There is a world of difference between nature and technology, however, for the latter is our own creation. To harness the sacred power of technology means to extend its reach over all of life; nothing can be excluded. But not all of human existence is so readily subject to technology.

Law and morality still place some constraints, which are rapidly weakening, however, on the technological manipulation of humans. Witness the debates on medical experiments on human subjects and the police use of electronic surveillance. The psychological and administrative control of humans (advertising, management, and self-help, for example) is not genuinely technical, for it requires human belief and participation to be effective. It is here that contemporary magic flourishes. Passing itself off as a kind of technology (as an objective process), but not formally recognized as such, psychological and administrative magic is allowed to cross the moral and legal boundaries that technology is still not permitted to pass. In the past century magic has come to imitate technology, acting to fill the gap that technology cannot— the psychological manipulation of humans. Technology, then, extends its control over human society by the magical control of human beings.

Magic, as Marcel Mauss noted, is about wish fulfillment.[1] Magic arises in the hiatus between the wish and its fulfillment. Magic represents the childish dimension of human existence that adulthood does not fully suppress. We wish for things, but reality intrudes upon our fantasies and frustrates their realization. Magic offers a way of influencing the desired outcome. Magic establishes a *symbolic* link between the magical practice and the desired outcome so that the magical practice is both responsible for the outcome and is its *operational indicator*. The power of the sacred is the middle term between the magical practice and the desired outcome. Magic is effective only in relation to humans and only when they believe in it. Magic succeeds as a self-fulfilling prophecy: belief in magic makes it seem efficacious. In relation to nature, magic is only apparently effective. If my bear-hunting ritual is invariably performed before I hunt bears, then it is associated with successful hunts. Hunting failures can always be explained away, e.g., we did not perform the ritual correctly. Magical healing can be effective, however, as a *placebo*, a kind of emotional self-fulfilling prophecy. Placebos often do work, if only temporarily.

Even though the main interest of modern magic is in technology, certain atavistic magical practices, sometimes referred to as neopagan, have survived. It was estimated twenty years ago that roughly 10,000 Americans identify themselves with the neopagan movement. Even now it remains a small movement. Neopagan refers here to anyone who belongs to a modern version of a polytheistic nature religion, or of a folk or tribal religion, or who practices some of their rituals. Some neopagans trace their ancestry to the mystery religions of Egypt and Crete, whereas others identify with some aboriginal group. Members may consider themselves to be witches, druids, or even gods and goddesses. The magical rituals sometimes include chants, dancing about a fire, casting spells, incantations, and burning candles and incense.[2] Whatever their specific religious identity, many neopagans pledge allegiance to a Mother Goddess, who is both a deity and the personification of the earth, "transformed and transfigured by its capacity for magic."[3]

Various practitioners agree that magic is a kind of spiritual energy received from the earth or the universe, but what that energy can be used for is the subject of debate. All neopagans believe that the magic leads to self-transformation, whereas only a minority believes it can change the world outside the self. One neopagan leader suggests that many neopagans are content to regard magic as mysticism (magic applied to the self) because of social pressures from the larger society and the prestige of science.[4] Indeed, most neopagans are "optimistic about the uses of science and modern technology."[5]

What are we to make of this attempt to employ traditional magic in the modern world? At a certain threshold of growth, technology comes to dominate culture and creates in its wake an entire civilization. At this point technology destroys the sense of mystery that historically seems essential to human existence.[6] Every technology as applied science is an objective, logical process that can be consciously communicated and replicated. Technology is rationality, but mystery resides in that which cannot be fully articulated and understood. Mystery resides in the realm of absolute meaning, which is beyond human control. The attribution of magic to human existence represents an attempt to "re-enchant" the world in an age of technical rationality. Other groups, such as New Agers and technopagans, draw upon traditional magic but largely as a backdrop to their main interest—technology. References to nature become a way of spiritualizing technology.

Our magical expectations for technology are not difficult to infer from the extravagant claims that are made for the computer, biotechnology, and medical technology. Some are more obviously magical than others, however, such as the claims that technopaganism makes for the computer. Technopaganism is one of a number of subcultures that have arisen around the computer. One can make the case that its views about the computer are at least tacitly shared by the others, such as ravers and "hippie hackers." Douglas Rushkoff characterizes the coming together of the computer and magic: "Computer technology fits in to cyberian spirituality in two ways: as a way to spread magic, and as a magic itself."[7] Mark Dery identifies technopaganism as the "convergence of neopaganism . . . and the New Age with digital technology and fringe computer culture."[8]

Thee Temple Ov Psychick Youth (TOPY) is an example of a technopagan group. It started as a fun club for Genesis P. Orridge who founded the technopagan band *Psychic TV*, but evolved into a network of devotees of magic and computer data. Its members believe that they form a single being comprised of information. As Rushkoff observes, this is a "metaphor for the postmodern

Gaian brain."[9] The universe is not biological but technological. Rushkoff describes the group:

> All male initiates to TOPY take the name Coyote, and all women Kali. The name is followed by a number so that members can identify one another. Kali is the name of a female sex goddess known as "the destroyer"; the coyote is found in many mythologies, unusually symbolizing wisdom and an adventurous nature. . . . The information passed about consists of "majickal techniques" from drugs and incantations to computer hardware and engineering tricks, as well as general TOPY philosophy.[10]

Other groups use the computer to play magical games. Role-playing games often make use of mythological and preternatural beings.

Technopagans perceive the computer to be a "magic machine." The computer is the final and most powerful kind of magic; it recapitulates all earlier forms. Dery notes that technopagans locate spirituality in the computer. The computer creates a *universe* of information and in so doing promotes a mystical identification with itself.[11] Its devotees become connoisseurs of information that at a certain level of ingestion provokes ecstasy. Technopagans are the high priests of the cult which believes that the universe and its deities are in the computer.

Technopagans, who often thumb their noses at scientific rationality, are not the only ones to spiritualize the computer. Proscientific types like artificial intelligence proponents, biotechnology enthusiasts, and information systems creators covertly and sometimes openly see the computer as a spiritual force and, in some instances, as a sign of transcendence. Jennifer Cobb's *Cybergrace: The Search for God in the Digital World* is likely the most extreme expression of the deification of the computer. This pretentious book is a paean to technology and the computer in particular. Invoking Teilhard de Chardin, Cobb places the computer and cyberspace within a Christian evolutionary perspective. "With computational emergence and self-organization," she reverently states, "we find divinity present in the digital."[12] The heart of her argument is the concept of emergence, that the whole is greater than the sum of its parts because something new is created in their interaction. As information systems become more complex and hierarchical, information that could not be predicted emerges. Cobb describes this phenomenon:

> In the relatively simple instances we have of emergent computation, the *product* of the emergent process can be mapped. The printouts will reveal the way, for example, that Deep Blue considered its moves before arriving at its brilliant strategy or the moment when the organisms began to reproduce. But the printouts are after the fact.[13]

The emergence Cobb discusses appears in many contexts in nature and culture. She admits as much in her book. But then why attribute transcendence to cyberspace when human language, art and literature, and human history better illustrate the concept of emergence? Given the fact that the computer cannot handle that which is truly qualitative (see Chapters 2 and 3), emergence in the computer is but an impoverished quantitative counterpart to biological and especially cultural emergence. Despite her discussion of God as transcendent, Cobb is an immanentist. Because the computer colonizes all human qualities and symbolic meanings, it is an absolute power. The technopagans better understand the computer than those who try to reconcile the computer with a transcendent God.

Most of us avoid the antiscience bias of groups like the technopagans and their explicit cultivation of magic. But are we any less magical in our orientation to technology? Consider for the moment the extravagant claims made for the computer: artificial intelligence, expert systems, and substantial improvement in student performance. The computer can be programmed to manipulate logical and quantitative information. The computer, however, *cannot* handle qualitative concepts and ideas that have been expressed symbolically and embedded in tradition and narrative. The computer operates according to Boolean logic, and therefore cannot think critically, reach qualitative decisions, or make moral judgments. But the computer can process an enormous amount of information rapidly, something humans cannot do. And because we worship quantity, speed, and growth, the computer appears to be omnipotent. How can we refrain from attributing to it magical powers and expecting a utopian future from its widespread use?

Our expectations for biotechnology and medical technology are equally utopian—the creation of a new nature and a perfect human being. Increasingly, molecular biologists and genetic engineers have turned to cybernetics for a metaphor of how biological systems work. Information theory is now applied to organisms and ecological systems so that they become "information systems." The computer with its negative feedback and programs becomes the model for life processes. With the help of the computer, we are told, the genetic code can be cracked and nature can be refashioned into a technological system.[14] But the code cannot be broken the way biological determinists desire, for heredity and environment are so interactive that there is, at times, an almost immediate impact of environment upon certain genes.[15] Furthermore, the more technology and chemical agents we introduce into the environment, the more difficult it becomes to ascertain the consequences of such changes.

Medicine too is exhibiting signs of magical thinking. Medical textbooks are beginning to use systems theory to analyze the patient, who becomes a collection of statistical errors. Medicine in this view would establish "optimal trajectories" for the course of one's life. The individual's total life has to be managed so that everything he does contributes to his overall health and that of society. The doctor becomes the leading member of a health care team that disseminates information to the patient and attempts to convince him to eat correctly, avoid stress, and eschew anything that is potentially unhealthy. Under such direction we would become "chronic patients." Such magical thinking is dependent upon a belief in the ability of the computer to measure health and illness from the level of the biosphere to that of the individual organism. Totalitarianism would flourish as mandatory health in the creation of a statistically normal human being.[16]

My principal argument is that today our expectations for technology are magical to the point that we have generated a multitude of imitation technologies that function as magical practices. This is an elaboration of Jacques Ellul's seminal idea that in a "technological civilization everything becomes an imitation of technology or a compensation for the impact of technology."[17] Psychological and administrative (managerial) magic's paramount purpose is to adjust humans to a technological civilization, to bring them in line with technical progress. The myth that organizes technology and its imitations into a coherent system of belief is technological utopianism. Advertising and television programs contain the basic themes and elaborated stories of technological utopianism.

Some of the psychological techniques (magical practices) that will be discussed in Chapters 5 and 6 appear to be New Age. The New Age movement is hard to pin down. The term "New Age" is so amorphous that it is virtually meaningless. And yet there are perhaps a few themes that tie together the disparate groups that are characterized as New Age. Like neopagans, New Age enthusiasts are concerned with self-transformation and hold nature in high regard. But they are more eclectic and experimental in their beliefs and lifestyles. Eclectic may be an understatement. New Age thought has the ability to synthesize almost any other set of beliefs and practices. Perhaps this is its hallmark—the absence of anything that is specifically New Age. New Age thought includes self-help groups, Eastern religious philosophies and meditation techniques, neopagan practices, the belief in the spirituality of the computer, and consumerism. Indeed, Theodore Rozak maintains that New Age devotees, like the hippies before them, combine an interest in nature with a fascination for technology.[18]

There is enormous variation in estimates of New Age group membership—from 28,000 Americans[19] to 12 million with another 30 million "peripherally involved."[20] The former estimate is restricted to New Age religious organizations such as the Church of the White Eagle Lodge, the Divine Word Foundation, and Scientology; the latter includes all sorts of loosely-structured groups that do not promote themselves as or are not regarded as religious: vegetarians, self-help groups, alternative medicine practitioners, and believers in extraterrestrial life. New Age thought is becoming synonymous with American culture in its emphasis on self-transformation. New Age thought is an amalgam of seemingly disparate beliefs. It regards change as progress and believes that the universe is in a state of flux so that objective knowledge of it is difficult to come by; consequently, truth becomes "personal and situational" and morality relative.[21] In the midst of this chaos, which can be good if one uses it positively, the only thing worth pursuing is self-growth and self- transformation. New Age groups offer a smorgasbord of psychological techniques and products to help one accomplish these goals. Like neopagans, New Agers accept technology more than science, but most do not overtly dispute the latter because of its great prestige. They borrow from it when convenient, e.g., chaos theory. Because New Age thought and practice is vague and widespread, and often is indistinguishable from the rest of American culture, it will not be singled out as a distinct category of magic in the chapters ahead.

Both technology and magic rest on a foundation of information. Technology uses its information as a logical procedure embedded in a tool or machine to realize a specific goal. When technology works, it works objectively. There are certain techniques, sometimes referred to as nonmaterial technology, that are based exclusively on information. Psychological techniques employ dramatized information (see Chapter 2), whereas certain administrative or managerial techniques use statistical information (see Chapter 3). Psychological techniques include advertising and the media, therapy, self-help, positive thinking, sales, human relations management techniques, and the plethora of how-to books about child-rearing, marriage, friendship, relating to one's boss, and the like. In each case the technique entails what is perceived as an objective process or set of steps to produce the desired outcome.

Wayne Dyer's *Real Magic* is a self-help book. The best-selling Dr. Dyer is the author of *Your Erroneous Zones, No More Holiday Blues,* and *Pulling Your Own Strings. Real Magic* is the "realm of human existence that transcends what we have come to view as normal or possible," and a miracle is "whatever you have considered beyond your ability to create for yourself because of limitations you believe you have."[22] Dyer identifies seven key beliefs that allow one to "tap the power of real magic":

1. There is an invisible but knowable life force within you.
2. Your thoughts are something that you control and they originate with you.

3. There are no limits.
4. Your life has a purpose.
5. You overcome weaknesses by leaving them behind.
6. When you examine what you believe to be impossible, you can change your beliefs.
7. You can go beyond logic.[23]

The rest of this pseudo-mystical, feel-good book involves a set of steps to achieve "real magic" in your relationships, in economic transactions, in transforming your personal identity, and in physical health. The book is a combination of warmed-over common sense and nonsense expressed in such a way that the key words have a vague, emotional meaning at the expense of lucidity.

There have been two major approaches to management in the twentieth century: scientific management and humanistic management.[24] The former attempts to measure and coordinate the activity of employees through statistical information, whereas the latter depends upon motivating employees through dramatized information. Servant-leadership is a humanistic management technique. Retired AT&T executive Robert Greenleaf authored *The Servant as Leader* in 1970 and later founded the Robert Greenleaf Center to disseminate his ideas about management. The Center's mission is "to fundamentally improve the caring and quality of all institutions through a new approach to leadership, structure, and decision making. Servant-leadership emphasizes service to others; a holistic approach to work; promoting a sense of community; and the sharing of power in decision making."[25] Greenleaf argues that administrators should act as servants to their employees, helping them to "grow as persons," so that they become "healthier, wiser, freer, and more autonomous." Ultimately, the employees will become, like their managers, servants to others.[26]

This psychological technique is actually a means of manipulating employees into being servants to their managers. The administrators *verbally* act as servants by providing the employees with cliches like "sense of community" and "shared decision-making" so that believing themselves to be part of a loving family employees will work harder and be more docile. Greenleaf frames his technique in the cloth of Christianity—he who would lead must first be a servant to others. Therefore, if employees are to be leaders, they must act as servants.

Psychological techniques such as these, I argue, are forms of magic. Technology employs scientific information in the service of a material technique that acts upon the physical world, but magic uses information that is symbolic to influence nature or human beings. Magic establishes an indirect or symbolic relationship between a set of practices and a desired outcome so that the magical practices become, as it were, operational indicators of the outcome. Psychological magic, it is believed, acts according to the principle of causality, or, in other words, it is thought to embody the sacred power of technology. Magic, then, works subjectively as belief. In the instance of psychological technique it functions as placebo. If one believes in Wayne Dyer's formulations for self-transformation or in Robert Greenleaf's about leading by serving, one's emotions and attitudes are temporarily altered. Underneath the facade of technology lies magic. But the creators of psychological magic often advertise their methods as an objective set of procedures (technology).

Administrative techniques that follow the scientific management perspective make use of statistical information. Used in both private and public sectors this approach goes by the name of systems analysis, strategic planning, management by objectives, cost-benefit analysis, and the like. It includes attempts to measure performance, measure employee work interactions, create decision models, and predict the future. Scientific management attempts to reduce all reality—present and future—to statistical information.

Peter Drucker created "management by objectives," an approach in the tradition of scientific management. He emphasized "clear objectives, both for the corporation and the manager, and urged translating long-term strategy into short-term goals."[27] Objectives and goals were to be rationally defined and capable of being measured. One of Drucker's innovations was to suggest that a company's organization should follow from its objectives and not (as was usual) vice-versa. To implement this the company should have an "elite group of general managers" who set the objectives for everyone else whose task was to implement them.

As we will see later, one of the chief characteristics of magic is the attempt to predict and control the future. That which is truly qualitative, however, cannot be measured and predicted. Management expert Henry Mintzberg has demonstrated that the most valuable kind of information in organizations is intuitive and holistic, in other words, informal and nonstatistical.[28] Moreover, evidence indicates that a considerable amount of organizational success is due to chance and contingencies beyond one's control.[29]

As with psychological magic, administrative magic creates an indirect or symbolic link between information and outcome.[30] Statistical information symbolizes technology and therefore administrative magic that makes use of it embodies the sacred power of technology. Because it is believed that statistical information is the operational indicator of organizational success, such information will be collected and used at some point to justify organizational decisions. Magic here acts as a self-fulfilling prophecy (a false definition that by our actions we make come true). If statistical information is always collected and used, it will invariably be associated with an organization's successes.

The most important magic today, however, is practiced by the mass media. Even though the mass media are comprised of hardware and machines, their influence on humans is through dramatized information. Advertising contains the key magical rituals of a technological civilization. It symbolically connects consumer goods and services to desired outcomes: success, happiness, and health. But these are not just ordinary outcomes, they are the chief symbols of technological utopianism. This myth suggests that technology will solve all our problems and make us permanently happy.

A recent ad for Datatel states that "life without technology isn't an option." "Imagine. *Technology as a friend*. A partner. A facilitator." "If you want to *do more than simply co-exist with technology*, there's only one option. Datatel." The ad claims that Datatel will "help you succeed." This ad suggests that technology is our fate and that it alone brings success.

An advertisement for air bags proclaims, "At 60 miles per hour a prayer is too slow." The power of technology is greater than that of prayer; consequently, it must be a god. Alcoa's slogan at one time was "We can't wait for the future." The meaning in context was not so much that we eagerly anticipate the future as that we must create the future now. Technology provides the means for a utopia now. One consumer recently proclaimed "McDonald's advertising makes me feel as if I died and went to heaven."[31]

If the content of advertising is sometimes explicitly utopian, its format or logic is invariably so. Following Neil Postman, I suggest that every commercial contains at least implicitly one of two interrelated themes: this product will solve a problem (success) and it will make you happy.[32] The product either directly makes you happy, e.g., a CD, or indirectly, e.g., Tide gets your clothes clean. Television programs illustrate in one way or another advertising themes. The programs dramatize one or more of the symbols that advertising attributes to consumer goods and services, e.g., programs that feature car chases and beautiful, wealthy people in automobiles are assigning power, prestige, and success to the automobile.

The mass media in both advertising and television programs are magical ritualizations that spiritualize every consumer good and service, including the psychological and administrative techniques previously described, providing them with a magical aura and a utopian cast. If my thesis is correct, then we live in a world that is at once both highly rational and irrational, both extravagantly technological and magical. The reason for this paradox is our childish, magical expectations for technology (that it will solve all our problems and make us permanently happy), which are expressed most vividly in advertising and the mass media. The mass media ritualize the myth of technological utopianism and thus envelop technology—both real and imitation—in a magical cocoon.

· 1 ·

Both Technology and Magic

We are unaware even today, as we study technique—the techniques that relate to men—that we are drawing on the great stream of magical techniques.

Jacques Ellul
The Technological Society

Magic has always been related to other social practices; therefore, it can only be understood in conjunction with religion, science, and technology, and within a historical context. Some of the controversies surrounding the interpretation of magic can be cleared up with the appropriate theory of history; every social phenomenon needs to be situated within its most general context. Social scientists, however, are still recoiling from evolutionary theory applied to society (social Darwinism) and from a Marxist view of history. Each of these theories of history, so apparently divergent, shared two assumptions: the continuity of history and the progress of history. Moreover, both were finalistic, that is, they assumed the final stage of history could be known in advance and that history proceeds according to a principle or a logic. Scholars have discredited both views; consequently, there is a reluctance to adopt a historical perspective other than that of relativism. Which is to say that we treat each historical period as self-contained and from a variety of theoretical perspectives without attempting to understand history in terms of the transitions between periods.

Somewhere between finalistic theories of history and historical relativism (in its full sense) lies a descriptive theory of history. It pretends neither to know the end of history nor its logic, but it does propose that history can be partially understood as an open process whose final stage cannot be scientifically predicted. A descriptive theory of history, then, assumes some modicum of human freedom, despite all of the biological and social determinisms at work. This freedom is not metaphysical. For it resides within longstanding social structures that appear frozen in relation to demographic and environmental changes it cannot control. Moreover, this limited, situated freedom rarely achieves its stated purposes. Yet it prevents history from being a closed system.

One of the major difficulties in developing a descriptive theory of history is finding the appropriate level of analysis. One can err by remaining mired in details that defy generalization beyond a specific period and culture, or one can generalize in too abstract a way so that the distinctiveness of history is lost. The key, I think, is in the relationship between history and sociology. Fernand Braudel[1] and Norbert Elias[2]—one a historian, the other a sociologist—argued that there is no difference between the disciplines, properly understood. Both take as their major subject society. History is the memory of human society, and society exists in the context of the changing narrative about itself.

What is required, then, for a descriptive theory of history is a historical knowledge of social environments. What constitutes a social environment? Are there certain similarities and differences among variegated individual social environments that are so important we can create categories of social environment set within broad historical periods? Does our theory reflect the fact that human societies move (if they do) from one category of social environment to another at widely divergent times?

The descriptive theory of history I will employ in this chapter in order to situate magic in a social context is French historian and sociologist Jacques Ellul's theory of the three milieus.[3] To my mind it represents the most accurate and powerful description of history we possess and is indispensable to those of us laboring in the social sciences. His theory of the three milieus has implications for everything social scientists study.

Ellul's Theory of the Three Milieus[4]

A milieu is an environment, at once both material and symbolic, in which humans face their most formidable problems and from which they derive the means of survival and the meaning of life. A milieu has three basic characteristics: immediacy, sustenance and peril, and mediation. We are in immediate and direct relationship with our milieu; it forces us to adapt, to conform, just as surely as we manipulate it. From the milieu we derive all that we need to live—sustenance for the body and the spirit: food, clothing, shelter, order and meaning. Concurrently, however, the milieu is the greatest threat to human existence, as in pestilence, famine, poisons, wild animals, political strife, war, and pollution. The milieu, then, is *ambiguous* in value and produces an *ambivalent* reaction on our part—attraction and revulsion, desire and fear.

A milieu is composed of two basic ingredients: meaning and power. Insofar as it is symbolic, a milieu is a human creation. The power of the milieu is harnessed for human ends; still, as an objective power, it is not largely under conscious control. The dominant power of a milieu assumes one of three forms: nature, society, or technology. In the first instance, the power is a given. We exist in relation to the power of nature, and about this relationship symbolization first occurs. The power of society and that of technology (as a system) are human creations, but they are experienced in holistic fashion as objective forces; they are reified.

Each subsequent milieu, e.g., society in relation to nature, mediates our relationship to the preceding one, rendering it an indirect force. The preceding milieu becomes an ideological *model* for the subsequent milieu, thereby providing an illusion of where power resides, e.g., the concept of natural law. In dialectical fashion, however, it is actually the subsequent milieu that is used to interpret the preceding one. For example, in the milieu of society, nature is actually read through society; it is anthropomorphized. Human society is projected onto nature in the form of divinities, social hierarchies, law, and a myriad of human passions.[5] Therefore, nature as a model for society is to a great extent a nature that is already a reflection of society.

The chronology of the three milieus can only be approximated, of course. Human societies do not make the transition to a new milieu at the same time, and even today societies are in different milieus. Once again, Ellul's theory is not a theory of necessary stages of development. The milieu of nature or the prehistorical period is the hardest to date, in part because one runs up against the problem of when the human species (in the modern sense of the term) emerged. Archaeologist Colin Renfrew argues that there is some evidence, although still fragmentary, that the extensive use of human language to interpret the world metaphorically and to think conceptually is linked with the development of *Homo sapiens sapiens*, at least 40,000 years ago.[6] *Homo sapiens sapiens* may have emerged in the physical sense even earlier, in some areas perhaps as far back as 90,000 years ago. If one uses 40,000 years ago as a starting date for the milieu of nature, the efflorescence of the milieu of society (the historical period) can roughly be dated to 3,000 B.C., the time of the rise of towns, agricultural civilizations, and literacy. The Neolithic period represents a transitional period from the late prehistoric period, the milieu of nature, to the historic period, the milieu of society. Finally, the posthistoric period, the milieu of technology, can be dated to the post–World War II period and the widespread use of the computer and television. The transition to the milieu of technology includes the last two centuries.

The milieu of nature

The first thing to note about the milieu of nature is that of the three milieus we know the least about it, for here we are limited mainly to archaeological evidence. Myth and ritual, as they are known to us, come from societies already in the milieu of society or in transition to it. Especially in the earlier stages of the prehistoric period, humans were overwhelmed by a nature whose power appeared unlimited. Both technology and language were relatively underdeveloped. By contrast, the practice of magic was extensive. One might characterize the human relationship to nature as largely magical.

Human groups were small and widely dispersed. The low population density helps to explain the apparent absence of warfare between the groups. Archaeological evidence indicates that the bones of those of warrior age did not suffer wounds.[7] Hunting and gathering groups are marked by a relative absence of internal violence as well. Backed by neither an economic inequality nor a centralization of power, authority is specialized and personal, peculiar to one's talents.[8] Such authority, moreover, is easily contested or ignored.[9] The relative absence of violence is short- lived, however, as population and the competition for resources increase in the transition to the milieu of society. Internal conflicts can sometimes be resolved by breaking up and regrouping.[10] Moreover, the redistribution of food in a situation of anticipated abundance mitigates some of the impact of internal strife.[11]

Ellul[12] argues that it is plausible to extrapolate to the prehistorical period certain characteristics present in the historic period. In this regard he applies Georges Dumezil's theory of functions (with the exception of the military function) to the milieu of nature, maintaining that the earliest principle of organization for the group was not that of kinship but that of function. The three functions, understood more as principles of classification which together form a system, include religious and political sovereignty, military force, and material well-being.[13] Everything else of importance—the family, groups, taboos, cults, myth, and ritual—was a way of facilitating the performance of the function.

Cave paintings which date beyond 20,000 years ago indicate that the creative process of symbolization was well-established in this period. The subject of many of these paintings was the animal, which represented simultaneously danger and sustenance. Humans appeared in only a tiny percentage of the paintings, and usually without arms. They appeared to be in a ceremonial relationship with animals and to be imitating them. It is only much later, in the Neolithic period, that humans come to dominate the artistic scene, both in the sheer number of human representations and in the representations of their tools and weapons.[14] The relationship between human and animal shifts in the transition to the milieu of society; the human slowly begins to dominate. But nature remains a formidable power throughout the historical period (milieu of society).

The human ability to symbolize in the milieu of nature shows little influence of social forms. Nature is such an overwhelming power and technology is so weak that humans regard themselves as participants in nature without a sense of being superior. Colin Turnbull's ethnography of the Mbuti Pygmies in the Congo demonstrates how a group in the milieu of nature views animals as their peers. For example, they speak of their brother the antelope.[15] The drama of nature centers around issues of life and death and the seasons of the year. There is no sense of the history of one's ancestors and even less of the ability to make history. Indeed, most of their songs and stories are about animals and their regret at having to kill them in order to survive.

Finally, there is no sense of good and evil in the milieu of nature. Moral evil was experienced in the same way physical misfortunes such as disease, famine, suffering, and death were experienced as "moments of the cosmic totality."[16] The Mbuti Pygmies argue that if misfortune occurs, because it is of the forest, then the misfortune must be beneficial. They believe that the negative and positive aspects of life are fully interconnected and interdependent; hence there is no trace of negative occurrences being perceived as a punishment for evil deeds.[17] Good and evil, as we shall see later, are categories that arise out of internal social and political conflicts that go hand in hand with increased social differentiation in the milieu of society.

The milieu of society

The milieu of society, or the historical period, Ellul dates to the emergence of towns around 3,000 B.C., although the Neolithic period represents a transition from the milieu of nature to that of society. He identifies several characteristics of this milieu.

The first is an increasing reliance on artificial means of action that allow humans a certain freedom from the determinations of nature. Voluntary action becomes self-reinforcing. Among those phenomena most responsible for the growth of the artificial and the voluntary are technology, literacy, law, and the entire range of social institutions. Technology allows humans both to distance themselves from nature and to master it. Literacy improves one's ability to think analytically, for now the ideas can be detached from their source, reread, and reflected upon. Writing permits a thought or decision to be applied to a variety of contexts. The absoluteness of cultural forms that functioned as archetypes can now be questioned.

Law was undoubtedly a central force in creating a society increasingly distinct from nature. A formal system of laws that begins by running parallel to the extant taboos and imperatives becomes increasingly important and at times is in conflict with religious norms. The creation and manipulation of law is a consequence of the main concern in the milieu of society: politics. Not just law, however, but all the social institutions as they become more rationalized and complex work to produce, at least among the elite, a sense of the artificiality of society. Politics is an implicit recognition of this development.

The second characteristic is the influence of one society on another. The emergence of towns facilitated this, as did literacy and the proliferation of and interest in artifacts. In the prehistorical period, by contrast, the human groups were too dispersed and their oral and visual symbolism too group-specific to afford transference to a different context. It is, of course, both the strength and the weakness of literacy that it gives rise to a higher degree of abstraction and objectification.[18]

Social hierarchy is the third characteristic. Hierarchy is almost the opposite of social stratification in the modern era.[19] Hierarchy assumes a view of society as an ordered whole so that each division within society, whether based on gender, age, class, occupation, or moiety, has a *complementary* relationship to its opposite. Moreover, a hierarchy, at least ideologically, is concerned more with status than with power.

Ellul speculates that the aristocratic class's claim to have an eponymous ancestor was the source of its authority. The eponymous ancestor provided the society with both a history and a hierarchy, for no social category exists alone but only in relation to its complement. The ancestor provides not only a history of descent but also a history of events and , finally, a theory of authority within society. As Ellul puts it: "The aristocratic families that preserved the memory of their history also had another essential role. As a frame for the whole people, they carried in effect the history of the entire society. Their history was the history of all. They were truly the memory of the society."[20] This confirms the idea that in a hierarchy the term higher in status is more representative of the whole than its lower status complement. Hence the aristocratic families are more representative of the society than the nonaristocratic ones.

The fourth characteristic of the historic period is the institution of law (previously mentioned under artificiality). Law as a general organizing principle is a consequence of the artificial and voluntary being brought to bear upon problems created by social hierarchy, problems that myth and ritual did not cover. Ellul argues that law was a response to three challenges: space, time, and human relationships.

Law allows humans to tame symbolically a section of the natural environment, to establish boundaries between natural space and social space. Law permits society to become the human life-milieu. Law likewise responds to the challenge of time: flux. Archaic man did not want to make history but rather to return to the time of creation.[21] And yet the more humans introduced technology, literacy, and rationality into their relationship to nature, the more unpredictable life became. There were unintended social consequences to every artificial and voluntary attempt to control nature. Law established the regularity in social relationships that myth and ritual were by themselves unable to provide anymore.

In the historic period the increase in the size of societies poses a threat to human relationships because one cannot personally know everyone else. Moreover, as politics is slowly disengaged from religion, the exercise of power is problematic. Law acts to regulate relationships between individuals and between kin groups.

Creativity and diversity in meeting the challenges of life is in particular a characteristic of the historical period. Not that every response is adequate. The diversity of responses in meeting the challenges of nature and society precludes any principle underlying history. The propensity to symbolize is the most important source of human creativity. This symbolization is increasingly directed toward human society, at times, as the collective memory of ancestors' accomplishments, and at other times, as an imagined future that was in part different from the past.

The most pressing and profound problems in the milieu of society are political—relations between groups, internal administration, and warfare. Natural problems such as wild animals, poisons, disease, and famine are still present and for a period can become the most dangerous; in the long run, however, the organization of society and relations between societies are the greatest concern.

Ellul maintains that each subsequent milieu mediates the preceding one rather than simply eliminating it. Therefore in the historical period, society mediates nature. Nature is interpreted as a society, a more powerful one, to be sure. In the milieu of society or transition to it, the principle of retribution was seen to underlay all of nature: every good deed is rewarded, every evil deed punished. The principle of retribution is the first theory of legal punishment and as such is projected onto nature, a bigger and better society.[22]

At the same time nature as a more perfect society becomes an ideological model, a model invoked after the fact to justify decisions and actions that are actually social (political). A good example is the concept of natural law, which emerges in the historical period.

The concepts of good and evil emerge in the transition to the milieu of society. They represent a growing perception that society and nature are different because humans are free to commit prohibited actions and they can be held accountable for them. Natural disasters and moral evil are no longer the same. In the milieu of nature an offense against another is simply an offense against nature. Now an offense against another is an offense against society.

The milieu of technology

The technological milieu creates the posthistoric period. By this is meant the decline of (1) the perceived need and desire to create efficacious symbols as a way of remembering the past and imagining the future, and (2) human autonomy in relation to technology (this will be further explored). For Ellul, technology or, strictly speaking, technique (in French *technique* refers to the actual method of doing, whereas *technology* refers to discourse about technique; in English *technology* tends to be used to refer to both practice and theory), is the "totality of methods rationally arrived at and having absolute efficiency (for a given stage of development) in every field of human activity."[23]

Modern technology fits Ellul's definition of a milieu: that which is concurrently the means of life and the greatest threat to life, that which is most immediate to us, and that which mediates all our relationships. The first point is abundantly clear today: we look to technology to solve all our problems. Yet in warfare, pollution of the environment, genetic and chemical manipulations, propaganda and the mass media, and bureaucracy, technology poses an enormous threat to our physical and psychological well-being. Technology is much more immediate to us than nature, for in modern societies our physical environment is one of plastic, glass, steel, and concrete, taking the form of an enormous diversity of technological objects and consumer goods.

The other side of this is that technology mediates all our relationships. Whether for purposes of production or consumption, technology mediates our relationship to nature. Material and non-material technologies reduce nature to one enormous industrial and amusement park. Even more importantly technology mediates our relationships with each other. Human techniques (techniques for the manipulation of human beings) tend to supplant morality, manners, and social institutions. Bureaucracy (a technique of organization), propaganda, advertising, public relations, psychological techniques (such as the how-to books on child rearing or becoming successful or having a positive outlook), and expert systems are only some of the most obvious examples.

The techniques used to mediate human relationships reduce the human being to an abstraction, the object of a method that makes everyone the same. But technology has deleterious consequences for the user as well as the recipient. As an objectified, rationalized method, technology does not depend upon one's subjectivity, one's experiences. As Ivan Illich has shown, all of life is given over to experts.[24] The wisdom of age and experience is given scant attention over against technical expertise.

Ellul's objection to technology is not philosophical; it is historical. Until the nineteenth century technology developed at a pace that allowed it to be integrated into culture; technology was subordinate to culture. Because of an unbounded faith in technology and a conscious intention to experiment with technology and find a diversity of uses for a single technique, technology came to dominate culture. Inappropriate uses are a consequence of the diffusion of technique into every sphere of life; that is, the effort to measure and rationalize that which is qualitative (dependent upon context for its meaning).

As technology proliferates, has generalized applications, and becomes coordinated (through the computer), it tends to form a system. Techniques are related to one another before they are adjusted to human use and need. Humans invent technology, but insofar as it has become a kind of system without true feedback, they allow it to function autonomously. Technology as a system (a system of techniques coordinated by computerized information) is superimposed upon human society, which at least in the milieu of society was organized by the symbolically-mediated experiences embedded in cultural institutions. In rendering culture ephemeral and transitory, technology foments a cultural crisis.

Technology's impact upon the milieu of society can be ascertained by examining what has happened to social hierarchy, the law, and the creation of symbols. Social hierarchy (in Louis Dumont's sense of the term) has disappeared in modern societies. Replacing it is that to which the concept of social stratification refers—a culturally unintegrated set of classes whose basis of domination is power and not status. Therefore, a set of classes exists without bonds of reciprocity and complementarity.

Because modern social classes are not bearers of cultural meaning, their importance is overshadowed by the mass society. Alexis de Tocqueville and Søren Kierkegaard understood this phenomenon well before social scientists of the 1940s and 1950s made use of the idea.[25] A mass society is one which is paradoxically collectivistic and individualistic at the same time. Cultural authority, which in historical societies resided in hierarchy, declines, along with kinship and the community as institutions that implement it. Thereupon, authority, which has become power, resides in the state and common opinion. The individual, isolated from and fearful of his fellow citizens, to whom he can no longer turn for aid, because in an age of equality obligatory norms of reciprocity wither away, turns instead to government for help. The power of the state and public opinion grow stronger and stronger with the collapse of hierarchy to meet the needs, demands, and fears of the isolated individual. At the same time, however, the individual believes that she can become an individual through the efforts of the state.

The growth of state power and public opinion has been made possible through technology so that the modern political state is largely technical, i.e., bureaucratic. Likewise, the formation and measurement of public opinion has become almost exclusively a technical phenomenon. Ellul has argued that politics itself has largely become a matter of rubber-stamping decisions actually made by bureaucratic and technical experts in the interest of efficiency.[26] Politicians' choices are always about what is technologically *possible*. On those occasions when politicians appear to resist technology, it is only by stopping technology from doing something positive, e.g., stopping the growth of nuclear power plants for civilian energy usage. But these occasional negative decisions are much less important than the positive commitment to technological growth. Yet traditional politics most often involved compromise, which is the antithesis of the solution, the goal of all technology.[27]

It would be absurd to claim that law has disappeared in the milieu of technology. If anything, it is proliferating at a geometric pace. But as numerous studies have indicated, this development has little to do with the value of justice.[28] All forms of law—not just administrative law—have become largely technical; their principal concern is efficiency. As Max Weber observed about bureaucracies, the rules are, strictly speaking, amoral, for they are technical in nature. Now all forms of law are technical, for the political state is fully bureaucratized.

The most problematic aspect of the milieu of technology is the erosion of the symbol as an *active* force in human evolution. This is a result of two interrelated phenomena: the technological system and the universe of material visual images.[29]

The visual images of the mass media have had a corrosive effect upon language. It is not due mainly to the speed and sheer quantity with which the images hit us. Rather it is a result of the formation of a pseudo-language accomplished through the logical sequence of visual images in a program unit and the subordination of the symbol to the material visual image.

The visual images of the media decontextualize reality by removing it from its existential, cultural, and historical contexts. (A symbol only has meaning in context.) The visual images impose upon us a strictly material and "objective" reality, but one that has been *selectively* represented. The visual images deconstruct and then reconstruct reality according to a spatial logic of signifiers: images of power and of possessions. We see objects to be possessed and consumed, the power of which becomes that of the consumer. These acts of power are spatially linked together in a television program or movie in a logical sequence that leads to an outcome—success or failure. Meaning is reduced to power.[30]

Visual images become the operational indicators of words. Advertising is adroit at reducing aesthetic and ethical qualities to consumer goods and services. Love is holding hands and drinking a Coke. Once again, a strictly material reality.

The use of symbols in advertising and political propaganda leads to a subjectivization of the symbol. For instance, the term "democracy" is used by politicians to refer to virtually every government that is on the side of their country. This is an enormous paradox. Natural language, which is being stripped of its traditional meaning and thus made subjective (in an emotional sense), is concomitantly made objective through its association with and subordination to material visual images. The fundamental reason for this incredible transformation is that symbols have lost their practical purpose in a technological civilization.

In the historical period, in the milieu of society, symbols served two related purposes. First, important historical events became symbolic of some action, characteristic, or quality a society wished to retain or to avoid by preserving the memory of its occurrence.

Symbols gave definition to and provided a cultural identity for a group. Second, symbols were the primary ingredients of social institutions along with the experiences they made sense of. Yet technology and the material visual images that represent it are now supplanting the symbolically-mediated experiences embodied in social institutions.

Just as the milieu of society reconstructs nature in its own image, so too does the milieu of technology remake society. Each subsequent milieu, then, overlays the previous one with its own worldview. Most telling perhaps is how the moral categories of good and evil are transformed in the milieu of technology: the dominant metaphor of evil becomes "social problem."[31] To use *problem* as a metaphor is to invoke mathematics and engineering. A problem is an obstacle, something to be solved or overcome. Social problems are not moral problems, but technical problems. But moral problems involve judgments that include the notion that evil is not something exclusively outside me but within me as well. Hence real moral issues cannot be objectified as external societal problems to be solved.

Ellul's theory of the three milieus in no way suggests that the technological milieu is the final milieu or that we cannot return to the milieu of society. It does, however, point to the major problem in the technological milieu—the eventual loss of freedom and creativity. For it is only within a vigorously symbolic language that humans imagine real alternatives and exercise moral freedom. Without this, the ability to make history declines: time becomes the repetitive time of technological progress.

Each milieu depends, of course, upon the reciprocal, socializing actions of humans to carry out the tasks of survival and the search for meaning. Humans are markedly different, however, in each milieu. Humans become distinctly human (with a sense of history and of the freedom to create a future) only when society and nature are viewed in dualistic terms and when society and technology are similarly perceived; this occurs only in the milieu of society. In the milieu of nature there is no sharp distinction in kind between human and animal; both are part of nature. Certain animals that are more powerful or more central to a group's survival become the emblems of the milieu (totem animals, for instance). In the milieu of technology as well there is in practice no significant difference between the human and the technological object. Humans appear only too willing to advertise products whose logo or picture they wear on their shirts, hats, and pants. The prestige and power of the technological product become that of the consumer. Here too certain powerful objects, such as the automobile and the computer, become representative of the milieu.

Magic in the Three Milieus

The following is a general theory of magic, one that takes into account how magic changes in the movement from milieu to milieu, including its relation to other institutions like religion and technology. The theory demonstrates that magic is the most adaptive of enterprises and does not operate according to a single principle or logic.

Magic changes according to what is perceived to be sacred. The sacred is, in the most general sense, the life-milieu. If the sacred is defined as ultimate power and reality,[32] what better fits this than the milieu? One's milieu is, as we have seen previously, both that which threatens life (material and spiritual) and that which sustains life. The sacred, then, refers both to positive and negative forces. This is the basic ambiguity of sacred value that social scientists from Émile Durkheim to the present have observed. Each milieu is organized around a different set of polarities: life and death in the milieu of nature, good and evil in the milieu of society, and efficiency and inefficiency in the milieu of technology.[33]

The key issue here is that a milieu is a dynamic totality so that both poles participate in the regeneration of the milieu and are thus internally related. Regeneration is the movement from the negative to the positive pole. For example, all living things depend for their continued existence upon the death of other living things. Life comes from death.

What is tacitly experienced as sacred is expressed in symbol, song, and story and lived out through ritual. Therefore, we can refer to the symbol-story complex as the theory of the sacred and ritual as its practice.[34] The most important stories describe the origin of the universe and (in the milieu of society) of one's ancestors, a "golden age" when things were perfect, or they describe a utopian future. The stories or myths organize the various symbols about the life-milieu so that they come to possess a larger meaning. Water, for instance, is almost a universal symbol of death and rebirth. This symbol gains meaning by being placed in the context of a story of a past creation and a future utopia. Rituals that have not been secularized allow humans to participate in or effect the movement of their life-milieu from negative to positive pole and back again to negative in a constant cycle of regeneration. Sacred rituals are invariably magical (at least as I define magic).[35]

The sacred, symbol, myth, and ritual comprise a cultural configuration that represents the deepest and most profound structure of any culture; it exists at a tacit or metaconscious level. We may comprehend its specific manifestations in word and action without understanding how they fit together. As we move from prehistoric to posthistoric times, this basic cultural configuration remains (although its content changes); but increasingly rational institutions like law and religion and political ideologies overlay this basic structure without supplanting it or fully grasping it.

Magic in the milieu of nature

In the milieu of nature, magic is both a way of life and a worldview. In this prehistoric period, magic operates according to the principle of creative persuasion. Anthropologist Stanley Tambiah has written extensively about participation (including persuasion) as a perceived view of reality that contrasts sharply with that of causality. In so doing he rejects the earlier view of Edward Tylor and James Frazier that magic is "failed science." Bronislaw Malinowski made two advances: that magic filled in the gap where technology was absent, and that magic was a kind of performance that involved magical words.[36] Tambiah and Michelle Rosaldo have both extended Malinowski's initial attempt to make sense of magical discourse. The former[37] interprets magical performance as a kind of speech act, whereas the latter[38] analyzes it as a linguistic code whose use represents an attempt to create meaning.

For Tambiah magical discourse is an illocutionary act (a saying that is also a doing, e.g., to promise, to apologize) that only on occasion attempts to be a perlocutionary act (a saying that brings about a result, e.g., frightening or annoying the listener). Tambiah plays down the perlocutionary aspect of magical talk that entails intended consequences, for it is here that magic is closest to technology. He argues that it rarely is intended to be objectively efficacious, but rather is largely intended to express meaning and at times to urge the transfer of the qualities of one object to another that is, in some sense, deficient. He uses the example of a Trobriand spell in which the participants attempt to persuade the taytu yam to put forth foliage the way a spider spins its web. The larger magical act involves both discourse and the manipulation of a surrogate yam and spider so that the power of the spider to "grow" a web will be transferred to the yam.[39] Tambiah claims that magical rituals should not be judged by the standard of causality, for the participants themselves do not expect their magical spell to be objectively efficacious. The key here is the difference between persuasion and causality, for persuasion necessitates participation, but causality does not.

Rosaldo emphasizes the persuasive aspect of magic too, but stresses its creative potential. Using illustrations from Ilongot magical spells, she argues that the restricted linguistic form encourages a creative reordering of experience and the world itself. Her point is that, like poetry with its specific forms, e.g., the sonnet, the magical spell follows rules that actually encourage a metaphorical comparison of things not previously perceived as similar or as connected.[40] I am not convinced by her structuralist explanation of creativity, but I think that her emphasis on the creativity of magical spells and other acts is important.

British philologist Owen Barfield has provided us with the key link between persuasion and creativity in his treatment of participation. He understood that in prehistory humans understood themselves to be part of a sacred totality in which they were participants. Beyond humans and their representations, that is, categories and concepts, was a reality that was similar to them in kind. Humans participated in this reality by naming and classifying the parts of nature; in so doing they helped to create and maintain it.[41] Humans did not control the power of nature but acted as its agents; hence, the necessity of persuasion as a way of attempting to realize the collective wishes of the group. Humans helped to create the world they lived in, but not in any automatic or causal way; for the power they attempted to make work on their behalf was mysterious and beyond their control. Magic in the milieu of nature was based on the principle of persuasion in which humans participated in creating that for which they wished.

Colin Turnbull's *The Forest People* perfectly illustrates the principle of creative persuasion. His sympathetic narrative about the Mbuti Pygmies reveals much about the milieu of nature and magic in particular. The Pygmies call themselves "children of the forest" and refer to the antelope they hunt as "brother." Their most important ritual is the Molimo Festival. The term *molimo* stands for the animals of the forest and the musical pipe they play either to soothe or to wake up the forest. The Pygmies maintain that the central activities of the Molimo Festival are eating and singing.[42]

As I have argued elsewhere, the feast is the principle of renewal in the milieu of nature.[43] Ritual eating signifies the movement from death to life, the polarities about which the milieu of nature is organized. All living things depend on the death of other living things for their continued existence; moreover, the death of living things, as with the fruit of plants and trees, is necessary for the plants to reproduce. Turnbull notes that the ritual eating of the Molimo Festival represents communion with others and most importantly with the forest.[44] The singing to soothe the forest and their stories and songs express their ambivalence—their regret over having to kill the forest in order to survive. By contrast, the singing to wake up the forest is their attempt to persuade the forest to provide a bountiful harvest. Taken together the eating and singing represent a magical act of persuasion, in which they creatively participate in the rebirth of the forest.

Magic in the milieu of society

The transition from the milieu of nature to that of society occurred after the onset of the Neolithic period. In the milieu of society, the principle by which magic operates is that of retribution: every evil deed is punished and every good deed is rewarded. In the transition to the milieu of society, and even after its establishment, the principle of retribution overlaps and eventually supersedes the principle of persuasion.

Anthropologists and historians take various positions about magic in part because they confuse the milieu of nature with that of society. Tambiah and Rosaldo have emphasized the persuasive and participatory aspects of magic (milieu of nature), whereas others have stressed the ways in which magic becomes more individualized and objectified in the milieu of society.

In the milieu of society, magic operates according to the principle of retribution. Clearly retribution represents the reading of nature by society. Now the gods interact according to this principle, and they reward and punish humans for their good and evil acts. Gradually magic is brought within the orbit of retribution so that successful outcomes indicate that one has performed the magical rite correctly or one has won the favor of the gods through self-control and an orderly life.

Persuasion and retribution coexist, however, because nature remains sacred, even if in a secondary way, in the milieu of society. This intertwining of nature and society creates an almost impenetrable ambiguity. For instance, Tambiah, who argues that magic is not based on the same principle as technology—causality—but instead is a form of participatory performance, notes that among Buddhist monks the blessing of a new house to ward off evil spirits is not expected to produce results. He suggests that the correct performance of the blessing is an end in itself with obvious religious overtones.[45] I am not convinced: Why associate the blessing with the driving away of evil spirits if one does not expect a happy outcome? My hypothesis is that in the transition to the milieu of society the principle of retribution becomes stronger over against that of creative persuasion the closer one gets to the milieu of society. Persuasion is stronger at first only later to be superseded but not eliminated by retribution.

Just as the principle of persuasion is inexorably linked to the feast as the central rite of renewal in the milieu of nature, so is the principle of retribution associated with the sacrifice as the rite of renewal in the milieu of society. Roger Caillois has observed that sacrifice is the "inner mechanism" of the festival, that which gives it meaning.[46] Anthony Wallace's *The Death and Rebirth of the Seneca* illustrates this point.

The Seneca were in transit to the milieu of society in the eighteenth and nineteenth centuries. Society had become sacred (along with nature) to the extent that the history of their ancestors was an integral part of the creation of the world. Indeed, the good twin and evil twin, who contended for control of the world at the time of creation, were born of a human mother. The chief gods were their ancestors. Their time, however, was still the time of nature—cycles and a circular return to the beginning. It is only in societies that have by various means freed themselves from the fate of nature that a sense of being able to create history emerges.[47]

The Seneca believe that the evil twin is both responsible for evil in the world and the one who can help them expel it. This demonstrates perfectly the ambiguity of sacred value: good comes from evil. Or in other words, order depends upon having an enemy to blame—a scapegoat.

I am following René Girard's theory of scapegoating, which argues that the evil twin in mythology all over the world was at one time a human scapegoat, who, after being killed, becomes elevated to the status of a deity. Ritual scapegoating in the form of sacrifice is a tacit acknowledgment that order is based first on a common enemy, the scapegoat, and only later on shared norms.[48] Society, based on the polarities of good and evil, is renewed by the expulsion of evil, just as nature, based on the polarities of life and death, is renewed by eating (the feast).

The Seneca are, in a sense, more devoted to the evil twin than the good twin. They formed the Society of Faces, in which virtually every adult was eligible for membership, that wore masks with a broken or crooked nose. This symbolized the struggle between the good twin and the evil twin for control of the world. The good twin won by moving the Rocky Mountains so that when his brother turned around he broke his nose. The contest, by the Seneca's own admission was about whose magic was stronger. And yet the Seneca were completely dependent upon the evil twin, for in their myth the evil twin had the power to undo some of the good work of his brother the creator, and had introduced misfortune, suffering, and evil back into the world.[49]

The very person responsible for evil would help them eliminate his handiwork. The white dog sacrifice and other sacrificial offerings, such as tobacco and corn meal mush, represent the renewal of society. The logic is: good (order) needs evil (disorder) because it depends for its existence upon the continued expulsion of evil. Unity is first and foremost a unity against the agents of evil; only subsequently is it a unity on behalf of the good. Girard has demonstrated that witchcraft and sorcery are cultural forms of scapegoating.[50] The witch or evil sorcerer is invariably someone who is to blame for one's suffering.

Perhaps now we can distinguish the principle of persuasion from that of retribution in magical practices in the milieu of society. In the milieu of nature, nature is an undivided totality. As the Mbuti Pygmies say, "There is darkness all around, but if darkness *is*, and the darkness is of the forest, then the darkness must be good"[51] The Pygmies trust the forest (nature); so, all of their magic entails a creative persuasion of their kindly parent or thanksgiving to him. The Seneca on the other hand live in a more dangerous and uncertain universe—a moral universe. They retain a sense of the goodness of nature, but this is balanced by the tacit perception that what happens to them is a consequence of their good and evil practices. Freeing themselves from the influence of evil and making it work for them becomes a preoccupation. Now they are not completely at the mercy of nature; they can "control" it by their moral actions, especially rites to expel evil. *Yet it is only by expelling evil that the goodness and bounty of nature can be guaranteed. Magical persuasion in the milieu of society is ultimately enveloped within the world view of retribution.* Some magical rituals such as sacrifice are directly based on the principle of retribution, whereas others like those of praise and thanksgiving are indirectly so.

The milieu of society, or the historic period, takes in almost all of recorded history. At one end it takes in the transition from the milieu of nature; at the other end it includes the transition to the milieu of technology. Changes in the extent and meaning of magic parallel those in the organization of human societies.

Mauss's work on magic is especially helpful here.[52] Building on it, we will examine the impact of the growth of individuality on magic, and the relations between magic and religion, magic and science, and magic and technology.

As we have already seen, the milieu of society is characterized by an increase in artificial and voluntary actions including the development of social institutions that indicate some reflection. Law and religion emerge as complete institutions, as does science much later in the period. Increased social differentiation, a growth of technology, and a greater reliance on reason combine to effect a slow movement toward greater individuality. The efflorescence of individuality awaits the concept of individuality. Mircea Eliade has argued that Judaism and Christianity furthered this idea in the West even more than did the Greeks with their emphasis on individual reason and the Romans with their concept of the legal individual.[53] What Jews and Christians introduced was the idea of faith, in which a personal God singles out an individual and establishes a relationship that leaves both parties free. Whatever the case, an increase in individuality is coterminous with the rise of civilizations. As a consequence, magic acquires an individual component. Magic still remains embedded in the collective rituals that celebrate the seasons of the year and the history of one's ancestors, but magic can now be tailored to the individual.

There is widespread ethnographic and historical evidence to support this contention. Every group at a certain stage of development has sorcerers, medicine men, and the like who cater to individual needs. The Seneca, for example, have a set of rituals that center on dreams or visions. They believe that dreams are the "language of the soul."[54] If the frustrated desire or fear in the dream is not realized, then the individual becomes sick. Members of the Society of Faces often perform magical cures; but, as we have previously seen, they also perform the critical rites of sacrifice during the collective seasonal rites.

Two developments converge to effect the individualization of magic. First, magic becomes partially separated from religion. Second, magic becomes more a practical way of understanding and influencing nature. Technology, literacy, and other forms of practical reason indirectly called into question a fully magical perspective. But magic as the most adaptable human invention affixes itself, so to speak, both to religion and to technology.

Religion in the milieu of society provides the world view that magic had previously established in the milieu of nature.[55] Religion relies more on the logical construction of philosophy and theology and less on the metaphorical construction of mythology. Religion theorizes about the gods, who direct nature but in the context of their society with its hierarchy. Religion is thus less about our relationship to nature than about our own social relationships projected onto deities, something Durkheim understood perfectly. Insofar as religion attempts to control the power of the gods, it depends upon magical rituals. As far as religion is concerned, magic is now exclusively a practical enterprise. It may still possess its theory about nature derived from the milieu of nature, but it is a theory that is on the outs.

Concurrently, however, to the extent that magic is demoted to a practical activity by religion, it becomes more like technology. As Mauss concludes, magic is somewhere between religion on the one hand and technology on the other hand. He likewise notes that magic "promotes and protects" technology.[56] Can we not say that it is a bridge between the two as well? By this I mean that magic insofar as it operates within religion's orbit, works according to the principle of retribution. The more individualized and secular forms of magic, e.g., dream-guessing rituals, especially function as a kind of practical activity, a technology. The principle of causality is, as Hans Kelsen has brilliantly demonstrated, the secularization of the principle of retribution.[57] That every good deed is rewarded and every evil deed punished is the forerunner of the idea that every effect has a cause. The causality of technology is not dependent upon rectitude, but both morally correct rituals and technology are perceived to be efficacious. At the same time religion as a worldview prevents technology from becoming fully secular, it permits magic to become more like technology.

Science emerges late in the historic period, and the subordination of science to technology even later, in the nineteenth century.[58] Just as magic and technology mutually reinforced each other as practical activities, so too in the beginning do magic and science, as evidenced by the scientists like Isaac Newton who were also alchemists. As Mauss observes, magic is at times both a theory and a practice.[59] Insofar as magic in its individualized and secular forms is like technology, the admixture of technology and science does violence to the archaic theory of nature embedded in magic. It is here that the transition to the milieu of technology begins, one whose road will end with the subordination of magic to technology.

Before beginning our analysis of magic in the milieu of technology, I wish first to discuss quite briefly two issues that are problematic to this theory of magic: (1) mysticism and (2) Judaism and Christianity. Mysticism can be viewed as a psychic state or as a technique. In the former case mysticism is a kind of ecstatic state that normally accompanies the performance of rituals or even strenuous or repetitive activity. In the latter instance, mysticism is cultivated as a religious experience. Mystical techniques develop and are refined in the milieu of society. Some civilizations, especially those in the East, become famous for their mysticism. Eliade suggests that those civilizations which have a pessimistic attitude, for instance, believing that nature is in a state of decline and the return to the time of perfection is infinitely far away, become heavily mystical. Mystical techniques become, then, a way of escaping the suffering of this world and uniting oneself with the spiritual forces of nature.[60] By contrast, those societies that became convinced that they could actively influence the course of nature were more magical in their orientation.

Judaism and Christianity are partial exceptions to the theory of the three milieus in respect to religion and magic. Some have argued that Judaism and Christianity were never intended to become religion and certainly were expected to eschew magic.[61] The key concept here is faith. As I indicated previously, faith assumes both freedom and individuality. In these respects it is the opposite of magical ritual, which is deterministic and collectivistic. French philosopher Paul Ricoeur, for instance, has demonstrated that the parables of Jesus are about faith. Few if any parables speak to all three stages of faith—encountering God, freely turning one's back on sin, and putting one's faith into practice—but taken as a whole they address the issue completely, despite being stated metaphorically.[62] It follows that a community of believers should first be a collection of individuals who freely have accepted the gift of faith.

This view of Judaism and Christianity rejects the idea of religion as an institution of the overall society and a form of societal control. Insofar as Judaism and Christianity subscribe to the concept of a transcendent God, both faiths reject in theory the concept of the sacred, tied as it is to the life-milieu of humans. A collective sense of the sacred is the foundation of culture by establishing an absolute value. Religion is the ultimate expression of the sacred in the milieu of society; it leads to the worship of one's society, whose ancestors are sacred, or of one's church (in a general sense), whose representatives have objectified God's will in ritual practices. Dostoyevsky called attention to the sacralization of the church in the "The Grand Inquisitor" section of *The Brothers Karamazov*. Now insofar as Judaism and Christianity have often functioned in practice as religions like other religions and became the paramount form of social control (Christendom, for example) or become absorbed by the larger society,[63] they can rightfully be considered within the theory of the three milieus.

Magic in the milieu of technology

The transition from the milieu of society to that of technology begins in the West in the late eighteenth century and continues until after World War II when the milieu of technology takes hold. The widespread use of the computer and television mark this event.

In the milieu of technology, magic acts according to principle of efficient causality. Science establishes the causal or probabilistic laws according to which it is believed nature and society are organized, and technology exploits them in the interest of efficiency. Technology, but only in the milieu of technology, is interested exclusively in an efficient outcome. In a technological civilization everything becomes "an imitation of technology or a compensation for the impact of technology." *Magic now imitates technology.* These magical or imitation technologies are the social form that our magical expectations of technology assume.

In the posthistoric period both society and technology are experienced as sacred, but now society is read through technology. The paramount political and moral problems are being transformed into technological problems to be solved by technical experts, e.g., the medicalization of moral issues. Technology is both power and reality today. Although at one level technology (as rational, efficient, objectified method) is abstract, at another level it is concrete—technological objects, consumer goods. These act as hierophanies (manifestations of the sacred).

A technological society is one whose chief value, purpose, or goal is efficiency, maximum production and maximum consumption. Over against rational technique stands inefficiency as instinct, the will to power. These opposite poles of a technological milieu are, however, at a deeper level related. For as Ellul notes, technology and instinctual desire form a dialectic: desire today can only be satisfied by technology, and technology can only advance by the constant stimulation of appetite.[64] Jean Brun first called attention to the paradox that the cold, impersonal, abstract force of technology does not finally appeal to reason and moderation but to our desire for power and possessions. Technology as a system is the "head of Apollo" superimposed upon instinct, the will to power, the "body of Dionysius."[65]

The more reason becomes objectified and collectivized in the technological system, the smaller the role for subjective reason based on symbolically meaningful experiences becomes. This tends to enlarge the play of irrational or instinctual forces. Moreover, the cumulative impact of technology acts as a repressive force; the more technology demands of us in terms of regulations, schedules, and coordination, the more we apparently need to escape this kind of rationality by plunging into the irrational, into random sensations.[66] The result is a society that is at once both extraordinarily rational and irrational.

The instincts most associated with the will to power are sexuality and aggression. As forms of inefficiency, sex and violence are the negative to the positive pole of efficiency (technology). If a milieu is comprised of two poles in tension, and the principle of regeneration involves the movement from the negative to the positive pole, then here the continuum between the poles is *excessive experimental consumption*.

The sacred power of technology becomes manifest in technological objects (consumer goods). These hierophanies of consumption become differentially sacred depending upon individual
circumstances. We have already seen, however, that technology,
while manifestly opposed to instinct, is perfectly suited to it at a
deeper level because both represent the will to power. Moreover,
advertising uses sex and violence to sell these consumer goods,
for instance, the eroticizing of the automobile. Even more important than advertising's direct use of sex and violence is its indirect
use: the consumer goods of advertising are placed in spatial relationship to the sex- and violence-saturated programs of the mass
media. In this sense programs are ads for advertisements. In consuming the technological object we are indirectly consuming the
instinctual power of sex and violence. Enlarge the sphere of the
instinctual, and the desire to possess and use technological objects
increases. The motto is: the more we consume (if only vicariously)
sex and violence, the more technological objects we will consume;
the more objects we consume, the more instinctual power we possess.

Caillois observes that excess is at the "heart of the festival."[67]
The more one pushes the negative pole, the greater the abundance
at the positive pole. In the milieu of technology the festival is
primarily centered in the excess of sex and violence in the mass
media. As the ritualization of the principle of regeneration, the
festival always begins with the negative pole—death, evil, the instinctual (sex and violence)—in the movement to the positive
pole—life, good, efficiency (abundance of technological objects).

In the milieu of technology, society is still sacred but in a secondary way. Societal power remains formidable and is organized
around the poles of the nation-state and revolution.[68] The technologization of society aggravates political problems by reducing
politics purely to a matter of power. With the disappearance of
hierarchy (in Dumont's sense), there is nothing left but competition for power among special interest groups only partially controlled by the political state. As Bertrand de Jouvenel has clearly
shown, political revolutions in the past several centuries have only
led to an increase in state power.[69] Just as technology effectively
operates outside the moral domain, so does politics today.

If nature provided the model of time for the creation myths in the milieus of nature and society (to a lesser extent), technology offers the model in the milieu of technology. As I will argue in Chapter 4, technological utopianism, which is our major myth today, is not about the past nor the future, as with the myth of progress, but about an eternal and perfect present that we can construct. The technological utopia is one where the inefficiencies or problems of nature and society have been solved, engineered out of existence, and humans have achieved optimum health and happiness. *The relationship of humans to the sacred is irrational; it is in the gap between the wish and its fulfillment that magic arises.* Our expectations for technology, our chief sacred, are magical. We tacitly believe that technology is omnipotent. A recent advertisement for air bags proclaimed, "When you don't have time for the answer to a prayer."

Yet technology has not allowed us to enter the promised land. Environmental problems and moral and political conflicts seem to be increasing rather than decreasing. This decline in the quality of life actually reinforces our magical relationship to technology: we desire even more to harness its saving powers. What is most disturbing, however, are the magical practices used on humans. These imitation technologies are used to manipulate humans in the interest of efficiency. This book is largely about these magical technologies.

What have we learned so far about magic in the three milieus as we work our way toward a definition? In the milieu of nature, magic was creative persuasion and provided a worldview. Technology was integrated within this magical perspective on nature. In the milieu of society, social institutions, literacy, law and other forms of voluntary rational action conspire to break up the magical world view; religion now provides the global perspective. Magic still remains potent, but it now exists in its collective capacity as part of religion or in its individualized applications as part of technology (as a practical activity in relation to nature). Magic has to compete with human reason and social institutions that more and more reflect deliberate action. In the milieu of technology, magic comes under the aegis of technology, and becomes either an imitation of technology or a compensation for it. Magic is now almost exclusively devoted to the control of human society.

Let us define magic, then, as a set of words and practices that are believed to influence or effect a desired outcome. The relationship is symbolic rather than objective. The symbolic words and actions work according to the principles of persuasion, retribution, or causality. The principle by which magic is believed to act is an imitation of the principle by which one's life-milieu operates. The sacred power of the milieu is thought to be contained in the magical practice, thus making the magical practice a more or less operational indicator of the desired outcome. In the movement from the prehistoric to the posthistoric period, magic becomes increasingly impersonal and objectified. Magic can be effective but only on humans. Magic works, when it is successful, when humans believe in it so that it functions as placebo or self-fulfilling prophecy.

In Chapters 2 and 3, I examine how technology is destroying the human capacity to symbolize our life-milieu. Discourse, I argue, is moving in opposite directions. Many terms are being operationalized and thus given a single definition for purposes of quantification; other terms are losing their common meaning and have become vague, retaining only an emotional connotation. Historically humans once lived in a symbolic reality, a world of shared experiences that came to possess symbolic meaning. If we live decreasingly in a shared symbolic reality, where is reality? Reality today is on television and in the computer. The former provides us with dramatized information (Chapter 2), whereas the latter gives us statistical information (Chapter 3). The computer is increasingly linked to television and the other media in its ability to provide visual representations, as with computer games. But I will be discussing the computer in relation to its ability to process and store statistical information. Dramatized information is the basis of psychological magic (Chapters 4 and 5); statistical information, the basis of administrative magic (Chapter 6).

· 2 ·

Dramatized Information: The
Basis of Psychological Magic

And man, this clever fellow, seems to have become sleepless in order to invent ever new instruments to increase noise, to spread noise and insignificance with the greatest possible haste and on the greatest possible scale. Yes, everything is soon turned upside down: communication is indeed brought to its lowest point with regard to meaning, and simultaneously the means of communication are indeed brought to their highest with regard to speedy and overall circulation.

Søren Kierkegaard
For Self-Examination

The nonmaterial technologies for the control of humans, which I have identified as psychological and administrative techniques, essentially consist of information. They are information technologies, in the jargon of today. I argue that psychological techniques, such as therapy, sales, advertising, mass media programs, and the like depend upon the dramatized information of the mass media for their effectiveness, whereas administrative techniques, like systems analysis and strategic planning, rely upon statistical information for their success.

Historically, most information was transmitted through language; today, however, much of it is in the form of visual images and statistics.[1] This could only happen concurrently with the gradual dissolution of language. The visual images of the mass media and the statistical information of the computer are now a central part of the magical practices applied to humans, along with language that has lost its symbolic force (in the traditional sense) at the same time it has acquired another "symbolic" function. Language is now subordinate to visual images and technology, whereas formerly it was their master. This incredible transformation of language, as we will see, renders magical all forms of discourse that are not truly technical. In this chapter we will examine the dramatized information of the mass media; in the next chapter, the statistical information for which the computer has provided a home and an outlet.

The Disintegration of Discourse

One could hardly imagine a worse time for serious discourse: the prodigious increase in noise, images, and information militates against it. Consider the following: Americans on the average listen to the radio twenty-two hours a week and watch television thirty hours a week; they spend slightly under six hours reading newspapers and magazines; the most popular magazine is *TV Guide* and the newspaper section most frequently read is the advice column; they purchase fifteen books a year, most of which, however, are romance and adventure novels.[2] Indeed, one survey indicated that the great majority of college students never read a serious book after graduation. If we add in the hours spent on movie videos, computer games, video games, and surfing the net, the time spent in the consumption of mass culture grows even larger. Parents spend under twenty minutes a day, some under ten minutes, in serious conversation with their children.[3] Parents spend little time reading to their children; much more time is spent watching television together.[4]

Just as important as the amount that is read, listened to, and watched is its quality. The importance and quality of dialogue in film has severely declined since the 1930s and 40s.[5] It is now secondary to special effects and action sequences. Consequently, plot and character development have suffered as well. Television has always been at a low level of character development and dialogue. But even here from the 1960s to the present there is a marked decline in the vocabulary and sentence structure employed by television news broadcasters and an increase in visual displays and short descriptive phrases in the broadcasts.[6] In a study of television news broadcasts, Thomas Schachtman concludes: "The language of the broadcast is tending toward complete union with the few thousand words that we utter in our everyday conversation. It refuses to consider as its base the much larger vocabulary of the written language—even of that vocabulary constituted by a dictionary recommended for use by grade-school students."[7] Talk shows on television and radio reduce dialogue to the level of street talk—emotional outbursts, simple assertions, and elliptic sentences.

Although the sale of books is down in some industrialized societies, it has more or less held its own in America. When one looks at what Americans are reading, however, there is little cause for optimism. Large chains like Barnes and Noble and Borders have an enormous variety of books on self-help, celebrities, sports, tourism, cooking, and how-to projects. The serious books in the literature or philosophy sections, for example, appear to be permanent museum exhibits. Neil Postman has written about the high-brow reading habits of Americans in the late eighteenth century and their continued decline to the present.[8]

Most damaging for the long-term reading habits of young people is the state of textbooks at every level of education. Publishers demand that textbooks be written at a level of comprehension well below that of its intended use. A textbook for college freshmen may be written at a ninth grade or even seventh grade level of reading comprehension. Complex sentences are to be avoided as much as possible; there are computer programs to disabuse the hapless author of any inclination toward hypotactic construction. Publishers claim that they are only meeting the wishes of teachers, who maintain that they are only responding to the demands of students.[9] Students and their unwitting parents want books, lectures, and class discussions that are simple and obvious. Commenting on British culture, and often American culture as well, Kenneth Hudson concludes that mass culture "is based on the creed that everything can and must be made effortless and immediately understandable."[10] Apparently, educators (like politicians) are afraid to tell the public what it doesn't want to hear:

that education involves struggling with ideas that are initially beyond one's grasp.

Conversation was once considered an art; today it is the release of a psychological pressure to talk—it has become pure impulse. Conversation can be the medium for the exchange of ideas and for rigorous discussion. Or it can be chitchat. Much of the conversation today is about shopping, television, sports, and relationships. Moreover, it tends to be superficial unless it is about the latter topic. The small amount of time adults spend conversing with their children suggests that the topics are rarely intellectual. Despite occasional arguments, parent-child conversations typically lack passion. M. P. Baumgartner's study of family and community life in a suburb in the Northeastern United States indicates that family members are for the most part not seriously involved in each other's life except when one becomes a problem to the others.[11] A lack of intellect and passion in conversation prevents one from conveying strong convictions and the rationale behind them to others.

The art of conversation peaked in the eighteenth- and nineteenth-century Europe; today it is everywhere in retreat.[12] Conversation requires time and silence, both of which are in short supply in a technological civilization. Serious conversation demands silence, not merely the inner silence with which to listen to others, but also the silence to prepare for the impending conversation. Technology's cumulative impact is to increase the tempo of life.[13] Research indicates that serious cultural pursuits such as conversation, reading, writing, and thinking are the first activities to be abandoned when time appears to be shrinking.[14] The level of noise has been increasing since the Industrial Revolution. Most revealing is the way we accept, even embrace, the imposition of noise upon us. Many of us apparently cannot function without music, the radio, or television playing in the background. This "white noise" has moved beyond our homes and is omnipresent in stores, offices, restaurants, and the like; it appears to be getting louder as well. Some of my students tell me they cannot work without noise and that silence frightens them. It would appear, then, that there is almost a conspiracy to prevent us from having the silence to think and that growing numbers of us do not wish to do so anyway.

Silence and noise serve radically different purposes. Silence is needed for meditation, reading, writing, reflection, and serious discourse; noise is useful for achieving a state of ecstasy, escaping self-consciousness, or escaping unwanted noise.[15] Noise is used to soothe the emotions or to excite them. Without silence our acquisition and use of language is stunted, and with it reason and freedom. The escape from silence is an escape from subjective reason, inner reflection, and a moral self into the foment of emotion and instinct. Noise, as Robert Pattison has argued, lies in the realm of vulgarity, that which is "common, noisy, gross," and most of all "untranscendent."[16] In a seamless environment saturated with media images, music, computer games, and an infinite number of distractions, where can serious discourse find an entry into human experience?

The consequences of this movement away from language toward images, noise, and abstract information are devastating. A study conducted at the University of Texas found that less than half of the sample of adults could understand a plainly-written paragraph.[17] Children who watch a lot of television tend to be poor readers.[18] Between 1971 and 1990 students' ability to read, write, and think, as measured on standardized tests, dramatically declined.[19] But it is even more shocking when one considers that the tests are being "dumbed down." Test-makers adjust the test to statistical norms of performance established by students. As students' ability to read declines the reading tests become easier, partially masking the true rate of decline. Controlling for the level of reading comprehension, Jane Healy discovered that a ninth grade reading test in 1988 was "demonstrably easier" than a fourth grade test in 1964.[20]

Speech and thought are similarly impoverished. Thought is of course central to reading, speaking, and writing. Students increasingly think in "nonsequential and visual ways."[21] This is largely due to the impact of media images, as we will see later. Speech is tending toward the "frequent use of semantically minimal generic words."[22] The most often used generic word appears to be "thing."[23] Not just objects, but qualities, actions, and people can be referred to as things. For some, especially group-oriented young people, using the word "thing" to refer to every object, person, or quality appears to be funny. The tacit motto of the verbally-impaired is: I don't know how to use language, but it really doesn't matter. Jane Healy argues that a considerable number of students diagnosed as having attention deficit disorder do not suffer from a medical disorder, but rather a deficiency in the ability to use and understand language. For those whose use of language skills is impoverished, lectures, discussions, and books may as well be written in a foreign language; consequently, their attention wanders.[24]

It doesn't matter how we use words if they convey little if any intellectual content. Having studied the everyday use of language in England and the United States, Kenneth Hudson concludes that language is moving in opposite directions: the first is the increasing number of scientific and technical terms with precise, operationalized definitions; the second is the proliferation of terms that have become vague to the point that they convey emotion but little thought.[25] Most of the words we use in everyday discourse are of the second kind. The meaning of words that we have previously used to impart a sense of purpose, belief, and value to others now appears to be evaporating.

The question of meaning is enormously complex. I will be referring to the term in two ways, a weak and a strong sense. The second sense will be discussed later in the chapter in the context of symbolism. The meaning of words lies in their use.[26] And words are typically used as utterances or statements (both written and spoken).[27] An utterance is a sentence or complex of sentences that is not just virtual, but actual as written or spoken. The meaning of the utterance derives from the social *context* of its use. That is, utterances refer to other utterances, past, present, and future. A statement (utterance) may directly refer to another statement someone has just made in a conversation, or may directly refer to historical statement; but all meaningful statements draw upon the various cultural contexts within which any use of words is typically embedded.

Let me illustrate this with the word "love." A young man and a young woman are discussing romantic love in light of their past experiences, in what they have heard, read, and witnessed. Is each one's understanding of love shaped by moral and religious discourse like Christian theology or Western moral philosophy, or is it formed by nineteenth century Romantic poetry, by contemporary romance novels, or by television shows like "Friends"? Does each have a largely ethical or aesthetical approach to love? Our understanding of love changes in light of the cultural experiences of others with whom we are in dialogue. Let us suggest, then, that meaning (in the weak sense) can refer to quantities, as with scientific and technical terms, or to the qualities that we attribute to or infer from actions, relations, and objects. Because qualitative meaning is becoming vague, the most serious linguistic problems reside with it.

Owen Barfield[28] and Henri LeFebvre,[29] among others, have called attention to the decline of referential contexts upon which discourse is dependent. What are these referential, cultural contexts? In traditional societies there are myths and religious narratives that provide a sense of ultimate meaning for human existence. Within that larger context, art, literature, and music work to clarify human experience. Political ideology, moral philosophy, and legal theory also offer interpretations of human action. Story, song, and folk wisdom (common sense) do much the same. These common discourses provide us with a sense of each key word in relation to others. Love takes on meaning in relation to beauty, to freedom, or to equality depending upon the referential context. Common discourses provide a narrative or philosophy in which key qualitative concepts become interrelated. These referential contexts are living, that is, they are reinterpreted by each generation in light of new experiences and renewed by additional discourses. Later in the chapter I will discuss why the source of these cultural contexts—symbolism—has become sterile and ephemeral, but for now I will simply note that these institutional contexts for cultural meaning have lost relevance in a technological civilization. Technology is supplanting shared symbolic experiences as the basis of order, as I indicated in the previous chapter. Theology, philosophy, myth, art, literature, history, and political theory have lost much of their power to inspire social action. The traditional humanities and related cultural expressions are irrelevant today; they do not address the lived experiences of people in a technological civilization.[30] For the individual, life is a matter of consumption: products, images, information, personalities. Traditional religious and moral discourse centered about the meaning of suffering and death, immortality, and moral decisions about how we treat others. Aesthetical expression took place within this larger religious and moral universe. Today we look to technology to eliminate suffering, perhaps even overcome death, create an earthly utopia, and eliminate moral and political problems. How could we not conclude that the meaning of life has become exclusively aesthetic and now resides in cultural experimentation (consumption, lifestyle, and entertainment) that mimics technological experimentation? Cultural meaning is thus inherently unstable and even random: there is no *common* referential context discourse can draw upon. (Deconstructionism is an ideological reflection and celebration of this cultural destabilization.)

As a consequence, the meaning of words that are not strictly scientific or technical tends to be vague. Academics and intellectuals often do not sense this because much of their reading and writing is informed by traditional (more or less stable) referential contexts provided in part by their intellectual discipline. The vagueness of language is reinforced by the propagandistic use of language in advertising and public relations.[31]

Meaning involves both sense (the *what* is said) and referent (the *about what*) of discourse.[32] Referent here pertains to the world beyond language as well as the cultural context. We live in a symbolic universe, but there is more to this universe than language. Words are related both to cultural (referential) contexts and to some part of the world that language points to (referent). Our experiences are shaped by language and everything that we encounter that is not exclusively linguistic. There is a natural ambiguity to all words that are not strictly scientific and technical (operationalized). The referential or cultural context within which words are used reduces some but not all ambiguity. This ambiguity is a strength of natural language in that it permits words to be used in a variety of contexts and be applied to differential experiences. Ambiguity, however, is not the same as vagueness. Vagueness in meaning can occur in two ways. First, the same word or statement can be used in regard to too many entities in the real world. The word "democracy" is used today to refer to virtually every extant government by those who champion its cause; any product in advertising can be called exciting. Second, the word may have nothing to refer to in the world beyond language. For example, Karen Horney observes that we talk so much about love because there is so little of it; the discourse is compensation for the absence of the action.

The aesthetical and ethical qualities that humans attribute to and infer from their interaction with nature and society arose within and are institutionalized in common discourses, such as myth, story, song, history, literature, and theology. When these common discourses lose their potency, the qualities that they helped to create begin to disappear from human interaction. Unlike material objects, qualities are created in discourse and in actions that embody them.

The sterilization of common discourses (referential contexts) means that words become abstract. As Owen Barfield has noted, the definition of a word is only its most abstract meaning. It represents a sketch of all the various uses of the word in discourse. If one only knows the definition of a word, not its various uses in the context of common discourses, one knows the word only as a "collective noun" or a name for a classification of existence. The more abstract a word becomes, the less meaning (context) it possesses. The computer reinforces the tendency of words to be used in an abstract way, for the precision of a program depends upon a word possessing only one meaning.[33] When one makes the words that refer to qualities of interaction abstract, one necessarily makes them vague as well.

One can measure and thus be abstract about a material object, but to be abstract about meaning is to reify it. The result is atomistic words with fixed meanings that function as self-contained entities. But because these atomistic words have to refer to something beyond language, their meaning will be vague. How can an atomistic word not be vague about a quality when those qualities are created in part by the context of common discourses?

Atomistic Words and Phrases

With the decline of common discourses that serve as a context for meaning, the meaning of qualitative terms becomes both abstract and vague. Scientific and technical terms are abstract, but their operationalization prevents them from being vague. In 1942, Stanley Gerr noticed the influence of technology on scientific terms:

> an operation is acceptable to technological science only when a device (tool, mechanism, instrument, apparatus) exists for carrying it out, and a process or physical property only when it can be measured; which is to say, only when a device exits for measuring it.[34]

All scientific terms must be capable of being measured. Lexicographers conclude that technology and science are the source of about half of the new words that have entered the English language in the twentieth century. Indeed, Raymond Gozzi made a context analysis of the dictionary *12,000 Words*, the 1986 addenda to *Webster's Third International Dictionary*, and discovered that 45% of the new words that appeared between 1960 and 1985 came from science and technology.[35]

Other words, in particular "plastic words" and jargon, mimic scientific and technical terms. "Plastic words" is Uwe Poerksen's apt term for a category of words that aspire to be scientific or technical but end up being amorphous. Typically they begin as ordinary words, transfer into science, often the human sciences, then return to the vernacular.[37] Science and technology, economics, and administration are the primary source of plastic words. If one broadens the latter two fields, economics and administration, to include all the applied human sciences, one is in keeping with the spirit of Poerksen's thesis.

Poerksen, a German novelist and linguist, maintains that these words have become universal in technological societies and appear frequently in the media. He does not pretend that he has discovered the identity of all plastic words and recognizes that he may have included some that are not yet fully "plasticized," but suggests that the following list[37] contains most of the plastic words:

basic need	identity	resource
care	information	role
center	living standard	service
communication	management	sexuality
consumption	model	solution
contact	modernization	strategy
decision	partner	structure
development	planning	substance
education	problem	system
energy	process	trend
exchange	production	value
factor	progress	welfare
function	project	work
future	raw material	
growth	relationship	

I would add the words "change" and "paradigm" to the list because they are now synonymous with "progress" and "model" respectively.

All the words are abstract nouns and possess an aura of neutrality or factuality. Plastic words are a special kind of abstraction. They replace vernacular terms that are more precise but still flexible enough to be used in a variety of contexts. Now we have "communication" rather than speech, writing, literature, art; we have "relationship" rather than friends and lovers. Such abstractions destroy precise discourse and leave behind only the most general and hollow meaning.

Plastic words, like other abstractions, are compressed sentences in that a predicate is implied in the abstract noun. The term "planning", for example, implies the sentence, "one plans for the future," or the like; the term "management" implies the sentence, "one manages the employees one is responsible for." An abstraction often turns a predicate into a substantive (a noun). It leaves us with a world peopled with nouns, a world infinitely materialistic, a world in which we have little room for free action. More than mere abstractions, plastic words are "frozen judgments," that is, they make scientific that which is normative. "Progress" and "development" seem neutral or factual, to follow from technological innovation. The "frozen judgment" here is that technology is good and our sole hope for the future.

Paradoxically, the more abstract a term becomes the more it appears to be an independent thing. Hypostasization involves turning an action, a concept, an attitude, a feeling, or a relation into a thing that appears to have a life of its own—autonomous and thus atomistic. "Education" becomes a thing apart from particular teachers, students, and ideas. Plastic words concurrently are like numbers in their abstractness. A number is equal to itself under all circumstances; so too is a plastic word. Education is always education. Plastic words perfectly reflect a technological civilization that demands that everything be reduced to a materialized state so that quality can be transformed into quantity.[38]

Plastic words are virtually interchangeable and can be used to generate sentences at random that appear to first glance to make sense.[39] Drawing from his list, I have created the following sentences: "Communication is the basic process by which information can be used as a model for management; planning is the key strategy for creating value in relationships. Management is the planned communication of information about relationships." Poerksen calls such words "Lego" words for they are the building blocks that experts and advertisers employ to form commonplace expressions (or catchphrases) and slogans.

Plastic words serve several functions, paramount of which is propaganda. Some experts use technology to remake the natural environment for purposes of technological growth. Other experts, administrators and applied human scientists, are needed to "engineer" society and to address the cultural disintegration and psychological stress that massive technological innovation produces. Poerksen suggests that the chief purpose of plastic words may be to "provide security and perform exorcisms."[40] Experts who use plastic words "cast a spell" of calm over a world in a state of constant flux and permanent anxiety. Technology mobilizes (Ernst Juenger's phrase) resources and people in the interest of its own continued growth. The helping professionals, applied social scientists, and administrators must be enlisted to help us adjust to a permanent state of crisis.

Poerksen argues that "people think less and less in sentences and allow themselves to be led more and more by words."[41] He goes on to demonstrate that plastic words are more or less meaningless, but they have an "aura" about them. He further states that plastic words are like visual images. May one conclude, then, that plastic words are symbols? But how can they be symbols if they have no meaning? We will explore these questions later in the chapter.

If plastic words express the unity of a technological civilization, jargon articulates its diversity. Jargon originates from two main areas: occupations and fashion and trends in lifestyle.[42] Jargon reflects the technological specialization that affects the world of leisure as much as that of work. Today leisure is stuffed with various technologies of amusement so that it does not provide a respite from the world of work. Indeed, both are highly specialized.

The less an occupation has a body of ideas and a set of skills that constitute professional knowledge, the more it proliferates jargon.[43] Jargon is, however, only a ghostly facsimile of technical or professional terms. It is for the most part devoid of meaning. Like plastic words, jargon terms are terms that can stand alone; moreover, they are personified abstractions that sometimes involve turning predicates into substantives. But unlike plastic words, jargon contains a substantial number of words that are nouns turned into predicates, e.g., quietize, problematize, bottom out. There are a significant number of jargon terms that take a noun and add the suffix "-ize" to create a verb. Either way, turning a predicate into a noun, or a noun into a predicate into a noun, the result is the same: the materialization of reality. Jargon is not neutral; it contains a tacit worldview, the same as that of plastic words: only experts count in a world whose fate is technology.

I have selectively compiled the following list of jargon terms from Walter Nash's glossary[44] of jargon:

ageism	couch potato	gender politics
attitude problem	counter-productive	golden parachute
bottom out	deconstructionism	hands-on
brainstorming	deskilling	headhunter
casual sex	distance learning	hyperactive
cohabit	digital	input
interface	proactive	smart money
lifestyle	output	sound bite

meltdown	quietize	throughput
over the top	quality time	trickle down
postmodernism	safe sex	up to speed
problematize	shelf life	zap

There is a group of jargon terms that almost requires a category of its own: "Bureaucratese," bureaucratic discourse. Often it is more laughable than regular jargon. Ralph Hummel includes the following examples from former Secretary of State Alexander Haig: "careful caution," "contexted," "definitizing an answer," "saddle myself with a statistical fence," and (my favorite) "epistemologicallywise."[45] The use of plastic words and jargon or buzzwords is so widespread in the business world that some employees now play "buzzword bingo." Although there are different versions of the game, the following is a popular one:

> Buzzwords—"incent," "proactive," "impactfulness," for example—are preselected and placed on a bingo-like card in random boxes. Players sit in meetings and conferences and silently check off buzzwords as their bosses spout them; the first to fill in a complete line wins. But, in deference to the setting, the winner typically coughs instead of shouting out "bingo."[46]

What are the purposes of jargon? First, it lends prestige, an association with technology, to one's endeavor. Second, it creates a sense of togetherness among its users. Third, it allows one's occupational or leisure activity to remain in part mysterious. Bureaucracy thrives on secrecy, both internally and in regard to the public.

There is no hard and fast rule for distinguishing plastic words from jargon. Poerksen's list of plastic words and Walter Nash's glossary of jargon contain a few common words, such as process, model, problem. Poerksen admits that plastic words are arranged in concentric circles from the most important in the inner core to the less significant in the outer circles. Some jargon terms, if they are used by the technological elite often enough, may pass into the realm of plastic words. Could we say, then, that plastic words are the most important expressions of jargon, those that best symbolize the promise of technology?

Our final category of atomistic word is atomistic only in a special sense. Even though the meaning of words lies in their use and the smallest unit of meaning is the sentence, individual words acquire abstract meanings of their own; moreover, they develop connotations. I am reserving a fuller discussion of symbolism for later in the chapter, but wish to explore the concept here in a preliminary way. I will simply call the class of words I am interested in "key words." These are words that have over time achieved unusual conceptual and symbolic significance in a culture. I would include among these, truth, equality, beauty, virtue, freedom, the individual, reason, and community. Because key words like other words depend for their meaning on the context of their use both past and present, the decline of serious discourse suggests that these words will have changed radically. Indeed this is what has happened: some of these words have been transformed into something akin to jargon.

Charles Weingartner's astute analysis of the words "freedom," "right," and "equality" is illustrative. These words, he demonstrates, are more or less vacuous in meaning and do not possess a common referent in the world beyond language. So what do they mean? They all mean *more*:

> "Freedom" means *more*—more latitude in avoiding responsibility for one's actions and their consequences; "rights" means *more*—more, better easier access to largely material comforts if not luxuries; and "equality" means *more* access, easier access, to the rights and freedoms that heretofore were privileges.[47]

Let us amend his analysis slightly and suggest that the meaning of freedom is consumer choice, aptly illustrated by the Wendy's commercial of the 1980s, which contrasts the old Soviet Union in which daywear, beachwear, and nightwear for women were identical with the United States where one can get his burger any way he wishes. Equality can be reinterpreted to mean possession of the same amount and kind of consumer goods and power that the wealthy have. "More" means more technological objects (consumer goods) and the power that goes with them.

Key words and other words that refer to qualities, which are embedded in actions, attitudes, thoughts, or beliefs, express the diversity of a technological civilization. Jargon reflects diversity at the level of specialization in work, key words at that of consumer choice. Freedom, equality, and love can be associated with virtually any consumer good or service. This is how advertising works: the association of products with key words and images. Plastic words express the unity of a technological civilization in the sense that all technology is ultimately related and leads to progress.

Understandably so, some readers may be questioning my analysis as extreme. Don't we still mean something besides consumerism when we talk about freedom and love? Certainly. We retain the memory of traditional meanings of key words and other qualitative concepts to some extent, but they act more as ideology than as effective motivation for acting. I have previously argued that institutionalized meanings become superfluous in a technological civilization; consequently, their common meaning disintegrates to the point that it becomes subjective. At the same time, in such a civilization everything is turned into a commodity (technological object) or a technique (objectified efficient means of acting). In subtle and unconscious ways the qualities, both aesthetical and ethical, that humans have lived by are reified in commodities and technology. This still permits the individual to hold onto a subjective understanding of love, freedom, and the like. When common or intersubjective meaning declines, words retain only a highly subjective and nostalgic meaning but still become objectified in technological objects and processes. The former compensates and conceals the latter. In not becoming aware of the loss of common meaning, we can pretend, as it were, that our subjective and ideological understanding is still an effective and common source of motivation for others as well.

Let us take love as an example. Parents retain a certain sense of love as affection and duty, but over time love has come to mean giving children certain technological objects such as toys, the best clothes, the best athletic equipment, the best computers, the best of everything that technology provides. Simultaneously parents sentimentalize their children and live vicariously through them to the point of turning them into consumable personalities. In the absence of cultural authority, parents increasingly use psychological techniques of childrearing to manipulate children into conformity.[48] Both through technological objects and technical processes parents create dependent children. At one time the end of love was to create free and independent children. Most parents, however, do not recognize the change in the meaning of love from ethical to sentimental and manipulative.[49] And yet with an appreciation and critical knowledge of past meanings of love, parents can make a heroic effort to live out some earlier meaning of love, but they do so at the risk of isolation.

Commonplace Expressions, Slogans, and Cliches

If words once derived their meaning from the context of discourse, today the "meaning" of discourse emanates from atomistic words and phrases. Commonplace expressions (catchphrases), slogans, and clichés dominate discourse. Commonplace expressions and slogans differ from clichés in that the former are rooted in the present and still lively, whereas the latter are residues of the past that fall off our lips effortlessly. Commonplace expressions *suggest* a course of action. Therefore, they all imply a slogan which is a call to action.[50] Slogans rarely stand alone and even when they do they all suggest commonplace expression. Consequently, we will consider commonplaces and slogans to be a unitary phenomenon. Commonplaces (and slogans) are expressed in political propaganda, advertising, and public relations. Because political propaganda and public relations are, at least today, forms of advertising, we will consider commonplaces and slogans as the language of advertising. I will explore Daniel Boorstin's prescient insight that "advertising is our folk culture" in Chapter 4.[51] Hence, my discussion here will be brief.

Every age has its commonplace expressions; they are the superficial expression of deeply-held beliefs that are mythological in origin. Commonplaces provide us indirectly with a worldview, an interpretation of the past and a sense of the future, and an implicit definition of human nature. Commonplaces are related to one another by a common myth; each one needs the others. Because commonplace expressions employ plastic words and other atomistic words, their literal meaning is both abstract and vague, or in other words, nonexistent. These expressions only *indirectly* refer to a larger myth; in this sense they act as a kind of symbol.

Leon Bloy ridiculed the commonplaces of the French middle classes in the late nineteenth century. Jacques Ellul did much the same in the 1960s but included the commonplaces of the working class as well in his treatment. Some of Ellul's examples are drawn from Marxist ideology: "You can't act without getting your hands dirty"; "We must follow the current of history"; "The Spiritual side of life cannot develop until the standard of living is raised"; "We don't want charity—we want justice." Others are drawn from middle class, capitalist ideology: "The main thing is to be sincere with yourself"; "Cultivate your personality: be a person!"; "Nobody can help anybody else." And yet, as Ellul brilliantly noted, beneath the conflict of communist, socialist, and capitalist ideology, lies a mythological unity—a belief in technological progress. All dominant political ideologies promise citizens a rise in the standard of living, more consumer goods and services, the American way of life.[52] Since the 1960s we have witnessed a waning belief in communist ideology even before the communist regimes in the Soviet Union and Eastern Europe collapsed. Consequently, today's commonplaces tend not to be overtly political and express the sentiments of global capitalism set within the technological system.

One of Ellul's commonplaces stands out, for it is still very much alive today; moreover, it reveals the magical nature of all commonplaces and slogans: "One must take a positive attitude."[53] This commonplace, this platitude of platitudes, is both the psychological foundation for accepting the others and a revelation of what all commonplaces are—incantations. Not only is this commonplace shamelessly conformist in telling us to accept things as they are, but also it is magical in suggesting that our attitude can change reality. One is positive seemingly not so much to accept reality as to transform it. And yet our attitude, if it does not lead to action, does not change reality. The ability of the individual to change a social reality under any circumstance is extremely limited. But if I change my "personal reality" by wishing away the social reality of, let's say, my job, I have only succeeded in adjusting to an unpalatable work environment. Positive thought may temporarily lower my blood pressure and prevent anxiety attacks, but it will not make my nasty supervisor and the intractable bureaucracy go away.

Some of the other commonplaces and slogans include: "You are worth it"; "Just do it"; "When you don't have time for...."; "Information (communication or technology) is the future"; "Nothing succeeds like success"; "Life is not possible without technology"; "Progress is our most important product"; "Volvo (Buick or any product), something to believe in"; "Communication (information or technology) is power." These empty expressions and slogans are the kitsch that sentimentalizes the brutal reality of a technological civilization. Indirectly they express the mythological beliefs of technological utopianism.[54] In abbreviated form, technological utopianism suggests that technology will permit us to solve all natural and social problems and to perfect the human body so that it is eternally healthy and happy. Technology is knowledge, powerful means of action, and objects; all three contribute to the perfection of nature, society, and the individual. Technology is our fate, and technological growth will allow us to realize a utopian future. One can readily see how the previously mentioned commonplaces express one or more of these core tenets. Technological objects are "something to believe in." That individual happiness is essential to a technological utopia suggests that "I am worth it." Technology is above all about the most powerful (efficient) means of acting; hence, don't hesitate to reflect, "just do it." If technology is our fate, then "life without technology isn't an option." And so forth, and so on.

In the above examples, there is only one naked slogan, "just do it," all the rest are commonplaces. Each commonplace, such as "you are worth it," contains a tacit imperative, "so go buy it." Other commonplaces suggest "do it," "use it," or "change with the times," and "be positive." We should note the plastic words in the commonplaces: "information," "communication," "future," "progress." I have just scratched the surface of the commonplaces. If we include commonplaces and slogans from political discourse and public relations, all of the plastic words receive a heavy work out. For example, politicians in Germany, Britain, France, and the United States go on and on about living in an "informational society" and about the need for "change, growth, development, and progress." Plastic words and their ancillary jargon words are the "building blocks" of commonplace expressions.

Clichés form a distinct category over against commonplaces. For the most part clichés are less important than commonplaces, more numerous, of greater variety, and older. Some clichés were undoubtedly once commonplaces. Because clichés are abstract and vague, they are similar to other atomistic words and phrases in that their abstractness suggests a certain corporeality.[55] The cliché "you know" is perhaps the most frequently used cliché in English. Others include: "hey, man"; "as far as I am concerned"; "peaceful coexistence"; "underprivileged children"; "self-esteem"; "cold war"; "last but not least"; "With friends like this, who needs enemies?" Clichés range from an apparently serious statement or phrase to one of little consequence. They are repeated so often in speech and writing that their use has become reflexive and unconscious.

Clichés serve the purpose of getting the listener (reader) to agree with the speaker (writer). Because the cliché is universally recognized, it is a common point of reference for speaker and listener. The cliché creates an emotional relationship between the two in the anticipation that the listener will not disagree. We all want people to agree with us and like us. Clichés in advertising and other forms of propaganda serve a similar function: create a bond of familiarity between product and consumer.[56] Anton Zijderveld argues that clichés form the consciousness of modern people because our relationships with others tend to be impersonal and because advertising and related discourses dominate what we hear and read.[57]

If my analysis is reasonably accurate, then apart from scientific and technical terms, modern discourse is replete with atomistic words and phrases, which are largely meaningless, and with discourse constructed out of them. Yet I have indicated all along that plastic words, jargon, key words, commonplace expressions, and slogans *indirectly* point to a belief in technology and its promise. The atomistic words and phrases are not linguistic symbols in the usual sense for they have no literal meaning. For an extant word to have an indirect meaning it first has to have a direct meaning. So what kind of symbol are these atomistic words?

Visual Images in the Media

An answer to this question first requires a detour through the world of visual images.[58] It is obvious that we live in an environment dominated by visual images: photographs, billboards, video games, computer games, virtual reality, advertising images, comic books, movies, music videos, and television. Advertising images, for example, are readily present in school hallways, gymnasiums, classrooms, and in the "educational" news that is broadcast during class time; some schools have seemingly adopted the logo of a company by allowing it exclusive rights to advertise its product in an event it sponsors. When one considers how much time we spend viewing images, how little time we spend reading serious books and having serious conversations, and what has happened to meaning of nonscientific words and discourse, one reaches the inescapable conclusion that we are enmeshed in and enthralled by the universe of visual images (especially those of the mass media).

Whereas language exists in time, visual images exist in space. All natural languages change to reflect the collective experiences of people in a historic period. The qualities that we attribute to and infer from human actions are the most important component of cultural meaning; but strictly speaking, qualities cannot be seen, but only inferred from a change of temporal context. Meaning is lived out as a narrative—as biography and as history.

The meaning of visual images is ambiguous. The cultural and linguistic context within which symbolic art is created provides the meaning the audience attempts to uncover through interpretation.[59] As we have seen the common meaning that resides in institutionalized discourse (narrative) and in words is disappearing. We are left with visual images that are autonomous and atomistic. Taken literally, visual images are precise and orient us to empirical (material) reality that exists in space. Sight allows us to see objects, manipulate them, and avoid dangers in our physical environment. In addition to the visual images our eyes provide we construct material visual images, e.g., photographs, drawings, televised images. With respect to both natural and artificial visual images, we assume that the image captures that part of the empirical word to which it points. Image and reality become one.[60]

We are witnessing the great reversal that has been several decades in the making: where once visual images were subject to language, now language is becoming subordinate to visual images. At the same time symbolic meaning becomes vague and thus subjective, it likewise becomes objectified in visual images. Qualitative concepts are "operationalized" in visual images. The turning of language into an accessory to the visual image suggests that every concept expressed in an utterance refers to an "object." The result is a thoroughgoing quantitative reality. When the protagonist on the soap opera says, "I love you," to the object of his affection, the "meaning" of love is the passionate embrace that accompanies the dialogue.

The domination of language by visual images could only occur if the reality people live ceases to be that created in part through discourse. What medium other than television provides an endless procession of visual images that dramatize information? Today people live in and through the dramatized information of the mass media. Television is the mass medium that most dominates our lives. The average American household has the television on fifty-five hours per week; the average individual, depending on age, watches television from just over three hours a day to over five hours a day. For many, television is the single most frequent and important leisure activity.

Television appears to the viewer to be a description of reality; moreover, reality is perceived to be on television. These two propositions—television is about reality, and reality is on television— are different but complementary ideas. There seems to be a one-to-one relationship between visual images and reality (actual or imagined). Television appears to be describing reality, particularly in news programs, documentaries, talk shows, and game shows. In effect, it is reconstructing reality by taking reality out of its temporal and cultural context. Reality as we live it still retains, no matter how small, some meaning, but television expunges this meaning and recomposes reality as a logical sequence of image fragments. Reality appears in televised images as a series of objects that encounter one another in space.

There are many other programs on television, however, such as soap operas and prime-time dramas and comedies that appear, cognitively, to be unreal. But emotionally they are real, just as real as the programs that appear more congruous with empirical reality. At an emotional level, all images are real: all images register their primary impact upon the emotions.[61]

Jerry Mander, in reflecting on his own child's inability to distinguish television from reality, remarks that "Seeing things on television as false and unreal is learned."[62] Just as with any other type of learning, this one may prove unsuccessful in certain cases. George Gerbner and Larry Gross's study of television viewing indicates that heavy watchers have a distorted sense of reality. Among other things, heavy viewers "overestimated the percentage of the population who have professional jobs; and they drastically overestimated the number of police in the U.S. and the amount of violence." The errors in the heavy viewers' judgments were congruent with the distortions of television. It is hard to escape the conclusion that the "the more television people watched, the more their view of the world matched television's reality."[63] Edmund Carpenter reports on an informal study of college students, who when told that television's report of an event was inaccurate, either accepted the inconsistency uncritically or doubted reality because television provides a more emotionally-satisfying reality.[64]

We have now reached the turning point: not only is television about reality, but reality is on television. This assertion suggests that, as spectators, we live vicariously through and in visual images, and that the medium of television is a principal epistemological authority that rivals the computer in terms of efficacy. When television momentarily focuses on an issue, it becomes a "real" issue; when television leaves it behind for a new issue, the old issue is eliminated from our immediate experiences and thus becomes a nonissue.[65] A society of the spectacle turns life into a visual drama, a show; and the most real show, the most "objective" show, is that on television. Television has become the most important authority of dramatized information among the various mass media. We are fascinated with the possibility of being on television or meeting someone who is on television (a celebrity), because it is only here—television—that our subjective experiences (which are experienced emotionally as real) can be made intersubjective. People spend a substantial amount of time talking about what appears on television, not just because they watch so much of it, but because this is the home of our *shared* experiences.

The visual images of television (and the mass media) are only images of power and possessions. The dialogue on television is an appendage to the visual images because discourse has lost its meaning. Autonomous visual images are about objects (possessions) and their relations (power), or, in other words, how some objects bring about the movement of other objects. The difference between human beings and products disappears: human beings are constantly being interrupted on television by advertised products and, more importantly, gain prestige by their association with these products.

The relations between products are relations of power: possession, consumption, manipulation, control, and violence. A world devoid of symbolic meaning as ethical truth is a world of raw power. Because symbolic meaning flows directly or indirectly from discourse, autonomous visual images are only about relations of power. For example, on television, a man and a woman embrace. Is this an instance of ethical love, sexual desire, or the desire to manipulate the other? The visual images by themselves make the first response impossible, for the visual image is about empirical reality. We are left with a choice between, or a combination of, the second and third responses.

Television creates a pseudo-language out of these images of power. Meaning in language is holistic in the form of utterances and narratives; words take their meaning from this larger context of meaning. A visual image, by contrast, is a *totality* by itself. It points to a material object and registers an emotion. Television programs (including the news) create a logic of images. Logic has no meaning; rather it is a set of rules about how to proceed in an argument.

The "meaning" of a television program is the final outcome—

success or failure, survival or death, possession or nonpossession; in other words, power. The content of the various programs are about objects to be possessed and consumed, the power of which becomes that of the spectator; more exactly, the content is about objects acting in relation to other objects—acts of possession, consumption, manipulation, control, or violence. These acts of power are spatially linked together in a television program or movie in a logical sequence that leads to an outcome—success or failure.

The subjectivization (sterilization) of symbols and their objectification in visual images effectively reduces meaning to instinctual power. Visual images hit us at an emotional level. When visual images are subordinate to language and symbolic meaning, as in traditional art, then the emotions unleashed are integrated by normative reason and made meaningful. When, on the other hand, visual images become autonomous, reified symbols, they leave the emotions under the control of the instincts: survival, aggression, sexuality, and so forth. For the individual (a spectacular reality creates a radical individualism) reality is emotional and meaning is instinctual. The implications of this are astounding. Technology is first and foremost an efficient or powerful means of acting, visual images are images of power and possessions, and the "meaning" of autonomous visual images is instinctual power. The circle is now complete: a reality of power, a reality without meaning.

Even when one allows for the discourse accompanying the visual images of television and the movies to provide meaning for the action, the primary mode of human interaction is domination/submission. In commenting on several media, Andrew Tudor argues, "Violent actions themselves are only the logical extension of this basically coercive image of human relations."[66] Television as a medium favors the more spectacular—peak events like catastrophes, wars, violence, death, sexuality, and conflict of any kind. This is the bias of the medium whose sole purpose is to entertain us. The more subtle forms of human interaction—compassion, ethical love, trust, and patience—cannot be transmitted through autonomous visual images; and even if they could be, they would not be as interesting. The expression of power is more spectacular than the limitation of power.

Visual images make a fundamental appeal to our emotions. Visual reality is an emotional reality. At this level, the intellectual credibility of the visual image is less important than how spectacular it is, the emotional response it can produce. Studies indicate that the most emotionally believable of realistic depictions on television are violent scenes. Violent images are the *most real* images because they provoke the strongest emotional response: they simultaneously give us a sense of being alive and of having control over our relations with others.[67] In an existence increasingly made abstract, impersonal, and meaningless by technology, unusual, spectacular, and frightening images allow us vicariously to experience a crisis, a turning-point in our lives. We are placed time and again in a crucible. This phenomenon is undoubtedly behind the popularity of horror films and action films.

Symbolism in the Milieu of Technology

Traditional meaning emanates from symbolic relations that humans perceive to exist even at the moment they create them. Symbolic creation in art, music, literature, poetry, myth, and story creates, renews, and recreates the institutionalized discourses that are the foundation of any culture. Without effective symbolism that people live out and put into practice, common meaning disintegrates. If discourse and words have become more or less meaningless, that is, abstract and reified, then symbolic creation must be nonexistent or ineffective. Clearly it is not the former with the proliferation of artists, musicians, writers, and new religious worldviews; so it must be the latter. So why has symbolism become sterile?

Meaning is both direct and indirect. Direct meaning is the obvious meaning of an utterance; it can be readily understood by anyone familiar with the words and their context. Indirect meaning is "grafted" on to the direct meaning. For example, I say, "Bill and Mary will arrive at eight o'clock tonight." The indirect meaning may be, "Please help me pick up the house." All metaphors possess an indirect meaning, for the literal meaning is invariably false: love is not a rose despite my saying it is. Indirect meaning may be nonverbal as well. Water in the form of a pond, lake, waterfall, or the like may suggest to a religious believer death and rebirth. Or the point on the horizon where the earth meets the sky may connote the union of man and woman. Following Tzvetan Todorov, let us refer to indirect meaning as symbolic meaning.[68] Now symbolic meaning exists both in language and in reality because language is the principal medium by which we infer from and attribute to the world certain relations, actions, and attributes that we imagine to exist. To the extent, however, that our lives are based upon these qualities, we help bring them into existence.

The farther back we go in time, Owen Barfield argues, the more metaphorical was human thinking.[69] The origin of meaning appears to be in the comparison of two seemingly unrelated actions or phenomena. Verbal symbolism expresses the tacit perception of indirect relations in the world. Every symbol (metaphor) requires interpretation. Once an interpretation is made, one enters the realm of conceptualization.[70] The metaphor, "love is a rose," gives rise to thoughts such "like roses love is prickly"; "like roses love blooms and eventually fades." Some of these interpretations eventually enter into the conscious perception and definition of love. Direct meaning emanates from indirect meaning.

The critical idea here is our intuition that the various relations between the forces in nature and between humans and nature are part of a larger organic unity. Symbolism, as Owen Barfield has brilliantly noted, depends upon the tacit perception that the world is an organic totality.[71] Unlike concepts, which differentiate, symbols express a sense of unity by perceiving relations of similarity between apparently divergent phenomena. This involves the attribution of "inwardness" or "consciousness" to a world believed to be alive. Meaning in the strong sense of the term is inwardness or that which is qualitative and takes the form of "feelings, states of mind, thoughts, relations, classes, moral qualities and so on."[72] The farther back we go into the milieu of nature, the more these qualities were believed to be a dimension of action, rather than having an existence of their own as "immaterial beings," like Platonic ideals.

The name for such action, according to Barfield, is participation. Humans feel both part of and subservient to that organic totality

called the world whose power is first spiritual. Participation involves an implicit recognition that humans are part of a world
whose consciousness is in part embedded in human consciousness. Language is a creative force borne out of the interaction between the spirit (consciousness) of nature and the human spirit.
There is a nonsensory or spiritual link between nature and humans such that in naming and attributing qualities (collective representations) to the world we participate in its creation; we are,
as it were, allowing nature to work in and through us. Therefore,
phenomena only fully come into existence when they are named.[73]
What I have just described is "original participation." I suggest
that this form of participation occurs in the milieu of nature; indeed, Barfield appears to have a tacit understanding of the three
milieus. As I indicated in Chapter 1, the principle by which magic
works in the milieu of nature is persuasion, but a persuasion in
which one is participating with the other in some action: "Can I
persuade you to help me find the antelope?" To kill animals selectively was perceived to be essential for the renewal of nature,
which was of course beneficial to both humans and the rest of
nature. In the milieu of nature, then, the world as an organic unity
was simultaneously a symbolic unity, for the inward relations between the phenomena of nature were spiritual and could only be
grasped metaphorically.

Original participation in the symbolic creation of nature did not
occur consciously. In the transition to the milieu of society, humans begin to think rationally about their world. Rational thinking for a long time, however, remains secondary to the symbolic
meanings in and by which humans relate to nature and to each
other. Myth, story, and poetry create the meaning that philosophy
attempts to define. As long as we retain a sense that the phenomena we perceive are created in part out of our own conceptions,
that we participate in the representations of the world, we avoid
the positivism of believing that concepts are a reflection of the
way things are in themselves.[74]

In the milieu of society (historic period), as we have already
seen, human institutions become more important than nature. Barfield notes that inwardness moves from nature to humans.[75] Nature comes to be a part of human consciousness. Humans become

increasingly dominant, but still possess a sense of a power beyond themselves, e.g., a pantheon of gods. Human qualities are projected onto nature. Rather than reading society through nature, we read nature through society. Nevertheless, nature and society are perceived to be organic unities so similar that they still form a larger totality. If we only symbolize that which appears to be an organic unity, the moral and aesthetical qualities of human society now become the paramount symbols used to make sense out of the rest of nature.

The vast symbolic edifice of nature and society starts to disintegrate in the milieu of technology. If only an organic unity suggests symbolization, the reverse is true as well: only a symbolic environment appears to be organic. Before examining the technological milieu and why it makes symbolization ephemeral and sterile, let us first examine the decline of human inwardness or meaning, the aesthetical and ethical qualities attributed to humans. We have previously seen that key words and other words that refer to human qualities have become meaningless, but some of these terms have disappeared.

Josephine Miles, for example, has demonstrated that the terms "goodness," "truth," and "beauty" have vanished in late twentieth century poetry (as they have in commentaries about the arts). In place of these natural and human qualities, poetry speaks a language of construction, of bodies and houses, to the effect that "man has more and more taken responsibility for making his own world."[76] Is it not apparent, the influence of technology, here? Insofar as values are a consequence of symbolizing a power (nature or society) beyond ourselves, they are superfluous in a technological civilization. For there is no power mightier than that of technology.

In a historical analysis of the English language, Geoffrey Hughes observes that terms like *"honour, virtue, temperance, modesty, chastity* . . . no longer form a central part of a meaningful moral vocabulary."[77] Instead the vocabulary centers about the concept of normality and includes terms like "deviant" and "mental illness."[78]

Speaking about twentieth century literature, traditionally a referential context for qualitative terms, Erich Auerbach concludes that much of the best European literature leaves us with a sense of "haziness, vague indefinability of meaning."[79] Literary critic John Aldridge makes the same point about American literature after the second world war.[80]

Traditional symbolism is declining because this mode of thought is incongruent with the technological milieu. The dominant mode of expression is harmonious with its milieu. For the milieus of nature and society, symbolic thought is the primary mode of expression (rational thought rests upon it); for the milieu of technology, technical thought is triumphant. The implication is that the technological milieu is not experienced as an organic unity.

In the milieu of society, nature remained a powerful enough force that it served as an ideological backdrop for understanding society until the early nineteenth century, as with the concept of natural law. But technology has become so pervasive and mighty that nature is reduced to a source of energy or an aesthetic retreat from the pressures of living in a technological society. The technological milieu is an abstract system of information that works to coordinate the variegated technologies at the level of practice (means of acting). Undoubtedly this milieu is also comprised of a multitude of technological objects or consumer goods. Still its ability to become a milieu is dependent upon the coordination of technical information so that each technology is both a means of acting and a source of information about other technologies. Each subsystem of the technological system, e.g., transportation, police, communication, industry, has to be coordinated with the others, and increasingly so as the system grows. This system of information is formed out of fragments or bits of information that are symbolically meaningless, but are necessary for establishing causal relations both within and between technologies. *The technological system exhibits holism at the level of causality, not meaning.* Technical thought, which is *"simplifying, reductive, operational, instrumental, and rearranging,"* creates the system.[81]

There is an inverse relationship between the power of technology and the power of symbolization. Historically, symbolization was a way for humans to gain control over their milieu. By enveloping it within their symbol system, even as they were acknowledging its greater power, they gained a sense of mastery. Ellul argues that the human ability to symbolize has been the single most important factor in the cultural evolution of the human race. Because technology is our own creation we do not perceive a need to symbolize it in the traditional sense. It is only when we confront a foreign power—nature—that we bring it within our symbolic net. Symbolization simultaneously creates a meaningful world and allows us to *distance* ourselves from this world. Without effective symbolization, we have no way to keep technology from invading and conquering culture.[82]

And yet we cannot help trying to provide technology with an inwardness or consciousness. In his analysis of *12,000 Words*, a dictionary of new words that appeared between 1961 and 1985, Raymond Gozzi demonstrates a pattern of "externalizing human qualities onto machines."[83] Computers now possess *brains*, *memories*, and have *languages*.[84] For some enthusiasts they have *souls*. Science fiction has even turned computers into living beings who wish to have sex with humans. Concomitantly, however, we mechanize human relationships.[85] Hence, today we create *networks* and *interface* with other people, and even *plug into* their life-styles or personalities.[86] We have created a closed system: we project human qualities onto technology but the human has already been rendered technological.

Symbolic thought, which is fundamental to the milieus of nature and society, employs the medium of language; technical thought, which is dominant in the milieu of technology, expresses itself in visual images, especially those of the mass media. Visual images are the language of technology.[87] Visual images in the company of atomistic words are meaningless, yet function as "symbols." They are in effect false symbols whose "meaning" is instinctual power. Technology symbolizes itself with these false symbols. Let us examine how this works.

In traditional symbolic meaning, as with a metaphor, there is a comparison of two words and what they represent. In saying, "love is a rose," I create a tension between the literal meaning of "love" and the literal meaning of "rose." The comparison is not to be taken literally and is pause for reflection. The meaning lies in the hiatus between the two words.[88] The meaning in this example is quite complex and includes the ideas that love has to be nourished, that it can hurt (thorns), that it is beautiful, and that it blooms and fades. Often a metaphor involves comparing something less well known and defined, *love*, with something better known and defined, *rose*.

Visual symbolism in the media does not exclude discourse and atomistic words, but incorporates and transforms them. I will use the example of a famous advertisement for Coca-Cola. It shows children of various cultures around the world holding hands and singing a song about friendship, "I'd like to teach the world to sing," and pictures of Coca-Cola being drunk. The symbolism involves key words and phrases, such as "peace," "harmony," and two sets of visual images: children holding hands and Coca-Cola. Peace or harmony is associated with hand holding and both of these with Coca-Cola. This material symbolism reifies the atomistic and more or less meaningless words "peace" and "harmony" so that hand holding equals Coca-Cola. The symbolism moves from less well-known to better known in the following direction: from *peace* and *harmony* to children holding hands to Coca-Cola. The meaning of peace and harmony resides in Coca-Cola, a product that has the power to give me pleasure (first-order importance) and the power to create world peace (second-order importance).

Not every act of visual symbolization has to involve a set of words and two dominant images. It can consist of a word an image, usually a product, or two images, like a logo and a product. Perhaps there is nothing more shocking and titillating than to see an advertisement dominated by the image of a product, like a diamond, with nothing else except the logo or name of the company in the background.

This visual symbolism, unlike the metaphor, creates no meaning, for it is created out of literal or material associations. That is, *peace* and *harmony* equal holding hands, and holding hands equals Coca-Cola. Life consists of material relationships to people and to products. But the "meaning" of life resides in that which is powerful—technological objects like Coca-Cola. This is how technology symbolizes itself; we are its unwitting agents despite being its creators.

We have previously seen that atomistic words other than scientific and technical terms have lost their meaning and become fully abstract. As such they have no choice but to act as symbols (indirect meaning). Visual images in the media have no meaning (in the traditional sense), and they too function as symbols. Visual images are more important than words in the symbolization of technology for they demonstrate the power and potential of technology. Not all atomistic words and visual images are equal as symbols, however, and not all symbolize the same dimension of technology.

Technology exists as information, means, and object. The first aspect of technology is its *abstractness*; each technology as well as the technological system is composed of technical information. The second dimension concerns its *power*. The third characteristic is its singularity as *product*. The chief symbols of the abstractness of technology are certain plastic words, those words used by administrators and applied human scientists all over the modern world. They signify technology as a organizing force that is infinitely adaptable. The most important plastic words are *information* and *communication* on the one hand and *progress, growth,* and *development* on the other hand. The former two words signify technology as a system, the existence of which is dependent upon the endless and quick *communication* of *information*. The latter three words signify that technology is always changing.

The various visual images of consumer goods signify technology as object. Technology appears to be our benefactor because it provides us with an infinite supply of new products and objects that are pleasurable. It is here that technology most dramatically turns us into consumers.

The violent images (and to a certain extent the sexual images) of the mass media signify technology as power. They constitute a reverse image: technology is abstract and rational, violence is concrete and irrational. But in another sense they are a direct image, for both technology and violence are expressions of ultimate power. We are in the presence of the sacred with violent images, for the sacred is always about power. The sacred power of technology is symbolized in the violent images of the mass media. *They are the paramount symbols of technology.*

All the other atomistic words and visual images symbolize in one way or another, through a series of associations with other words and images, one of the three aspects of technology. The myth of technological utopianism unifies the various symbols of technology and permits each one to imply the others. The myth of technological utopianism is better represented in the visual images of the mass media than in language. Chapter 4 will address this in some detail.

What are the consequences of a culture permeated with false symbols that provide no meaning? It transforms our sense of truth, freedom, and reality. The concept of truth is radically altered. Traditionally the concept of truth is ethical and implies some universal standard of goodness, whether natural, historical, or transcendent, according to which one's life is judged. Is my life true or false in regard to what I claim to believe? Do I keep my promises? Do my words accurately describe what happened? True and false belong to what Ellul calls the order of truth. A lie is only a lie if there exists a standard that I should tell the truth. Language is the only medium through which questions about truth and the ethical standard it leans upon can be raised.

The order of reality refers to empirical reality, that which can be observed and measured. Visual images best allow us to orient ourselves to empirical reality, to grasp it, manipulate it, and adjust to the movement therein. Visual images, unless they part of symbolic art, root us in the empirical world. Now the fundamental question about empirical reality considered as a self-contained reality are those of power: manipulation and adjustment. I manipulate that which is less powerful and adjust to that which is more powerful. With the decline of symbolic meaning, there is no effective way of raising ethical questions about the exercise of power. The evidence of truth now becomes, "success relative to reality."[89] Because technology guarantees an efficacious outcome, it is the standard of truth.[90] Not science but technology. This is a completely materialistic conception of truth that equates power with truth.

Freedom is dependent upon symbolic language. Without symbolism it is impossible to distance oneself from one's milieu. Technical reason will not lead one to reflect critically on the conditions of life. Technical reason keeps our attention centered on questions of possibility and probability, thus blunting our moral judgment. Language may be a "prisonhouse," encapsulating us for the moment in a web of ideologies, but every natural language harbors within itself a potential revolution of new meanings and liberating thoughts.

Only a symbolic universe gives us the experience of living in a concrete reality.[91] When language becomes too abstract, we are cut off from empirical reality and inhabit a world of personified abstractions. When language loses meaning, we live in a completely material world of instinct, sensations, and power. And this is a frightening world of raw power, wherein one must be suspicious and distrustful of others. It is a world that always appears on the verge of apocalypse.[92] It is only symbolic language that allows us to experience and create a world that possesses ethical meaning and thus appears to be consistent, coherent, and worthy of trust. Concrete reality is a unified reality; only a symbolic universe can provide us with experiences that unite the abstract and the material.

Without effective symbolism, concrete reality becomes schizophrenic. Part of reality is lived in the dramatized information of the mass media, and the other part of reality is experienced in the statistical information housed in the computer. Reality is on television and in the computer.

Atomistic words (nontechnical terms) have lost their meaning, become vague, subjective, and emotional, and fallen under the influence of visual images whose primary impact is emotional. These words and images function as symbols, but false symbols whose meaning is instinctual power. As such these words and images become magical terms. They can be associated with each other and technological objects in an infinite and random number of ways. Anything can be transformed into anything else by its association with an image. Peace is holding hands, holding hands is Coke, peace is Coke. Magic can go no farther than this. Without symbolic and ethical limits on magical representation, it tends toward unlimited power—technology. Abstract words and material images become the foundation of magical techniques of manipulation.[93]

Chapter 4 examines the use of dramatized information, especially the images of the media, as the basis for the magical practices on television. Chapter 5 discusses the role of dramatized information, especially language, in the magical acts of therapy, self-help, and positive thinking. But because language is subordinate to visual images, we will need to ascertain how the media affect the practice of therapy and self-help. Before doing this, we must first examine the significance of statistical information, which creates half of our bifurcated existence, for a different set of magical practices—management techniques—that are described in Chapter 6.

· 3 ·

Statistical Information: The Basis of Administrative Magic

Everything has to increase, has to acquire more speed, has to achieve greater numbers. Quantity is the purpose. If another million souls has been reached there is a speech; a eulogy over a disaster. If another hundred thousandth inhabitant of a city is born there are flowers for the mother and a saving certificate for the child; premiums on our misfortune. The number, our misfortune. The number, our idol.
J. H. Van den Berg
Divided Existence and Complex Society

For over thirty years visual images and numbers have been replacing language as the primary means of sharing knowledge.[1] In the previous chapter we examined how the visual images of the mass media have captured and objectified the meaning of qualitative terms. In this chapter we study how the quantification of everything human has likewise led to the erosion of the symbolic capability of language. Statistical information relies on the visualization of existence as much as dramatized information does. Visual images and numbers help us locate, separate, and count objects in space. As Henri Bergson noted, "Every clear idea of number implies a visual image in space. . . . Every number is a collection of units."[2] Logic too is based on sight. Logic and mathematics, after Descartes, are inexorably linked. Speaking of a neo-Cartesian view, Stanley Rosen observes:

> The heterogeneous appearance of nature, and so too of applied logic, is subjected to the uniformity of logical space. This is the

assumption underlying the mathematicizing of nature. Mathematics is the universal articulation of logical space. . . .[3]

As we have previously noted, discourse exists in time and while it can be employed to refer to objects in space, its genius is to permit us to create symbolic meaning and to explore the idea of truth. But autonomous dramatized and numerical information chain us to empirical reality.

Not all visual images lend themselves to quantification. Before visualization could be placed in the service of quantification, it had to be liberated from its religious (symbolic) context. After 1100 A.D. the Church increasingly relied on visual images to communicate biblical events and religious ideas to an illiterate laity.[4] Religious leaders believed that architecture, sculpture, stained glass windows, frescoes, and later holy cards "efficiently" transmitted the faith at a time when many villages were without a priest to preach the word of God on a regular basis. Early on these images were symbolic and expressed the Christian figural view of reality.[5] This view was organized around two poles: figure and fulfillment. The figure was a historical event or person that anticipates or prefigures another historical event or person, the fulfillment. Figure and fulfillment are not connected logically or temporally. Instead the fulfillment completes the meaning of the figure. God's providence, not to be understood in deterministic terms, coordinates the free activity of humans to bring about the desired state or fulfillment. For example, the story of Abraham and Isaac in the Hebrew Scripture was understood by Christians to be a figure for the relationship of God the father to his son Jesus Christ. In the figure the son's life is spared; in the fulfillment the son is killed.

Dante, Erich Auerbach argues, was the last major Christian writer to express the Christian figural view of reality. But by the "autumn of the Middle Ages" the realism of his descriptions were becoming disconnected from their symbolic context. His portrait of human characters such as Farinata and Cavalcante, whether they end in heaven, purgatory, or hell are so vivid, so compelling, that the figure of earthly passions and conflicts overwhelms the fulfillment, even that of heaven. Eternity becomes a backdrop for human action. "The image of man eclipses the image of God."[6] Aesthetical values such as pleasure and beauty come to the foreground in the Renaissance: visual images are no longer fully subordinate to a religious worldview. Eventually visual images will become free of symbolism itself.

The medieval fascination with logic finally broke the nexus between visual images and symbolic meaning. Christians argued of course that logic came from God, and Thomas Aquinas produced the great synthesis of scripture and Aristotle. Nature was perceived to be a logical creation. As Georges Duby observes, "The universe ceased to be a code that the imagination strove to decipher. It became a matter of logic, and the cathedrals were to restore the pattern of it by situating all visible creatures in their respective places."[7] The logician paved the way for the mathematician and the engineer.

From the thirteenth century on, the West brought together two previously separate disciplines: abstract mathematics and practical measurement. Alfred Crosby argues that this was the West's unique intellectual contribution; it was made possible by the assumption that underlying the rich panorama of nature was a uniformity of space and time.[8] The technological applications of measurement and mathematics in the form of the clock, the cannon, the crossbow, *Portolano* marine charts, perspective painting, and double-entry bookkeeping reinforced and furthered the assumption of uniformity.[9] Behind all this was the emphasis on sight. If Greek and early medieval culture had emphasized intuition based on hearing and touch, culture from the late Middle Ages to the present stresses visual insight.[10] The symbolic reality of Greek, Romans, Jews, and Christians was in each instance unique, but common to all was a sense of the heterogeneous nature of reality. The new model of reality, as Crosby describes it, was practical:

> Reduce what you are trying to think about to the minimum required by its definition; visualize it on paper, or at least in your mind, be it the fluctuation of wool prices at the Champagne fairs or the course of Mars through the heavens, and divide it, either in fact or in imagination, into equal quanta. Then you can measure it, that is, count the quanta.[11]

The synthesis of visualization and quantification relied first on geometry, later on algebra, for the technological mastery of life.

Statistics Everywhere

The quantification of nature eventually led to the quantification of human existence. The result is the proliferation of statistics. The word "statistics" comes from German into English near the end of the eighteenth century. It derives from the Latin word for state (political) and suggests as well information that can be scientifically acquired and analyzed.[12] Thus we arrive at: the scientific information of the state. Statistics need not be numerical, for as a description of reality it can be based on a single or typical case. Descriptive statistics require little more than a knowledge of arithmetic. Prior to the widespread use of the term *statistics*, the phrase *political arithmetic* was often employed to refer to the facts the state collected about its citizens.

David Landes has identified three stages in the collection and use of statistical data for economic purposes: the proto-statistical era, the premodern or first statistical era, and the modern or second statistical era.[13] The first stage goes back to the Middle Ages and includes health surveys and a count of victims of the Plague but mainly includes the seventeenth and eighteenth centuries and early nineteenth century; the second stage (first statistical era), variously referred to as the "era of statistical enthusiasm" and "the avalanche of printed numbers,"[14] begins in the 1820s with the realization in government, business, and industry that the collection and analysis of statistical data must be numerical and systematic. The third stage (second statistical era) begins after World War I and features the growth of and experimentation with sophisticated aggregative and analytical indicators of economic changes, such as input- output tables.[15] Statistical data collected for non-economic purposes roughly follows this path of increase.

Government, business, and industry all perceive a need for vast amounts of statistical information for the coordination and control of products, markets, workers, and citizens. The growth of statistics is commensurate with the growth of and centralization of power in the political state and with the advance of industrialized capitalism. Behind both of these stands technology. Indeed, "statistics is a social technology" that serves the interests of control and coordination.[16] James Beniger has observed that just as in-

creased information is needed to facilitate more efficient processing of matter and energy, so too there are various information
systems required to coordinate the proliferation of information.[17]
In this chapter I will discuss the increase in statistical information
about products but especially about people; in Chapter 6 I will
examine the various systems of management.

We will briefly examine the use of censuses, surveys, administrative data, accounting and actuarial data, opinion polls, and
examinations in the public and private sectors, especially since
1820, roughly the time statistics became largely numerical.[18]

Censuses go back at least to the time of the Hebrews as described in the Book of Numbers in the Old Testament. Beginning
in the sixteenth century, European societies often inaugurated censuses of their colonies before they did the same of the home country.[19] The mercantilist and cameralist governments of Europe
desired economic growth and increased revenues to facilitate their
increased activities; consequently they promoted censuses as a
way of ascertaining their tax base.[20] The interest of the state in
censuses varies directly with its control of the national economy.
In the seventeenth and eighteenth centuries Spain, for instance,
exercised more direct economic control over its colonies than did
England, which relied heavily on its merchants; hence, Spain insisted on a strict economic accounting of the activities of its col-
onists.[21] The English state was almost blase about censuses
compared to many of its competitors; indeed, the Anglican
Church conducted censuses of England from 1800 to 1831.[22]

Apart from economic interests, politics sometimes played a decisive role in the number and kinds of censuses taken. Although
the French state was more directly involved in promoting economic growth than the English state in the seventeenth and eighteenth centuries, the quality of its census data was questionable
because its citizens were smarting from perceived tax inequities
and administrative corruption.[23] The relation between democracy
and the census is paradoxical. A census can provide government
with crucial information that enhances control over its citizens. At
the same time, however, official statistics, if they are published,
give citizens a more informed basis for making political decisions
and help legislators better evaluate the competing demands of

special interest groups.[24] The United States was the first country to institute a periodic census beginning in 1790.[25] James Madison wished to expand the categories of response—restricted to race, sex, and age—to include occupation. He argued that such information would help citizens and legislators balance the claims of competing groups. Not everyone was convinced, however; for some argued that the concept of the common good should not be reduced to a balance of special interests, but emphasize what was best for society as a whole.[26] Throughout the modern period the chosen path is for censuses to ask more questions of its citizens and to perform ever more statistical manipulations of the data. Moreover, special surveys are often used to supplement and update the census. This serves the interests of the state much more than it does those of citizens who remain largely ignorant of the census unless organized into large special interest groups.

Hand in hand with the increase in the number and complexity of censuses has been the collection of data for administrative purposes within government and in business. Rates of unemployment, crime statistics, health statistics from hospitals and HMOs, rates of poverty, marriage rates and birth rates, divorce rates, rates of automobile accidents, rates of mental illness, and death rates are only a few examples. Ian Hacking has demonstrated the preoccupation with gathering statistics on crime and deviancy in nineteenth century Europe. "Moral statistics" were likened to physical statistics because both occurred in lawlike frequencies and were indicators of health of the physical or the social body.[27] In the early nineteenth century in France, for instance, the Ministry of Justice competed with the Ministry of Health to publish statistics on suicide. Was it a disease or a crime? Eventually a new category of problems emerged—social problems—that were now regarded as problems common to both legal and medical specialists.[28] Entire bureaus of statistics were created within some governments, as in Prussia in the late eighteenth century.[29] Thus began our intoxication with statistical information, a state from which we are still not sober.

Although double-entry bookkeeping began in the late Middle Ages, accounting techniques did not dramatically increase until the middle of the nineteenth century.[30] At that same time the profession of accounting begins in Great Britain. In an economy of small businesses, on-premise owners, and no income tax, there was scant need for external accounting consultants. The accounting profession had to wait until joint stock companies, bankruptcies, and taxes became widespread.[31]

Cost accounting, which originated in American corporations in the late nineteenth century, did not become central to the British economy until World War I.[32] That same American penchant for technology produced the cash register in 1879, which allowed retail stores to keep an accurate account of their income. Prior to this the owner could only guess at his intake, especially given the unknown amount of petty theft.[33] Cost accounting went well beyond the cash register in its attempt to provide an accurate measurement of the cost of everything: raw materials, other overhead expenses, labor, and the processes by which raw materials became a product. After the turn of the century, scientific management applied to the factory provided a boost to accounting, for now every aspect of a complex industrial process could be measured.[34] Scientific management, according to Taylorism, involves breaking every task and complex process into its smallest relevant units, studying each unit as to the most efficient way of proceeding, and reconstituting the units into a system of relationships and flows. Once one could reduce production to a logical process, one could then measure its various steps in terms of time and effectiveness, and, already knowing the cost of materials and labor, assign a cost to the overall process. Eventually the principles of scientific management would be applied to virtually every kind of labor— including intellectual labor—and to management itself. This story will be taken up in Chapter 6.

Rivaled only by government in its appetite for statistics, the insurance industry generates an enormous amount of data on death, sickness, and accidents. From the late seventeenth century to the nineteenth century insurance and gambling were not yet separate activities; indeed, insurance was a variation of gambling insofar as it involved an exchange of risk. In the eighteenth century, lotteries took Europe by storm. Gambling was so widespread among all classes that Lorraine Daston maintains it had "become a metaphor for civil society itself.[35] Insurance followed suit. The insurance market in London permitted one to purchase insurance against adultery, lying, and gambling losses. Some less reputable London underwriters "issued policies on the lives of celebrities like Sir Robert Walpole, the success of battles, the succession of Louis XV's mistresses, the outcome of sensational trials . . . and in short served as bookmakers for all and sundry bets."[36] The insurance industry by and large resisted the application of mathematical probability to empirical statistical data in part because long-term life insurance was only a small fraction of the business, in part because mortality statistics were unreliable, but mainly because it was making money without doing so. Common sense probability worked just fine for individual risk.[37] By common sense probability I mean probability that is both deductive, e.g., the equal probability of getting a head or a tail with a two sided coin and inductive, e.g., formulating the probability of death from mortality statistics. One used one's own experiences rather than official statistics, and concurrently assimilated the risk to a gambling scenario, e.g., over any six month period (most life insurance before the nineteenth century could only be obtained for a period of a year or less) there was an equal probability of living or dying.

Daston argues persuasively that insurance came to rely more upon mathematical probability in the sense of statistical frequencies when the growing middle classes started to demand security for their families.[38] Rather than risk they wanted certainty—the relative certainty that statistical regularities such as mortality statistics provides. What is the life expectancy for a male at age forty? A specifiable degree of certainty in facing life's adversities as a member of a statistical category replaced the risk of going it alone.

Before life insurance became widespread in the nineteenth century, annuities were a popular but risky substitute. European governments were in the business of selling life annuities. Great Britain attempted to ease its large national debt of £900 million by selling life annuities at extremely low rates. Unfortunately for the government, the going standard of mortality was based on the statistics recorded in the city of Northampton in the eighteenth century. The expert Richard Price had estimated mortality at twenty-four years when it was actually close to thirty years. John

Finlaison, chief actuary of the National Debt Office of Great Britain, objected to the continued use of Price's "law of mortality", for he knew the data to be unrepresentative.

Even more strenuous were Finlaison's criticisms of Price's attempt to formulate a law of sickness. The latter estimated that until he was thirty-two years old, a man would be home sick a week per year, whereas by the time he was sixty years old he would miss work two weeks per year. The Equitable, Britain's first life insurance company, used Price's laws of mortality and sickness.[39] Yet not everyone believed you could formulate a law of sickness from limited empirical data given the fact that some jobs self-selected healthy workers whereas some jobs made people sick.[40] Insurance companies had depended on their own employees to assess the health and stability of prospective customers on a case by case basis, but the spotty quality of such judgments made company managers seek more ever secure medical and actuarial advice.[41]

The Institute of Actuaries in England was founded in 1848, and in 1853 a Select Committee on Assurance Associations attempted to regulate the insurance industry to reduce the bankruptcies and fraud. The new actuarial profession claimed that an insurance company's success depended on the skill of its managers, in particular its actuaries.[42] Only gradually, however, did actuaries, who were originally secretaries and bookkeepers, begin to apply national statistical tables and mathematical probability. First, they had to be trained to do so.[43]

Obviously America was not the first country to offer life and health insurance to its citizens, but it was the first to make insurance a "democratic, universal institution."[44] Maritime accidents in particular had been insured for centuries, but the proliferation of technology and its products in the eighteenth and twentieth centuries produced new risks: gas lines, electrical wiring, plumbing, and automobiles.[45] Casualty or accident insurance rose to make these new risks less uncertain. Actuarials were now required to ascertain the statistical regularities of myriad accidents and their resultant injuries and deaths.

Public opinion polls began with market research in the nineteenth century and later included political polls and academic surveys. "Public opinion" refers to both attitudes and reported behavior; in the latter sense it overlaps with the administrative data that the political state collects about its citizens: crime; birth, marriage, and death rates; income and occupation; and so forth. Politicians came to realize in the eighteenth century that public opinion (as attitude) had become a powerful force; he who controlled public opinion was a mighty leader indeed.[46] With the rise of the mass media beyond newspapers—radio and television— politicians and administrators could easily have surveys and polls taken. The unanticipated result was the realization of how ephemeral public opinion often is. Propaganda and advertising in the service of government, politicians, and business provided the solution. If the mass media allow for the expression of public opinion, they concurrently provide the means for its control.

In the nineteenth century, market research in America started with discovering the audience for magazine advertising.[47] The breakthrough came in 1911 when an advertising representative convinced Cyrus Curtis, publisher of *Ladies' Home Journal* and *Saturday Evening Post*, that he should know more about the products advertised and the customers the advertisers desired to attract. Charles Coolidge Parlin coined the term "commercial research" for the surveys Curtis had hired him to conduct. Perhaps his greatest contribution to market research was his 1914 five-volume study *Automobiles*, which included information on production, distribution, and consumers. Among other forecasts, he predicted the growing influence of women on men's automobile purchases.[48]

By the 1920s market research "compiled indexes of buying power in various areas, cataloged media coverage, and tabulated brand preferences at representative retail stores." The typical way advertising copy was tested was through a coupon the customer returned for a sample or premium; the coupon was "keyed" to reveal the kind of media, magazine or newspaper, kind of artwork, or kind of copy that had moved the customer to cut it out and send it in.[49] Of course no one really knew if returned coupons were related to future sales.[50]

Market research gradually became more sophisticated in the kinds of questions that were asked consumers and the directness of approach. Samples of consumers were sent complex questionnaires with the expectation that many consumers would reply. Americans were being asked their opinion about so many things that they felt it was both a duty and a right to share their consumer preferences with others.

Jonathan Robbin was one of the founders of niche marketing. A cheaper and more effective alternative to mass-market advertising, niche marketing involves matching a product to a less inclusive group using demographic data to construct the group, whether wealthy teens, wealthy retirees, ecological-minded professionals, or urban cowboys. The final step is to associate the product to be sold with images and slogans known to "touch" the defined or niche group. "Ads for organic ice cream and environmental banking, for example, grace the pages of the socially conscious lifestyle magazine *Utne Reader*."[51] There have even been attempts to create a typology of lifestyles. One study identified nine American lifestyles based largely on patterns of consumption (in the broadest sense of the term).[52] Obviously niche marketing operates to a certain extent as a self-fulfilling prophecy. The more advertising limits what it is selling to a specific group, the more that group's buying patterns will resemble the advertised lifestyle.

Political advertising employs a variation of niche marketing in its use of demographic lifestyle data to match political slogans to a statistical group (urban cowboys) so that a politician can be marketed like toothpaste. John F. Kennedy was the first politician to successfully use niche marketing to sell himself.[53] The politician becomes a moral chameleon who adapts his message to the views and interests of his audience. Never before have pollsters and social scientists asked people their opinion about so many products, issues, and events in the hope of manipulating their apparent predispositions.

From Nielsen ratings, first in radio and later in television, to the constant polling of viewers, listeners, and readers by the mass media, ascertaining public opinion has now become a form of entertainment as well as a business. Our view is only real if it has been recorded as a part of public opinion. As Tocqueville ironically observed in the nineteenth century, public opinion saves the individual the trouble of making up his own mind.[54] Our attitudes, behaviors, and life-styles must fit into measurable categories so that we can be persuaded to consume the images, goods, and information offered us. Each of us can belong to an almost infinite number of statistical groups according to either our social characteristics such as age, sex, class, ethnicity, and occupation or our patterns of consumption (lifestyle). Advertising aims to make the latter a function of the former and to reduce the former to the latter: a statistical group is what it consumes. Individuality is nothing more than the mishmash of statistical categories and consumer choices peculiar to each person.

Testing has been a growth industry throughout the twentieth century. One can make a distinction between authenticity tests that attempt to get at moral character, e.g., lie detector tests, and qualifying tests that strive to measure "innate" intelligence, acquired knowledge, personality, or vocational aptitude.[55] I am concerned here with qualifying tests. Medieval and Renaissance universities gave oral examinations to degree candidates. The exam or disputation consisted of the candidate defending his answers against the criticisms of a group of faculty. Perhaps the first written exam, in mathematics, occurred at Cambridge University in 1702.

American universities began to employ written examinations in the nineteenth century. As long as a uniform classical curriculum prevailed, exams were identical for all students and infrequently given. Once the elective system was introduced separate exams for each program of study and eventually for each course had to be provided.[56] The multiplication of exams brought with it the realization that exams were not merely a means of discovering what students had learned but also a way of controlling students. The threat of pop quizzes and endless exams was a stick to poor motivation. Studying for tests rather than to learn was an unintended consequence of the proliferation of exams. By the middle of the nineteenth century written exams had entered American public education.[57] All of education had been brought under the technology of testing.

Vocational aptitude tests emerged in the early twentieth century. With their penchant for the practical, Americans seemed especially devoted to the measurement of aptitude. The basic idea was to match the individual's talents, personality, and interests to the jobs available. Sometimes the latter took precedence over the former. Later in the twentieth century came the view that one might need to wait to administer vocational aptitude tests until the test taker had matured.[58] This idea suggests a tacit recognition that matching individual to job required little more than common sense.

The Scholastic Aptitude Tests (SAT), the bane of every aspiring college student in America, was created in 1926 by the College Entrance Examination Board. The scaling was revised in 1935 and assumed more of its present-day form; moreover, the tests could now be mechanically scored and taken on-line. In 1947 the College Entrance Examination Board merged with other groups to form the Educational Testing Service. Its stated goal was to classify the "nation's personnel" and to predict success in college.[59]

The testing of intelligence according to reasoning ability begins in 1904 with Alfred Binet in France. Dissatisfied with "medical" approaches to intelligence, he anticipated that by experimenting with divergent tests, each of which gets at a different intelligence, e.g., mechanical or abstract reasoning, he could arrive at a psychological method that would provide an index of a child's general potential. He repeatedly warned against the use of IQ tests to scale ordinally some single entity called intelligence. Aware that previous learning contaminated any measure of "innate" intellectual prowess, Binet insisted that scores on his tests did not measure anything that might be thought of as permanent intelligence. And he strongly urged that the scores only be used to point to a learning problem, not to stigmatize a child. His advice was roundly ignored in America, where to compound felony with felony, American educators in the main subscribed to a hereditarian theory of IQ earlier in the twentieth century. Stephen Jay Gould notes the paradox of a hereditarian theory of IQ (an American creation) in a country promoting equality.[60]

Nowhere did intelligence testing catch on as it did in America.[61] Indeed America was the home to and source of more tests than any other modern society. This is not surprising given America's tendency to define itself in terms of technology.[62] If the nineteenth

century witnessed an "avalanche of printed numbers," the twentieth century has been party to a continuous monsoon of statistics
about everything conceivably human.

Statistics: Moral and Normal

The widespread collection and use of statistics was assisted and
justified by the growth of the discipline of statistics. Moreover, the
coming together of statistics and mathematical probability created
an entirely different conception of human society and the individual. This new conception of normal people that replaced Enlightenment and Christian views of human nature is based on the
assumption of statistical equality. The collection of statistics is especially important because the underlying assumptions about
how to classify humans that govern their use are made real by
their use.

Classical probability theory was applied to mathematical problems and to gambling, but its entry into the moral sciences, such
as political philosophy (later called political economy), did not at
first lead to a redefinition of human nature. The Enlightenment
view of man, whether as hedonistic (Adam Smith) or naturally good
(French *philosophes*), was that he was rational. Most of them believed as well in some variation of natural law theory if only in
the principle of utility. But what united virtually all of the Enlightenment thinkers was the view that some humans, the cultured
elite in particular, were reasonable. Humans should be reasonable,
rational about acting in moderation, rational in anticipating the
consequences of their action, and rational about the grounds of
their beliefs. To be reasonable was to exercise common sense. The
latter is invariably a practical as well as a moral guide. Rational
humans would choose to obey the law and follow the dictates of
social morality if they were based upon reasonable beliefs and
held in place by reasonable punishments (theory of deterrence).

Probability theory was applied to the degree of certainty of
proof in legal proceedings during much of the eighteenth century.
What is the probability that a corroborated eyewitness is giving
accurate testimony? Or a witness who has vested interest in the

outcome? Some anticipated that their research into the "art of conjecture" would allow them to establish beyond jurisprudence the degree of certainty of proof for all beliefs. One could thus construct a reasonable basis for belief.[63]

The Enlightenment theory of human society was atomistic: rational individuals choose to enter into a social contract. The laws of society were natural laws: universal and discoverable through reason. The difference between the laws of nature and those of society resided in human freedom and reason. The laws of nature were necessary and involved no choice; the laws of society had to be gradually discovered because reason was imperfect, and they could be violated. Whether one based the moral order upon human rights (French version) or upon the principle of utility (British version), the seminal idea was that rational self-interest and a common moral order could be reconciled, indeed made one. Probability theory was essential to the establishment of a rational social order, that is, a society based upon reasonable beliefs. In sum, the Enlightenment belief reduced human society to the subjective reason of the individual who, even when looking to nature for guidance, creates the social order in concert with other like-minded individuals but always remains capable of violating its moral laws. By the mid-nineteenth century the moral laws of the Enlightenment were in transit to becoming statistical regularities if not statistical laws.

Simeón-Denis Poisson and A. A. Cournat, two nineteenth-century French probability theorists, made a sharp distinction between probability and chance. The former referred to the "degree of reasonable belief," whereas the latter pointed to "an objective property of an event," that is, the frequency of its occurrence.[64] Adolphe Quetelet advocated the latter view in his relentless attempt to prove that society was not merely a collection of individuals but a separate reality. There were two approaches to the concept of the normal distribution of frequencies that peaks around the mean (often referred to as the "bell curve"): the first was from coin-tossing, the second from observational astronomy. Quetelet became a social astronomer. He took the idea that errors in astronomical observation were distributed normally so that the best guess is most often the mean (the standard deviation is used as a measure of accuracy), and applied the normal curve to bio-logical and sociological phenomena. As Ian Hacking notes, *"he transformed the mean into a real quantity."*[65]

This act of reification has two aspects. First, Quetelet provided his readers with the "average man," who, for example, has been divorced 0.17 times and who has 2.2 children. Even though the average man does not exist, Quetelet situated him within a specific society, which makes the abstraction more concrete than if he had only been talking about the average of the human race. Second, and more importantly, he turned the probable errors of measuring unknown astronomical quantities into the "theory of measuring ideal or abstract properties of a population."[66] The abstract prop-erties of a society became as real as the unknown quantities as-tronomers attempted to measure. Now society could be studied as an entity that possessed abstract properties—not just crime rates (a favorite of the nineteenth century) but also public opin-ion—capable of being measured. Once that was accomplished there was nothing to prevent subdividing any population into a number of subpopulations or groups that are homogeneous ac-cording to some property. Hence we can place those labeled as having attention deficit disorder or the homeless into a population to be contrasted with those who do not have ADD or are not homeless by calculating a mean and standard deviation for each subpopulation in respect to the property being measured, e.g., crime. This leaves open the possibility of creating new categories or kinds of people that were not perceived as such previously.[67] We will come back to this issue shortly.

Once society was perceived to be a whole greater than the sum of its parts, attention turned to the patterns of society: statistical regularities, statistical laws, or social laws. Quetelet believed that the statistical regularities in society constituted statistical laws, but he explained these laws, e.g., a rate of crime over time, in terms of a multitude of "petty" causes acting upon individuals. The in-numerable little causes pressing upon someone to commit a rob-bery, for instance, was compared to the way gravity presses upon all objects. Some objected to the idea of statistical law because it contradicted the value of freedom. G. F. Knapp had an answer to Quetelet and his critics, however. He pointed out that despite

Quetelet's disavowal of the Enlightenment atomistic conception of society, his understanding of statistical law was atomistic: Quetelet had no proper concept of culture. A concept of culture allows one concomitantly to locate the causes of statistical laws in society and to permit human freedom. A culture gives meaning to and limits what its citizens can do but does not determine it (in the strong sense of the term).[68]

There were other social scientists, like Auguste Comte, who believed in social laws but concluded that they were nonstatistical. For Comte, society was an organism and could be studied much the way biological organisms had been in terms of description and classification. Émile Durkheim, the French sociologist, synthesized the views of Comte and Quetelet. Durkheim possessed an evolutionary, functionalist view of society. Culture was reduced to servicing the needs of society for order; if culture began to break down, society became pathological. Except in times of evolutionary transition to a new form of society, whatever was most widespread or normal in terms of social organization was likely to be functional to the maintenance of order. Durkheim believed statistical laws were an epiphenomenon of social laws. For example, he argued in *Suicide* that societal rates of suicide may be either normal or pathological when compared to the rates of other societies in a similar phase of evolution, but the causes are cultural forces, such as anomie or egoism, that affect societies and groups within society differentially.[69] Durkheim retained Quetelet's idea of the normal as a statistical average, but he applied it to a group of societies instead of individuals within society, and he placed it in an evolutionary context. Culture becomes exclusively a means of adapting to evolutionary pressures by maintaining order within society.

Culture for Durkheim is more about social control than meaning, for the latter necessarily involves the individual. Although the use of language is social, the meaning of discourse is malleable enough to be applied to both individual and collective experiences. Indeed individuals create new meanings through metaphorical comparison.[70] Despite his advocacy of individualism, Durkheim denied the full existence of the individual in his theory. Even his support of individualism was in the context of his belief that it is the final stage of social evolution—an individualistic society. Meaning is only collective meaning and functions exclusively to maintain order. Because Durkheim reified society and regarded it in functional terms, culture too is objectified to a certain degree; he failed to appreciate the potential in individuals and in language for radical change. Max Weber, his German counterpart in helping establish modern sociology, did not make this mistake.

Not everyone, however, believed that social laws were behind statistical regularities. Sir Francis Galton championed the idea of statistical laws. This great British statistician did not suggest that statistical laws, frequencies and correlations between frequencies could not be reduced to some underlying scientific principles. But he rejected the idea of deterministic social laws because they invariably regarded the statistical average as good. For Galton, who believed in individuality, what was good was the exceptional, the statistically abnormal. Galton asserted that statistical laws were autonomous (free from psychological and social laws). As Hacking notes, *"Statistical laws became autonomous when they could be used not only for the prediction of phenomena but for their explanation."*[71]

Sir Francis Galton often reflected on the topic of inherited traits. There appeared to be a normal distribution, albeit with some small change, of traits from generation to generation within a species. Outstanding families, however, seldom produced exceptional children, who in fact were often sired by ordinary parents. He understood this as a "reversion towards mediocrity," a mathematical consequence of the normal curve.[72] In effect he had explained a physical, psychological, and social phenomenon—reversion towards mediocrity—as a statistical law.

Galton was interested, among other things, in criminal identification, an application of anthropometry. One of his rivals had collected a set of measurements, height, length of arm, length of foot, and length of finger, that could help the police and criminologists identify criminals. Galton immediately recognized a correlation among the various measures, for short people would tend to have short feet, arms, and fingers; subsequently, he tested the idea with empirical data. The traits were correlated. An empirical measure of correlation could be computed, and this in turn was closely linked to the normal distribution. Galton believed "that from certain statistical laws about the distribution of traits one would deduce general phenomena about how traits are correlated."[73] The correlation that the statistical law explained now took on a life of its own; it become reified.[74] Galton's main contribution to the applied human sciences lay in the measurement of intelligence. Correlation, however, became so real to certain statistically-minded social scientists later in the twentieth century, as C. Wright Mills observed, that they often shopped for concepts to "explain" their empirical correlations as if the concepts were an afterthought. In such instances the concepts chosen were so concrete, so like the atomistic, empirical findings themselves, that they were of dubious value.[75] Correlation had become as real as the statistical average.[76]

The concept of normal is exceedingly complex, and is by no means an inherently statistical idea. Yet in a paradoxical way the statistical sense of normality eventually won the day. From the mid-nineteenth century to the present, there appear to be at least three meanings of normal, each of which is connotatively ambiguous. The term "normal" means, among other things, that which is typical. Now in the Enlightenment, "typical" was a moral concept and referred, at least for the French, to "man in general," that kernel of a good human nature that existed in all times and places. Man in general was only imperfectly realized in cultures that were superstitious and did not depend upon reason. For the French *philosophes*, the cultural elite who followed reason, represented a minority, who with the progress of the human race would some day become the great majority.[77] By the middle of the nineteenth century "typical" meant that which is common or usual. Man in general as an ideal that had now apparently materialized.

A second meaning of normal is that of a norm or an ideal state (notice the overlap between the first and second meanings). "Normal" means that which is perfect.[78]

Finally the term "normal" means that which is average, in the statistical sense. As we have seen, Quetelet championed this meaning. The statistical average refers to the mean, but "normal" here encompasses both the mean and the normal distribution. The statistical average or mean is good, for it represents that which is most general or widespread. The normal represents power and success.[79] The interweaving of these three meanings takes place within the context of medicine and the belief in scientific and technological progress.

Dispute about the normal and the pathological in nineteenth-century medicine centered about the following question: "Is the pathological merely a deviation from the normal, with both residing on the same continuum, or is the normal the complete absence of all symptoms of disease?" In the first instance the normal comes first, whereas in the latter the pathological comes first.[80] Comte credited Francois-Joseph-Victor Broussais with the idea that there is an empirical normal state from which pathology is a deviation. For Comte, society is an organ for which science can establish standards of normality or health. No need to refer to the Platonic world of ideas or a Christian philosophy for a concept of the normal state. Although Comte rejected a statistical conception of the normal state, he accepted the functionalist view that just as disease is not always fatal, but may in fact strengthen the organism that has to overcome it, so too deviancy may reinforce the social order.[81] Comte was a utopian as well. He believed that "positive" knowledge (scientific knowledge) would allow us to create technologically (applied science) the positive society of the future. He anticipated that industrial administrators and sociologists as "engineers of the soul" would set the technical norms for the perfect society of the future. The Comtean concept of the normal expresses a belief in technological progress.[82] What is normal today is "pathological" over against the perfect utopian state of the future society, but it is good insofar as it is necessary to create that future state. Progress implied continuity from past to future: the normal is improving. Comte rejected probability theory and Quetelet's statistical average, for he understood that statistics introduced an element of indeterminism into the social universe. For him science established deterministic laws.[83] Durkheim argued that one could retain a sense of statistical uncertainty (statistical law) only if one explained it as a function of social law.

Durkheim borrowed from Quetelet the concept of the normal as the statistical average and from Comte functionalism and an evolutionary perspective. As we have seen, Durkheim believed that that which is most general was in most instances successful (good). From an evolutionary perspective improvements in the species should be represented in the average member. Some have pointed to Durkheim's cultural conservatism and his critique of the twin pathologies of industrial society—egoism and anomie—as reflecting a desire to return to the past. Durkheim may have looked to the past, to Aristotle's concept of the golden mean, but he did so only in a formal way.[84] He was clearly a utopian in his vision of individualistic societies as the apex of social evolution and of professional ethics as a solution to anomie.[85] Evolution led to a future different from the past; otherwise it was not evolution.

Sir Francis Galton provides a final gloss on the term "normal." Galton believed that the statistical average as normal represented mediocrity. Truly exceptional members of any species "are to be found at the right hand end of the Normal curve of talent or virtue."[86] Not that which is most general but that which is unique is most valuable to a species or a society. On this point Galton opposed the social statisticians. On another he differed with Comte and his followers. Comte and Galton were interested in improving the human species—Galton through eugenics, Comte through social engineering—but each had a different unit of analysis. Galton was interested in the individual within the species, Comte with society. Ultimately, however, both were technicians and utopians. The normal for each expressed the tension between what is—the statistical average—and what is possible—technological perfection. The traditional conflict between what is and what ought to be had been subverted.

The two approaches vie for attention today. We vacillate back and forth between reducing society to a collection of biological organisms and treating society as the ultimate organism. Sociobiology and biotechnology turn the human being into just one more animal species, subject to the same genetic determinisms or, should I say, statistical regularities. Culture is an epiphenomenon of biological evolution. At the same time modern medicine has merged with the applied social sciences. If the social sciences early on promoted the view of society as a self-sufficient organism that moved between the poles of the normal and the pathological, modern medicine has increasingly adopted a systems approach in which human culture is a subsystem within the hierarchy of living systems (the biosphere is the largest subsystem). From this perspective the individual is a "unique collection of statistical errors" who needs to be reconstructed according to "optimal trajectories" of living.[87] These include biological, psychological, and organizational techniques that produce the healthiest, most efficient human being. All of life must be reduced to a technique, techniques to deal with stress, techniques to be happy, techniques to rear children, techniques to manage people. The doctor here becomes the team leader of a group of applied human scientists whose goal is nothing less than the management of *every* aspect of human existence.[88] Biotechnology plays a larger role in this endeavor to the extent that psychological and organizational techniques (the subject of Chapters 4 through 6) do not work efficiently.

Equality: Statistical and Social

Ian Hacking argues that normality is a metaconcept, a way of making sense out of people and their actions, and that the concept of normal people has replaced that of human nature.[89] The former is a statistical concept, the latter a moral one. I maintain that equality is also a metaconcept and that the metaconcept of normality is dependent upon it.

Before examining statistical equality, let us briefly look at the historical movement toward social equality. Population increase in the eighteenth century and ease of travel and communication made public opinion a formidable obstacle for every head of state. Public opinion was now perceived as power,[90] and the ruler's task was to control and guide it. Public opinion is a great equalizer, for as an abstract and thus impersonal force it makes everyone's view equal.

Industrialization gave rise to the equality of standardized, mass-produced consumer goods, but it was accompanied by bureaucracy, which made humans equal in applying the same procedural rules to customers and to coworkers. Indeed, Max Weber maintained this to be one of the characteristics of bureaucracy:

formalistic impersonality.[91] Equal treatment in the application of an abstract rule made everyone identical. It fostered both equality and efficiency at the expense of individuality.

As public opinion became more powerful, there was a cry for greater social and political equality. Tocqueville brilliantly observed that the discrepancy between the norm of equality and the fact of equality worked to create a passion for equality. This passion proved insatiable, for each step toward greater equality made the still extant inequalities, no matter how small, appear to be momentous. Whereas political and social equality (equality in the cultural conditions of life) did not necessarily occur simultaneously, in the United States both were being promulgated. Tocqueville observed that the political state also favored social equality because it made the citizens easier to govern; he appreciated the paradox—both citizens and government in favor of the same principle, but for totally different reasons.[92]

Perhaps no one has had greater insights into equality than Søren Kierkegaard. His discussion of "leveling" unites public opinion at the collective level with envy and moral resentment at the individual level. Due to a failure to act morally, by only reflecting on life's possibilities, the individual, who is already envious of those who accomplish more or have more, becomes resentful and brings the other down to his level by denigrating and ridiculing him. Leveling is transformed into a collective phenomenon; it becomes the "negative unity of the negative reciprocity of all individuals" through its expression in public opinion.[93] This is the main reason we delight in the downfall of celebrities.

The decline of Western moral communities in the nineteenth century is behind an extreme pluralism that necessitates equality as compensation. Because of their great achievements science and technology become identified with objectivity and truth. Religion and moral values in turn are gradually perceived to be subjective, a matter between the individual and God. Consequently, moral values become so ambiguous that they lose their unifying force. Moral ambiguity threatens the tacit trust that makes any group of people a community; human relationships as a result become vague, competitive, and dangerous. Now everyone is an individual without the mitigating influence of a moral community. Extreme pluralism is the result, so J. H. Van der Beg argues. A common morality united people without making them equal, for it required authority and individual discretion in applying it. Without it we need "equalizers" such as television, radio, newspapers, automobiles, and the like to create a pseudo-unity by objectifying our experiences.[94] Aesthetic communities organized around consumption supplant traditional moral communities. Behind all these forces that are creating an ever greater social equality, despite all the manifestations of a shallow and false individualism, is technology. Technology is the great equalizer, for it reduces both user and recipient to identical abstractions.

Only within a social milieu that was already predisposed to social equality could statistical equality have enjoyed such immediate success in the nineteenth century. Statistics creates social categories, and social categories have become statistical. The former is illustrated by the creation of the category *Hispanic* for purposes of collecting official statistics related to the census. Cuban Americans, Puerto Ricans, and Mexican Americans, among others, suddenly become Hispanics. Official recognition of this category helped to create a special-interest group in the political arena.[95] Prior to 1900 unemployment was the province of the individual, but upon collecting statistics on unemployment, the social category "unemployed" was created.[96] Unemployment was now a social problem. Every category creates the phenomenon it purports to classify and measure, or at least recasts it.

Hacking uses the term "human kinds" to refer to categories of humans defined according to some behavior or attitude seen to be characteristic of the person. The social sciences, especially sociology, helped bring human kinds into existence in the nineteenth century. Human kinds often reflect judgements about the normal and the deviant, and suggest acquiring greater knowledge to control the latter.[97] For example, Hacking has written about how the human kind "child abuse" was created sometime around 1960. Prior to this time "cruelty to children" was usually considered to be an individual act not a social problem.[98] Other examples include homosexuality, multiple personality disorders, alcoholism, autism, teenage pregnancy, and attention deficit disorder: all our human kinds created in the nineteenth or twentieth century. They are statistical types as well as human kinds, for each represents a statistical deviation from the mean—the average human being. The statistical social sciences have created human kinds, "statistical persons," who are either normal or deviant.

Just because some behavior or trait is statistically deviant is not sufficient to transform it into a human kind. Statistical regularities are not merely the product of statisticians who create categories; they reflect as well a certain kind of culture and social structure. For example, teenage pregnancy has been widespread in many parts of the world where young people married early. Teenage pregnancy is perceived as a social problem today because many are unmarried (traditional morality sometimes overlaps with the more recent statistical morality), because some are poor and likely to enlarge the welfare rolls, and because teen pregnancy is associated or correlated with additional problems such as dropping out of school and child abuse. As we have seen, statistical correlations are now perceived as real, so the search for correlations between deviant human kinds is relentless. Any human kind can be perceived as either an indicator of or cause of another. Child abuse now "appears" to be the root cause of other deviant human kinds.

Even traditional social categories, e.g., age, sex, and social class, are readily transformed into statistical categories because they are operationalized for research purposes, that is, taken out of their cultural context and treated as variables or things. Social class is often operationalized in terms of income, occupation, and education with little thought given to the culture of a class. Age and sex in one sense mean what they seem to mean; but, again, taken out of their holistic, symbolic context they become variables. Social scientists sometimes compound the problem by correlating social categories with the behavior of human kinds so that we may attempt to discover how much child abuse is explained statistically by class, sex, and age. Ultimately society becomes nothing more than a collection of statistical regularities and statistical categories. It makes little difference whether the category is a traditional one of *social structure* (age, sex, class) or a *kind of person* (child abuser, homeless) because the statistical category is the great equalizer—

it strips the meaning from a social category and the individuality from a human kind. Society is statistical and so are the individuals who comprise it.

With the triumph of statistics, the individual vanishes. First, the statistical category makes each individual equal in the possession of some trait or in the performance of an action. All the homeless are equal in being without a home. The meaning of the trait, behavior, or situation is not explored on either the cultural or individual level. In some instances, as with intelligence, we measure how much of a trait or characteristic one possesses, but all are equal in the possession of the same property. As we saw in the previous chapter, however, that which is truly qualitative does not exist on a continuum so that it can be scaled. Love is not an entity that we possess more or less than others. Each person's understanding of and ability to love is *different*. Qualities take on their meaning from the context, cultural, historical, and individual, of derivation and application. Gould's incisive criticism of IQ tests demonstrates how one of the most pernicious acts of reification works. Despite Alfred Binet's warning, American test makers believed that intelligence was singular, rather than being plural (multiple intelligences for reasoning, visualization, creativity, and so forth) and that intelligence was the same in kind for everyone so that our intelligences differ solely in terms of quantity.[99] Psychologists and sociologists have come up with scales to measure just about everything: intelligence, aptitude, love, charisma, and religiosity. Individuality is reduced to quantity. Second, the individual now becomes a collection of statistical categories, e.g., senior citizen, Buick owner. Uniqueness is my set of statistical categories, which never overlaps perfectly with anyone else's set of categories. The individual is stripped of his qualities and then reconstituted in terms of quantities.

Perhaps a better way of coming to the issue of the individual is through literature. In reflections on Don Delillo's *White Noise*, John Frow observes that conventionally the literary type, e.g., the miser, is preceded by a social type of miser. In one sense social reality precedes its representation in literature. Now realistic literature only imitates reality to a point beyond which it creatively reinterprets this reality. But both the social type and literary type are "embodied universalities"; they are holistic and concerned with the meaning of the person's actions and attitudes that are dramatized.[100] Too many details would cause us to lose sight of how the type is both general and particular. A social type is expressed differently in each culture according to particulars, but is recognizable as a literary type across culture because of what is general or universal.

Frow proceeds to demonstrate how Delillo shows that television simply provides us with details, particulars without meaning (fragmented types). He does this at times through overly-detailed description. One of the characters, Murray, proclaims:

> " 'He drove an orange Mazda.' You know a couple of useless things about a person that become major facts of identification and cosmic placement when he dies suddenly, after a short illness, in his own bed, with a comforter and matching pillows, on a rainy Wednesday afternoon, feverish, a little congested in the sinuses and chest, thinking about his dry cleaning."[101]

In its reliance on visual images, television only provides us with fragments in respect to holistic meaning, but totalities in regard to power. Each visual image, when language has become its subordinate, is a self-contained unit of power (what one person or thing does to another person or thing) whose impact is emotional. The individual represented in literature as a social type is buried in a sea of details on television. It is too concrete.

Statistical categories move in the opposite direction: they destroy the individual by making him general (in the sense of abstract, not of holistic meaning). Statistical categories reduce the details and complexity of an individual's life to one behavior that becomes a category. You are now one of the homeless. What is too abstract, however, as with abstract words, tends to become a substantive. Without meaning, each image, each word, each statistical category becomes concrete, a thing. Such words, images, and categories conspire to kill the individual.

Mark Seltzer has noted how the novels of Stephen Crane create characters at times who are generic or average. In satirizing the preoccupation with statistics, he adds types, like the prostitute or gambler, who sometimes have no names and little that is specific about themselves; in effect they are abstractions.[102] Honoré Balzac ridiculed the obsession with statistics in his own day. In *Physiology of Marriage*, Balzac humorously provided sixty-two pages of reflections on "conjugal statistics."[103] Although he attempted to classify humans the way animals are classified in zoology, he remained too much a student of history and morality to create statistical categories of human types.[104] In the twentieth century Don Delillo realizes what the logical conclusion of the proliferation of statistical information is: the self becomes a random collection of statistical categories and information. As one character says in *White Noise*, "you are the sum total of your data."[105] Delillo likewise recognized that the individual had become what he consumed: "I shopped with reckless abandon . . . I shopped for its own sake, looking and touching, inspecting merchandise I had no intention of buying, then buying it. . . . I began to grow to value and self-regard. I filled myself out, found new aspects of myself, located a person I'd forgotten existed."[106]

Daniel Boorstin talked about statistical communities and consumption communities supplanting moral communities in America in the late nineteenth and twentieth centuries.[107] Of course, what we consume and how much lends itself to being counted and placed in statistical categories. Only a moral community can provide one with a unified moral self, without which one cannot be a full individual, consistent, coherent, and free. An aesthetical approach to life places no limitations on experimenting with life except those of boredom or pain.[108] The aesthete can become anything and do anything as long as it is interesting and pleasurable. But for the individual with a moral self the limits are the respect for and love of others. Statistical categories and statistical frequencies define consumption—we call it fashion and lifestyle. It is the ephemeral and shallow freedom that a technological civilization provides in compensation for the disintegration of symbolic meaning, and with it culture and individuality.

The normal is now an epiphenomenon of statistics, which when applied to human culture and the individual turns quality into quantity and imperialistically imposes the equality of standardization upon the individual and society. Behind this is technology, which demands a statistical equality for everything it encompasses. In order to create a technology one has to construct a logical process; every logical outcome is subject to measurement.

Humans must be reduced to quantities, statistical categories and regularities; for that which is qualitative cannot be turned into a logical process or outcome.

I am mainly if not exclusively concerned with statistics as applied to cultures and individuals. Statistics can be misapplied to economic and demographic issues[109] and even to technological objects (consumer goods).[110] Pressure to make decisions even when the available data is misleading and to use propaganda to manipulate public opinion sometimes leads one to choose statistical indicators that are accessible but not easily justified. But statistics applied to human qualities are always wrong.

The technological system relies on statistical data so that every individual technique is both an efficient means of acting and a source of information for the coordination of related techniques. The technological system exists fundamentally at the level of information. Only through statistical information can technologies that are separated spatially be made to work together. Jacques Ellul has persuasively argued that the technological system is imposed inadvertently upon human society because of our blind faith in technology. Nothing can be allowed to remain outside the system; nothing can be excluded from statistical measurement; no knowledge, no judgement that is not technical can be permitted. The computer with its enormous ability to store and process information rapidly is the "nerve center" of the system. Without it technology could not have become a system.[111] Today the computer and statistical information are perceived to be synonymous. The system relies exclusively on information that is internal to its functioning; hence, it attempts to be a closed system. Yet the system butts up against human culture and the human personality; it provokes, represses, and in many ways creates a need for escape and compensation. Consequently, the technological system does not govern perfectly adapted individuals.

Magical Numbers, Magical Words, Magical Images

No one can doubt the power of numbers: the majority, the statistical average, the normal distribution. Nathan Keyfitz claims that "Numbers provide the rhetoric of our age."[112] But more than this they are the foundation for a set of magical practices that we variously refer to as administration or management. All attempts to measure goals and performance, all attempts to objectify decision-making and to predict the future are magical, imitation technologies applied to humans. We have no choice in the absence of shared symbolic meaning and common sense. There is nothing left but technique. When language has been tamed, when it is not in the service of creating and renewing symbolic meaning, it becomes an adjunct to visual images and numbers. We increasingly live in a materialistic world, for abstract words and numbers end up functioning like things. We vacillate back and forth between the abstract and the materialistic—our reality has become schizophrenic. Only the symbolic capacity of language can help us create an integrated concrete existence. Reality is on television (and related media) and in the computer. This is the main reason so many of us perceive the real world to be somewhere where we are not. Unable to integrate our experiences, we are susceptible to the magical practices described in the following chapters. The myth of technological utopianism provides the symbolic link between these magical techniques and the desired outcome: statistical information, which forms the basis for administrative magic, symbolizes *success*, whereas the dramatized information that is the foundation of psychological magic symbolizes *happiness* or *health*.

· 4 ·

The Mass Media as Magic

It was sometimes lonely in the grid of one, alone. People reached out toward their home, which was in television. They looked for help. . . . Celebrities have an intimate life and a life in the grid of two hundred million. For them, there is no distance between the two grids in American life. Of all Americans, only they are complete. . . . The most successful celebrities are products. Consider the real role in American life of Coca-Cola. Is any man as well loved as this soft drink is?

George W. S. Trow
Within the Context of No Context

He realized that all the things around him, the planes taking off and landing, the streaking cars, the tires on the cars, the cigarettes that the drivers of the cars were dousing in their ashtrays—all these were on the billboards around him, systematically linked in some self-referring relationship that has a kind of neurotic tightness, an inescapability, as if the billboards were generating reality.

Don Delillo
Underworld

Advertising and public relations are intimately related, and both are heavily dependent upon the mass media for their effectiveness. Television is the most important vehicle for the dissemination of advertising and public relations. Yes, advertising is omnipresent on the Internet, in magazines, and on billboards; but Americans, and increasingly members of other societies as well, spend more time watching television than participating in any other leisure activity. For now anyway, television is the home of advertising and public relations. In this chapter I will be examining the complex of advertising (public relations) and television programs as the center of magical images and practices in a technological civilization. The mass media are a hybrid of technology and magic. Insofar as they consist of machines, e.g., cameras, computers, and recorders, the media are forms of material technology. In their reliance on dramatized information, however, they act as forms of magic or imitation techniques whose chief purpose is to control public opinion.

The Fabrication of Images

Advertising can be dated to the onset of markets (milieu of society), but it only becomes a major force in the life of society late in the nineteenth century. The rise of advertising to a prominent position in society was aided by the newspaper. New techniques for printing and a growing readership provided fertile grounds for the growth of advertising. For a time newspaper advertising was held back by the tiny size of the agate type that had long been mandatory. Large department stores, which were the largest employers of newspaper advertising and were already using display presentation and illustration techniques in their in-house brochures and flyers, were pressing newspapers to do the same.[1] Joseph Pulitzer with the acquisition of the New York *World* in 1883 and William Randolph Hearst with his newspaper chain permanently changed the form and content of newspaper advertising. The display presentations in advertising aped the sensationalistic headlines: the newspaper and its ads were becoming one. Expenditures on advertising, largely in the print media, increased from $15 million in 1870 to over $140 million in 1908.[2] Newspapers claimed the largest share of advertising revenue.

Magazines, however, shortly began to rival newspapers in the competition for advertising income; indeed some magazines were expressly created for the purpose of advertising.[3] Religious periodicals, numbering around 400 in 1870, dominated the periodical advertising market for at least a decade and received a large percentage of advertising revenue. The N.W. Ayer and Son advertising agency was established by profits from the solicitation of advertising for religious magazines. With no sense of irony, Frank

Presbrey observes that at the same time these periodicals often rejected patent-medicine ads they accepted those from insurance companies. The latter industry proved to be the major advertiser in religious periodicals.[4]

By 1890 women's magazines had surpassed religious periodicals in the acquisition of advertising. Cyrus Curtis, founder of *Ladies' Home Journal*, did more to promote magazine advertising than any other publisher. By 1888 the *Ladies' Home Journal* had at least twice as much advertising as its women's magazine competitors; by 1892 its circulation exceeded that of every other periodical whatever the subject matter.[5]

In 1897 Curtis acquired the *Saturday Evening Post*, a literary magazine from the early nineteenth century (which even earlier had ties to Benjamin Franklin's *Pennsylvania Gazette*). Freely mixing popular culture with high culture (as in his claim to have the "best poems in the world" and "great speeches of famous Americans" side by side with stories of "American money kings" and "practical sermons by the great preachers"), Curtis increased the circulation of the *Post* from 2,000 to 200,000 in three years. By 1928 the circulation had risen to nearly three million and its advertising income exceeded $48 million.[6]

Just as Pulitzer and Hearst had helped narrow the difference between news and the ads by making each spectacular, so did Curtis with mass-market magazines. But it was more than headlines and personal interest stories. The very *tone* of the popular magazine was that of advertising. Creating an amalgam of "plain talk" and "tall talk" the mass-market magazine effectively used a simple, direct, yet persuasive, style that resembled a "pitch." Concurrently there was an editorial emphasis on stories that glamorized the commonplace and everyday, that in effect created a "romance of real life."[7] The advertising style present in the *Saturday Evening Post* and the *Ladies' Home Journal* found an eager group of imitators in the magazine trade.

Radio advertising had to await the formation of national networks of affiliated stations to take off. The percentage of weekly programs that had regular sponsors followed the increase in radio stations that became nationally affiliated. Between 1937 and 1947 the percentage of stations that were members of a network in-

creased from 46 to 97. National ad agencies and the largest businesses effected this dramatic change and until 1941 controlled
radio programming directly.[8] The radio soap opera, a tremen-
dously popular genre, was the brainchild of advertising agents
who realized that people were bored with information presented
all day in a matter-of-fact way. The use of music in both programming and advertising further cemented the relationship between
communications media and advertising style.[9]

Of course nothing captured the public's attention more than
television. As it became apparent that people read less and
watched more, that they took their news from television, and that
the visual image was a more effective advertising tool than the
written or spoken word, advertising agents and advertisers found
a variety of ways to realize television's enormous potential as an
advertising medium. None of the other media was able to make
its stories or programs so completely blend into the style and content of advertising as effectively as television.

Even more than television soap operas, game shows exploited
the very tendency toward consumerism that advertising preyed
upon. But it is the common style even more than content that has
united advertising and television: camera angles, dialogue, acting,
and music. "Advertising uses television programming as a system
of reference; returning the favor, programming uses advertising
as its framework and in some cases its exemplar. 'Sesame Street'
adopted the pacing of advertising to the task of teaching pre-
schoolers."[10] The reverse is that some television advertisements
imitate the music video format with its fragmentation of time and
space and resultant dream-like mood.[11]

The movement of new media into the arena of advertising did
not pit medium against medium in a winner-take-all war for advertising revenue. On the contrary, each time a new communications medium took hold, there was a sizable increase in the total
amount advertisers spent for advertising. Magazines, radio, and
televison successively added to the overall fortunes of advertising
agents and the communication media.[12]

If the amount spent on advertising by advertisers increased, so
did the reliance of the mass communications media on advertising
revenue. Today radio and television are almost totally dependent

on advertising money for their operating expenses; newspapers receive about 75 percent of their income from advertising and magazines between 60 and 100 percent.[13]

The advertising agencies rationalized the relationship between advertisers and the communications media. Until 1875 the agencies' clients were the media: they assisted in the location of advertisers. Once the power of advertising was widely recognized, the ad agencies found clients among the advertisers.[14] After 1875 the shift in clientele was more or less complete: now the agencies worked for the advertisers. At the bidding of the major businesses, agencies helped the media better understand their respective audiences and shape the form and content of programs to sell products more efficiently.[15] At the same time the agencies explained to businesses what media best served their needs. The agencies were information brokers between two clients: the first (the paying client) had a manufactured product or consumer service to sell; the second had an audience and a communication medium to sell to the first.

Undoubtedly the most profound change in the ability of advertising to persuade people to consume more was the increased reliance on the visual image. After 1910 there was a steady decline in the text and a great increase in display and illustration in print advertising.[16] In his study of magazine advertising between 1920 and 1940, Roland Marchand identified the "visual cliché" as the critical form of advertising appeal. The visual cliché is a set of visual images that form a familiar scene at once both idealized and desirable. By associating a product with the scene, advertising encourages the viewer to transfer the qualities of the scene to the product. The earlier "parables" of the advertising text, such as the "democracy of goods," were being translated into "more emotional, icongraphic forms."[17]

The public relations industry, born in the twentieth century, developed much later than its advertising sibling.[18] Earlier, companies sometimes hired "press agents" to provide advertisements and publicity to newspapers for a minimum price, even free when possible. These early public relations practitioners were flamboyant characters, at times con artists and drifters, who wheedled their way into the confidence of newspaper men. Some came from the ranks of underpaid reporters, who already knew something about the newspaper trade, even to be disillusioned about earning a living at it. Their reputation was so low that in 1911 Will Irwin referred to them as "the only group of men proud of being called liars."[19] At this stage, public relations was almost exclusively concerned with publicity;[20] image was still to come.

Edward Bernays, the self-proclaimed founder of public relations, attempted to ascertain the impact of publicity on the public. To do so he turned to the applied social sciences, especially social psychology. Bernays argued on behalf of the scientific manipulation of public opinion—propaganda—as necessary to stabilize a society riven by a series of social problems. He often used public opinion polls as a way of influencing opinion leaders. For instance, he commissioned a poll of doctors about breakfast. Discovering that they recommended people eat a "hearty breakfast," he sent the results to 5,000 physicians with the message that bacon and eggs constituted a hearty breakfast.[21] Bernays was an image-maker: bacon is an essential part of a doctor-recommended hearty breakfast. Among his other feats, he organized the march of New York debutantes, lighting and smoking cigarettes, in the 1929 Easter Parade. George Washington Hill, President of the American Tobacco Company, maker of Lucky Strikes, hired Bernays, who of course not only took credit for the subsequent increase in the sale of Lucky Strikes, but as well claimed that his genius fostered the growth of the public relations industry.[22]

Advertising is so pervasive today that it is the background for everything we do. Taking into account billboards, logos, and labels, as well as television, radio, and Internet advertisements, some studies estimate that we are exposed to 16,000 ads each day.[23] Some cable stations are devoted exclusively to advertisements, and infomercials seem increasingly prevalent. Public relations is omnipresent as well. Several public relations experts estimate that over 70 percent of information disseminated as news is actually public relations.[24] Entire sections of the newspaper are virtually the province of public relations: entertainment, real estate, automotive, food and beverage, and home repair. PR people, whether trained as journalists or not, know how to write publicity that apes news stories. "Video news releases," complete news stories that appear to be the actual thing, are transmitted by satellite to TV stations in various countries. A public relations executive claims that most of the TV news is a "canned PR product." This remark might appear self-serving except that in 1995 the number of public relations practitioners outnumbered reporters by 20,000— 150,000 to 130,000. Furthermore, expenditures on public relations in America are at least 10 billion dollars a year.[25] As public relations experts have turned their attention to the image of celebrities and brands, advertising and public relations have fused. Indeed, virtually every major New York ad agency owns or has an agreement with a large public relations firm.[26] One group of analysts views advertising as a speciality within the field of public relations;[27] another views advertising as "paid media" and public relations as "free media."[28] Public relations sometimes involves covert and disreputable activities that go beyond media coverage of an event: "crisis management, industrial espionage, organized censorship and infiltration of civic and political groups."[29] Yet advertising and public relations both attempt to create an image for a product, a company, or a celebrity through the use of the mass media.

Daniel Boorstin terms the image a "pseudo-ideal," for it is "synthetic, believable, passive, vivid, simplified, and ambiguous."[30] In other words, an image is aesthetical rather than ethical: it only has to be believable and interesting. And what is believable includes almost anything in an age of rapid technological innovation, the politicization of life, and a loss of belief in language and the concept of truth. Witness the proliferation of paranoid conspiracy theories and the absurd rumors that abound on the Internet.

Advertising and public relations create images for products, people, and organizations in a variety of ways. William Leiss et al. have identified four approaches to advertising: product information format, product image format, personalized format, and lifestyle format. The product information format was the dominant approach to advertising throughout most of its history. It provided consumers with information about the product: sizes, colors, cost, effectiveness. Often it worked like a scientific demonstration, proving that the product was effective or more efficient than its competitors.[31]

After 1925 American advertising discovered that consumers were equally irrational; approaches that appealed to desire competed with the product information format. The visual image became more dominant in advertising; the text was now its adjunct. Visual images whose primary impact is emotional, were better suited to demonstrate consumer satisfaction than product efficiency.[32] Increasingly advertisers relied upon the appeal to desire to motivate consumers.

The product image format, personalized format, and lifestyle format depend upon "symbolic" associations. The product image format makes the product come alive by placing it in a natural or human context. The product acquires life and power through its association with nature and human beings. The personalized format stresses what the use of the product will do for the consumer—make one happier, more successful, more admired, and so forth. The power of the product works on behalf of the consumer. The lifestyle format associates a product with a collective style of life that includes friends, activities, and products. The collective lifestyle is supposed to be one that the targeted group of consumers will wish to emulate, e.g., college age beer drinkers playing sports in the mountains.[33] Given that lifestyle is largely a matter of consumerism, the product to be sold is the center of the lifestyle with which the lifestyle is associated. The product is associated with itself and other products. In a sense, the personalized and lifestyle formats explain the product image format. The latter format makes the product come alive and acquire power, which means the power to fulfill the consumer and to create an entire lifestyle. If the product begins by acquiring power from nature and humans (product image format), it ends as a more powerful force (personalized and lifestyle formats). Because it is an awe-inspiring force, the product can eventually stand alone in the ad. As ads for both Volvo and Buick at different times have proclaimed, "Volvo (or Buick)—something to believe in." We may scoff at such claims, but emotionally what is interesting and exciting is believable.

Advertising and public relations experts are so aware of the primacy of the image in communications that they have fashioned companies that specialize in creating images. In 1991 Chuck Pettis created a company that creates "technobrands" for clients. Part of the motivation was the perceived need to differentiate Floathe Johnson from other advertising/public relations firms.[34] Clive Chajet, Chairman and CEO, Lippincott and Margulies, refers to his company as America's oldest firm that features "identity and image management." He describes his company's handling of Nissan's venture into the luxury car market. Rarely does a company have the opportunity to create an "integrated image" for a product several years before its manufacture. Here was an opportunity to create the name and logos as well as to work with the design team on the car's image. Lippincott and Margulies created the name *Infiniti*, which they believed met the following criteria to convey the image of a luxury car:

1. It must project the notions of luxury and quality; be consistent with the idea of an international, "world-class" product; and connote state-of-the-art technology. Top of the line. None better.
2. It must nourish the idea of exclusivity—prestige—status— and signal all of these to discerning, differentiating car enthusiasts.
3. It must project the image of uniqueness and of those timeless/ excellence attributes that we associate with the best of Japanese culture, as well as the personal enhancement to be gained from purchasing the product and having that purchase appreciated within one's social set.
4. It must project the image of a product keyed to provide customer satisfaction, beginning with the "human engineering" design of it, and carried through in the way it is sold, in personalized owner care, and in hassle-free service.
5. Beyond these, the name would have to be proprietary—not a dictionary word, but sounding as if it were, and conveying the idea that the product so named would be the ultimate car you could buy.[35]

One can readily discern the product image, personalized, and lifestyle formats in the above list of criteria.

The manufacturing of celebrities is an area of specialization within the advertising–public relations complex; it is now referred to as an "industry." It is difficult to ascertain the expenditures on creating, promoting, and transforming the image of a celebrity, but the entertainment industry would disappear without it.[36] The history of the celebrity industry parallels that of public relations so that it is largely a post–World War I phenomenon. Within the industry, the question arises, "Can people be shaped into products?" Several enthusiasts argue that the "limits of stretchability are expanding all the time." "It may be that people are becoming more easily transformed than traditional products are. After all, Heinz ketchup cannot be turned into Lipton tea."[37]

The transformation of singer Olivia Newton-John's image in the 1980s is an apt example. Record sales were off; her career was declining. The task was to alter her image of the girl next door to that of a "smoldering seductress." The strategy worked on several levels. First, instead of photographs of her kindly holding kittens, there now were photographs of her in tight pants lying on a "red satin sheet surrounded by flames." Second, her agent arranged to have the "news" of her marriage to a much younger actor released to the media along with quotes that she and her husband were behaving like children all over again.[38]

One of the main goals of a political candidate is to become a celebrity. One needs a public relations director to insure free media coverage and an advertising agency to work on political advertisements. The political sound bites get shorter and shorter, which hurts the few candidates who really have something to say but helps those who have nothing to sell but an image. The world of politics is encapsulated in the universe of media images.[39] The media inadvertently acknowledged this in the 1988 presidential campaign when the networks spent more time on how politicians create their images than on their views and programs.[40]

The Culture of Advertising

Daniel Boorstin has called advertising the "omnipresent, most characteristic, and most remunerative form of American literature." It was "destined to have an intimate popular appeal and a gross national influence without parallel in the history of sacred and profane letters."[41] At another time he referred to advertising as America's folk culture.[42] This folk or popular culture is the only living culture today, because high culture survives only as nostalgia for the few remaining serious readers. If advertising is the American culture, then consumerism is its way of life. Advertising both reflects and stimulates consumerism. If culture is both a set of symbols and a way of life, then the advertising-consumerism complex is the American culture, the American Way of Life.[43]

Culture has always been based on a set of lived or primary experiences that were symbolically mediated through language in a way that left those experiences with their subjectivity still intact. Not so today. Our skills are increasingly objectified in technology, at the same time our experiences are objectified in the mass media. A technological civilization conspires against the individual by making public opinion supreme. But public opinion can only be expressed through the mass media. Advertising and public relations attempt to manipulate public opinion, but have to serve it as well. The reason is that both the former and the latter reflect the deepest beliefs of a technological civilization. Technological societies are best characterized as mass societies, societies that concomitantly promote collectivism (bureaucracy and public opinion) and a pseudo-individualism (the shallow, aesthetical freedom of consumerism). It is here that advertising becomes the dominant culture.

The culture of advertising can best be understood in relation to public opinion, the spectacle, and the celebrity. Public opinion is based on second-hand knowledge rather than on experience or readily intelligible facts.[44] Public opinion is a necessary component of a mass society; it is a substitute for interpersonal knowledge that arises from practical, everyday life in the context of intense familial and friendship relations. The mass media provide us with ersatz experiences upon which opinion rests. If, as Boorstin notes, personal knowledge is phenomenal, public opinion is epiphenomenal;[45] it is concerned with what most of us know little about through experience or serious thought. Therefore public opinion is secondary both in regard to its source—the mass media—and its type of knowledge—epiphenomenal.

Just as obvious as public opinion's artificial character is its fragmentation.[46] There is no coherence nor continuity to the totality of opinions. A sure sign of fragmentation is the inconsistent if not contradictory quality of many opinions. For example, American opinion supports preserving the environment and economic growth simultaneously. Opinions are always out of context, for issues are presented to the public consecutively as self-contained entities; they resemble facts that appear to be autonomous. The fragmentation of opinion is a reflection of the fragmentation of information conveyed through the media.[47] Infatuated with the new and the sensational, the media unintentionally destroy the memory of the past.

In part as a consequence of fragmentation, public opinion is based on simplified issues.[48] Complex and profound problems can only be resolved, and even then only rarely, through long and arduous discussion. Because opinion forms (or is pressured to form) on an enormous number of issues, many of which are outside of most people's personal expertise, the media must simplify the issue. Only then can public opinion emerge. Criticism of American politicians, for example, sometimes centers on their tendency to simplify issues, when the problem is actually much more a result of the mass media that can only operate profitably through simplification and of the public, which, no matter how well educated, due to technical specialization, is ignorant about most issues. Inefficient bureaucracy, for instance, comes under attack from the political right in its assault on bloated government, when the evidence is rather strong that bureaucracy under certain circumstances is highly efficient and that big business is itself highly bureaucratized.[49]

If public opinion is knowledge (albeit simplified and secondary) at one level, it is desire and fear at another. This is evident in the very terms under which opinion is solicited—"agree or disagree," "yes or no," "approve or disapprove," "like or dislike." The relationship between technology and public opinion rests largely on the titillation of desire. Public opinion, which is founded upon desire, is receptive to technological possibility because technology as illustrated in advertising promises the good life now. Technology modifies desire just as public opinion demands the realization of the desired technological goods and services.[50]

Public opinion is decidedly ephemeral.[51] Because it is based upon desire, envy, and fear, public opinion is an aesthetical phenomenon. Its "norms" change as everyday life changes and new objects of desire emerge. Public opinion is tied to current events and technological possibility. Current events are often the least important aspect of political life, but the part most amenable to dramatic presentation in the media. Current events are transformed into political spectacle.

The symbiotic relationship between advertising and public opinion is recognized in the spectacle. This idea is so important than we must consider Guy Debord's theory.[52] In technological societies all of life has been transformed into an image/object for immediate consumption. The spectacle includes both commodities as visual images and material visual images of commodities. The spectacle is the "language" of the commodity; it is the visualization of the commodity for spiritual consumption. The spectacle idealizes reality by turning it into a speculative universe ruled by a kind of logical concept—the commodity form. Moreover, it strips existence of both experience and meaning and thus makes it abstract. Concurrently, however, the spectacle reifies existence in the visual image and therefore makes reality thoroughly materialistic. The spectacle is the "apologetic catalogue" for the totality of technological objects; in consuming an object, one consumes the whole.[53]

Human beings become objectified as commodities, and as such are equal to their image. The spectacle turns existence into "appearing" over against being and doing. As the spectacle tends to eliminate the distinction between image and reality, there is less difference between living and vicarious living. Ultimately the image becomes more important than lived reality itself. Life becomes a picture show, a screen onto which images are projected. Life as spectacle is a purely aesthetical existence; everything is judged as interesting or boring. Advertising attempts to make consumer goods and services spectacular, and public opinion demands that which it has been conditioned to desire—the spectacle.

The celebrity is "the spectacular representation of a living human being." The celebrity "embodies the image of a possible role," and only exists to act out certain lifestyles.[54] Every celebrity plays a variety of roles and thus becomes the "center where general tendencies meet."[55] That is, the celebrity is an *average* human

being, but one whose life has been glamorized and romanticized.[56]
This makes it easier for the audience to identify with the celebrity:
the celebrity is just like me. At the same time, however, the celebrity is infinitely far away, dwelling in the "promised land of total
consumption."[57] The celebrity is only an image, if a spectacular
one, and as such can be created and transformed arbitrarily. The
celebrity is a caricature of the human, a visual stereotype. But
there are other celebrities—products—who are the real stars of
our advertising culture.[58] As we have seen in advertising formats,
the symbolic approaches to advertising all stress the power of the
product. If human celebrities are crucial to advertising, celebrities
are themselves first and foremost commodities.

The devotion of fans to celebrities is highly irrational; clearly
many people have a tacit need to live vicariously through a star.
At the same time, however, the public delights in the scandal, the
expose, the idol with feet of clay. This paradox is best explained,
I think, in terms of the decline of moral communities and the rise
of a mass society. Only a moral community can provide citizens
with common purpose and a minimal level of trust. Without this
our relationships to each other become vague and dangerous;
moreover, our existence becomes lonely.[59] J. H. van den Berg
terms modern psychopathology "the science of loneliness."[60] As
compensation for this loneliness and as a way of masking it, we
exhibit a "pseudo-cheerfulness" toward each other, like that of
the used-car salesman, pretending to overcome the almost insur-
mountable gulf between us.[61] And with celebrities (including
products) we develop a "pseudo-intimacy." For only celebrities
have both a public life and a private or intimate life. But if our
private lives are driven by anxiety, mistrust, and loneliness and if
an ideal reality is in the media, then what is public (the celebrity)
has to fill the void of our private existence.[62] Our pseudo-intimacy
with celebrities still leaves us detached observers or spectators. It
is here that our ambivalence toward celebrities and others takes
root. Better than anyone else, I think, Søren Kierkegaard has made
sense of this ambivalence.

Among Kierkegaard's most penetrating insights is the idea that
the public is formed not only by the mass communications media
(the newspaper and pamphlet in his day) but also by individuals

becoming detached observers of others.[63] This condition of being an onlooker to life involves a complex of intellectual and psychological processes: reflection, envy, and moral ressentiment (destructive envy that desires less to imitate the other than to see him brought down to one's level). Kierkegaard opposes reflection first to passion, then to action.

In a period of moral dissolution, relationships between individuals become ambiguous in that the aesthetical interests of each party are in conflict and yet remain partially concealed both to self and other. It is not polite to admit one's selfish motives. This leaves the individual in a state of "reflective tension." Rather than an inward relationship regulated and given meaning by moral qualities such as trust and self-sacrifice, the relationship has become external. In Kierkegaard's formulation, passion can only be expressed by those whose relationship to others is inward, that is, ethically qualitative. With the decline of inwardness and passion, one's relationship to the other becomes concurrently that of aesthetic possibility and ethical indifference. As such the relationship must necessarily become abstract, the object of theoretical reasoning (reflection). Life in a "reflective age" assumes the characteristics of a game in which one plots one's moves in advance in order to maximize one's chances for success.

Reflection itself, Kierkegaard maintains, is not the problem, but rather reflection that does not result in action, reflection that becomes an escape from action. When reflection is not accompanied by inward moral commitment, envy ensues. The powers of reflection are at the disposal of selfish desires. One envies others, their possessions and accomplishments. "Selfish envy" actually deters the individual from decisive action; instead time is spent ruminating about one's possibilities or what it would be like to be someone else. At this point Kierkegaard draws a startling conclusion about the modern reflective and passionless age: *"envy is the negative unifying principle."*[64] This envy has both individual and collective manifestations, for the envy within the individual has its counterpart in the envious attitudes of others. As we shall shortly see, the chief way in which this collective envy is expressed is through public opinion.

When the envy that is present in reflection as aesthetic possibility is not punctuated by decision and action, it spills over into moral ressentiment. Assuredly ressentiment is present in every age, but what makes it different in the modern era is "levelling." By this Kierkegaard means the attitude that no one is better than I am. Because of a lack of moral character, the individual denigrates and even ridicules those who have distinguished themselves. It is not enough to admire and envy the other: one must tear him down. Levelling to be effective must be done in concert with others; it is essentially a collective phenomenon. Whereas it was once the province of a social class or occupation, in a reflective and passionless age it is accomplished by the public. The public is an abstraction in that the members do not interact with one another; therefore, the public's opinion must be expressed through the mass media. Because moral ressentiment takes the form of levelling in a time of passionless reflection, and because levelling is expressed through public opinion, public opinion both creates and is an expression of the "negative unity of the negative reciprocity of all individuals."[65] Kierkegaard's brilliant insights help us to better understand the tendency for the media, even more so today, to "level" every politician, movie star, and celebrity. And, to follow Kierkegaard again, because we have become onlookers to life, we can't get enough of the expose, the scandal, and the conspiracy. The individual has become a "fractional part" of the public and as such delights in levelling. Public opinion, in Kierkegaard's formulation, expresses desire (positive up to the point of selfish envy) and ressentiment. Our pseudo-intimacy and pseudo-cheerfulness conceal envy and fear that can only safely be expressed in public opinion.

The American culture of advertising is a culture of propaganda.[66] Advertising and public relations play a large part in making language a servant to visual images and thus freeing words to be used more readily for purposes of manipulation. Truth in a technological civilization becomes equivalent to success or power. But what "truths" does advertising promulgate, and what myth undergrids it? If advertising is a culture, then like all cultures it must organize symbolically the collective experience of the sacred.

Technological Utopianism: Myth and Ritual
of an Advertising Culture

Every culture is anchored by a sense of the sacred (the life-milieu) that is expressed in a narrative or myth about the origin of the world and its future; moreover, these mythological beliefs must be put into practice or ritualized. This complex of myth and ritual help to unify a society and to control both individual and social diversity. Willem Vanderburg terms this the "dialectic of culture," the tension between the pressures toward unity and conformity and those toward the diversity of individuals and groups.[67] Too much unity results in totalitarianism, whereas excessive diversity creates anarchy. We will come back to this point later, but only observe now that the major etiological myth of a society normally maps out a normative relationship between unity and diversity. What do men and women, young and old, share in common? In what ways should they be different? Myth attempts to provide an answer.

Technological utopianism[68] is the myth of a technological civilization, and it resides in advertising and the programs of the mass media. We will first look at advertising by itself and later in relationship to television programs. The mythological values of advertising culture have been identified by a host of researchers. Advertising poses to and answers for the consumer the fundamental question: "How can I be happy through consumption?"[69] Advertising sells "well-being and happiness."[70] Happiness is the paramount value of advertising culture and as such is the most general; it implies and is related to all the others. Happiness is portrayed in advertising as pleasure, increased consumption.[71] Leisure time is the opportunity for consumption and pleasure; hence leisure activity predominates over work in advertising.[72] Happiness is located in the ecstatic expressions on the faces of the actors or models. Even the family when portrayed in advertising is the locus of or background for paradise.[73] By 1940, the American Dream, as expressed in advertising, suggested that "you can have it all."[74]

Second only to happiness and directly related to it in the general idea of well-being is health.[75] Allied to the value of health are those of beauty and youth. All three refer to dimensions of the human body: health refers to the perfection of the body or at least its general maintenance; beauty refers to its pleasing external appearance; youth, to a combination of health and beauty, to a perfected state of existence. In advertising, youth is reality.[76] "Women are the chosen victims of the 'youth cult,' " in part because they were identified earlier in the twentieth century as the major consumers.[77]

Success and high status as advertising values appear less frequently than the above values. Even here, because of the preponderance of leisure over work in the ads, high status and success are realized in consumption.[78] After 1965 there was a marked emphasis on lifestyle in advertising.[79] The lifestyles portrayed are, of course, those of successful and higher status people engaged in activities rather than merely using a product. The activities are leisure activities and are thus presented as consumer services.

Friendship and love appear even less frequently than status and success.[80] If one makes a distinction between sex and love, this finding is not surprising. After 1930 the sensual appeal of products received much greater attention,[81] as did the use of sex to sell the products. Then, too, love and friendship are subtle qualities, difficult to visualize. They are not well matched with the medium of television.[82]

Advertising depicts freedom in two related ways: the free world with its plethora of goods, and the enormous number of choices consumers have. A Wendy's commercial of the 1980s plays this to perfection. In the ad, a small group of Russians sit watching a fashion show in which a stout woman stylelessly attired wears the same garment to show the audience the latest in daywear, beachwear, and nightwear. Quickly the scene changes to the United States where freedom is shown to be choosing what to put on your burger while at Wendy's.

All of the above mythological values are an expression of consumerism and can be reduced to consumer pleasure and choice—happiness and health. Yet the mythological symbols of technological utopianism are better understood in the context of the structure or logic of advertising than in terms of its atomistic content.

I refrain from calling this a narrative structure because of the predominance of visual images in advertising.[83] Neil Postman has exposed this logic admirably in his interpretation of a classic ad, "The Parable of the Ring around the Collar." The ad finds a married couple who normally get along well in a commonplace setting, a restaurant; the waitress notices the husband's dirty shirt collar and calls attention to it. The husband is upset and the wife embarrassed. The next scene shows the wife using the correct detergent that eliminates the unseemly ring around the collar. Finally the couple returns to the restaurant enveloped in ecstatic rapture. [84] In Postman's analysis there is a narrative in the ad that takes this form: problem, solution, ecstasy. The problem is the dirty collar along with the husband's anger over the social embarrassment; the solution is the advertised brand of detergent; ecstasy is the satisfied expression on the faces of the couple in the aftermath of the solution.

I think, however, that there are two distinct but closely related logics at work in this single ad. Moreover, I maintain that all ads contain either one or the other and often both of these logics. Finally, I suggest that these two logics illustrate perfectly the two dimensions of the myth of technological utopianism: the objective power of technique and its subjective impact upon the consumer. The two logics are: problem to solution and discontent to content. The problem-solution logic was dominant in advertising until the early twentieth century in a product information format. After 1925 advertisers began to use approaches that appealed to the consumer's desire to be happy. Therefore, the personalized and lifestyle formats emphasize what the product can do for the consumer in terms of pleasure. The second logic, then is discontent to content. Sometimes the discontent is explicitly shown, as in "The Ring Around the Collar" ad. The husband is angry, the wife is embarrassed; both are humiliated. The use of the correct detergent produces emotional satisfaction if not ecstasy. The two logics, problem-solution and discontent-content, correspond to the two major story lines of the myth of technological utopianism. Each logic implies the other, whether made explicit or not in the advertisement. The overall myth unifies the two logics.

This utopian "narrative" is straightforward. Science and especially technology are leading us to a utopia of maximum production and consumption. Technology insures our collective survival and success in allowing us more efficient control of life and providing solutions to all our problems. This promised land is likewise a world of total consumption. In it people have perfect health, are beautiful, eternally youthful, free to do whatever is pleasurable, and thus completely happy. The myth of technological utopianism is promulgated through the liturgy of advertising. This myth (in the strong sense of the term) is as much a myth as that of any archaic people.

If the world of advertising is truly a mythological world, then it exists outside of the dialectic of truth and falsehood. For the world advertising creates is not actual but only possible. As with all mythologized rituals, advertising can withstand the negative test of reality for there is always a next time: the possibility of perfection and total fulfilment in the newest commodity. Myth likewise works to overcome contradictions that we experience in the everyday world. The technological system, as we saw in Chapter 1, creates cultural meaninglessness and intense psychological stress. This system does not rest easy upon human society. As well, technological growth threatens the physical environment. Consequently, some of technology has to be directed toward helping individuals adjust to the system and toward repairing the damage to the environment. But this can only be done if adjustment is brought within the symbol of happiness, and repair (survival) is contained within the symbol of success. As part of the myth of technological utopianism, all four symbols are interrelated; moreover, each one implies the rest. The value of success was gradually transformed from an individual to a collective phenomenon. Success became by the late nineteenth century the success of the organization. The equation of the American nation with technology meant that national progress was insured by technological growth.

The value of success is related to that of survival: both are expressions of collective power turned into a value. Survival is minimalist success. If success today is most epitomized in technological growth, then survival is related to the destructive aspects of that same growth. The value of survival grows increasingly important as we become acutely aware of problems such as pollution, overpopulation, and potential nuclear catastrophe that require repair. Success (as technological growth) stands in a contradictory relationship to survival (as technological repair).

As success is collectivized in technology, it is redefined for the individual in terms of well-being (happiness and health). During the twentieth century happiness and health have each come to possess two distinct meanings. Happiness refers to the consumption of goods and services and to adjustment to one's circumstances in life; health refers to the perfection of the body through consumer goods and services, e.g., vitamins and organized exercise, and to adjustment, defined as emotional or mental health. (The most prevalent criterion of mental health for much of this century has been adjustment.[85]) Therefore, happiness and health have a common meaning in adjustment; concurrently happiness as consumption and health as the perfection of the body share the common meaning of physical well-being. Happiness and health (taken together) have two overall meanings: physical well-being and emotional well-being (adjustment). The overall meanings, moreover, are related. First, a consumption-oriented lifestyle is a major part of adjustment to the technological system. It is our compensation for the diminution of moral responsibility and individual freedom. Second, physical well-being and emotional well-being are increasingly perceived to be interdependent. But just as success as technological growth can threaten survival, happiness as consumption can impair one's physical or emotional health.

The mythological symbols are arranged in an hierarchy: success and happiness are higher in value than survival and health (as repair and adjustment). The latter two symbols indirectly reflect technology's inability to carry through on its utopian promise. Between the former two symbols, happiness is higher, at least from the individual's viewpoint. That is, technology can grow indefinitely, but if it does not lead to individual happiness, what good is it? Keep in mind, however, that if technology because of its interconnections has become a system and thus autonomous, it is not directed toward individual happiness but only its own continued growth and survival. In the mythological world the various symbols are compatible; in the real world their realizations are often at odds.

Earlier I suggested that television programs are an advertisement for advertising. Only now can the full meaning of this be explicated. Television programs and television advertisements form a complex, not merely because many ads occur within the period of a program, but mainly because both express the myth of technological utopianism. In one sense the programs are the ritualization of the myth expressed in advertising. That is, an advertisement, which tends to be brief compared to a program, contains the essential story lines of problem-solution and discontent-content. These are akin to the moment of creation in a traditional etiological myth about the state of perfection in the past (golden age) to be once again realized in the future. Success (solution) and happiness (content) are the moment of creation, the time of perfect bliss.

The programs are a longer dramatization of the myth of technological utopianism that is already dramatized briefly in the commercial. In another sense there is no difference except length between commercial and program, for the myth of technological utopianism is a *spatial* myth. The dominance of visual images in ads and programs and the more general subordination of language to visual image eliminates the conventional distinction between myth and ritual. The former was a kind of discourse, whereas the latter was its dramatic enactment. The visual image here is both word and action. Perhaps the relationship between ad and program is better understood as the *visual* relationship between the central theme and its elaboration in a story. Here, story needs to be thought of as the entire set of television programs. The various programs illustrate one or more of the four mythological symbols of technological utopianism. No program embodies all four symbols, but taken together television programs enact the full range of symbols. Moreover, certain programs illustrate one symbol in its pure form.

Earlier I concluded that happiness and health each had two distinct meanings with overlap in one of the meanings: happiness and health as physical well-being realized through consumption versus happiness and health as emotional well-being realized

through adjustment. For purposes of convenience I will refer to
happiness as consumption and health as adjustment. The following is a chart of genres of television programs and the main symbols they represent:

Genre of Program	Mythological Symbol
Sports	Success
Children's Shows Game Shows	Happiness
News (serious)	Survival
Soap Operas	Health
Dramas	Success and Health
Situation Comedies	Happiness and Health
Talk Shows	Happiness and Health

One should note how well represented the symbols of health
and survival are. One of the major functions of television programs is to help us accept survival and health as utopian values,
to make us believe that reality as we live it is actually part of a
technological utopia. Remember that watching television is enjoy-
able so that even problems of survival and health can be vicariously experienced as pleasurable. Advertising, however, is
exclusively about success and happiness, the strong symbols of
technological utopianism.

Largely because of television, sports has become spectacle. It is
not enough that the game be well-played, there must be additional
drama to that which is on the field—pep bands, gymnastic cheer-
leaders, dancing girls, marching bands, and the increasingly violent gesticulations of the participants. All of this aims to work the
fans into a state of ecstasy so that they mirror psychologically the
violence in the arena. The spectators vicariously experience the
success or failure of the team they support.[86]

Sports enthusiasts and critics appear to agree that winning is
the "nucleus of the sport."[87] Most often cited is the remark of
Vince Lombardi, former coach of the Green Bay Packers, that
"winning is not everything—it's the only thing." There is little
disagreement about this in the ranks of coaches and players today.

No better indicator of the supreme emphasis on winning exists than the decline of sportsmanship. One sees this especially in the sports that draw the largest audiences—soccer worldwide, and football and basketball in the United States. Players are taught how to get away with certain rule violations and when to use them strategically. Even more obvious is the increase of "trash talking," the attempt to intimidate one's opponent. Gary Gumpert argues that television replay plays a part in the effacement of sportsmanship by emphasizing and normalizing rule infractions (whether intentional or not).[88]

Modern sports is technique-driven. The incessant experimentation with superior training techniques, better equipment, more efficient organization of practice, and more complete control of athletes' minds and motivation are indicative of a preoccupation with winning and with records.[89] Under these circumstances the distinction between amateur and professional is blurred. At an ever younger age children are subjected to professionalized sports instruction. Sports is no longer a game; it has been transformed into a technique of winning.

Children's shows are about happiness in the form of toys. Until age seven or eight, children cannot distinguish between commercials and television programs.[90] When they finally can distinguish between the two, it makes little difference; for many of the programs center about figures that exist as toys, sometimes before the program was created. Tom Engelhart referred to the process of creating a cartoon show around a set of toy characters that market research had indicated would be well-received as the "Strawberry Shortcake Strategy." Cartoons like "Strawberry Shortcake," "The Care Bears," "My Little Pony," and "Rainbow Brite" with toys to match the main characters were produced to reach a young female audience; cartoons like "Teenage Mutant Ninja Turtles" and "Slimer and the Real Ghostbusters," to reach a young male audience.[91] Sometimes the characters in cartoon shows are not toys, but characters that are already extant in video games: Donkey Kong, Jr., Pitfall, Dragon's Lair.[92] In one instance the cartoon was based on a candy—Gummi Bears. Under these circumstances, children's cartoons are simply infomercials.

Game shows are children's shows for adults. That is, the stars of the game show are the prizes. This is less true when the prize is only money. Most of the game shows involve some minimal level of skill to emerge victorious. But the success is less important than the ensuing happiness. This is in perfect keeping with the gradual redefinition of individual success. In the late nineteenth century in America success began to be more the province of technology and organization than individual skill. Consequently, success was increasingly defined in terms of individual happiness—job satisfaction and the leisure activities one's income or geographical location permitted.

News programs, serious news not just public relations announcements, are about survival. Despite self-conscious attempts to have an uplifting story in each program, the news is invariably bad news: tornadoes, oil-spills, nuclear waste management, ethnic conflict, political corruption, and wars. The news is about who and what survives. Survival is a kind of minimum success, and it receives emphasis when the perception of crisis abounds. Elias Canetti defined survival as the "moment of power"; I survive, the other does not.[93] The significance of the news is that it indirectly and sometimes directly points to the need for technology to repair the damage in nature or society. The very episodic nature of the news favors a technological rather than a moral or political approach to a crisis.

Soap operas appear to be about everything imaginable, but mainly they are about personal relationships and "life-adjustment problems." The characters on soap operas express their feelings about what goes on around and to them and expect others to do likewise. The illnesses, deaths, crimes, and intrigue are the background to the foreground of personal feelings and needed adjustments. Moreover, many personal problems are "cured" by psychological insight.[94] At the same time, soap operas feature an inordinate number of wealthy and glamorous people.[95] Perhaps this is a way of showing that the distance from health (adjustment) to happiness (consumption) is not too great.

Talk shows and situation comedies illustrate the symbols of health and happiness. Talk shows vacilitate between shows featuring celebrities who shared their consumer-oriented lives with the audience and shows featuring ordinary people in various stages of distress (e.g., drug addicts, wife-beaters, incest victims) who are attempting to make a "life-adjustment." Some shows like Oprah Winfrey's feature both kinds of guests. As with soap operas, the message is that one can move from mere adjustment to happiness.

Situation comedies tend to be about relationships: parent-child, marital, friends, and coworkers. Shows like "Grace Under Fire," "Seinfeld," and "Friends" are apt examples. There is an emphasis on feelings and problems of adjusting to the other's expectations and demands. All relationships are essentially aesthetical, and moral conflicts invariably lend themselves to a quick and happy resolution. As well, the programs stress the joy of group consumerism, as the entire family or group of friends enjoy a ball game, a meal together, or shopping together. Once again the problems of adjustment are never far from happiness.

Dramas range from those that emphasize the power of technology to those that emphasize interpersonal conflicts. The former are often action programs in which the police, detectives, and the military battle criminals. The emphasis is on cars, guns, missiles, electronic eavesdropping devices, and the like.[96] Technology, violence, and special effects are the stars of the show. Other dramas center on the problems of everyday life, the stress of making a living, raising a family, and maintaining a romantic relationship. The symbol of success is the focus of action shows; technology as machine and organization wins the day. The symbol of health (as adjustment) is the theme of melodramas. Is not the indirect relationship between the two kinds of drama that technology is the final solution to serious problems of adjustment?

Where do music videos fit into this scheme? On the one hand they are advertisements for records, as well as being advertisements for themselves since they can be purchased. On the other hand, they are the content of programs. Like children's shows they are about happiness, the immediate pleasure of music and a visual dramatization. One of the major themes of music videos is the rapid transformation of self: characters change role, sex, status, class, and occupation in rapid succession.[97] Madonna is a virgin, then a prostitute, a girl, then a woman. This suggests the mystical power of technology as an agent of self-transformation.

Violent and sexual images supply the final piece in the myth and rituals of technological utopianism. By violence I include psychological violence like coercion, as well as physical violence, whether directed against nature or humans. Sex without ethical commitment and affection is a form of violence. To a lesser extent in advertising than in programs, television provides a surfeit of violent and sexual images. Most observers and critics miss the point. It is not principally directed against traditional morality. Rather it is positively related to consumption.

As I argued in Chapter 1, the sacred is, in the most general sense, the human life-milieu. Each milieu is organized around polarities: life and death in the milieu of nature, good and evil in the milieu of society, efficiency and inefficiency in the milieu of technology. It is in the movement from the negative pole to the positive pole that the regeneration of the milieu occurs. The sacred power of technology resides in technological objects or consumer goods. Technology represents the principle of efficiency; violence and sex, the principle of inefficiency (as powerful human instincts). At a deeper level, however, both represent the will to power. The continuum between the two poles—technology and violence—is *excessive experimental consumption*. Sex and violence in advertising and television programs are used to sell consumerism as a lifestyle. Most important is the juxtaposition of violence with consumer goods; the spatial relationship suggests an association. In consuming the technological object, we are consuming the instinctual power of violence. As our instincts are given free reign, the more technological objects we will consume. A technological utopia is one of total consumption, both technological objects and the rapacious instincts of sex and violence that generate them. The violent images of the media are a ritual for the regeneration of the technological milieu. They are responsible for the movement from problem to solution and discontent to content. Success and happiness are the utopia, the golden age. One moves from mere reality to the utopia through the ritual of regeneration as it is dramatized in the violent and sexual images of advertising and television programs.

In summary, television programs are elaborations of one or more of the symbols of technological utopianism that are enacted

in advertising. Television programs enlarge the sphere of technological utopianism to take into account reality and improve it:
survival is a kind of success, health a kind of happiness. The violent images of the media help move us from a reality/utopia of
survival and health to the full utopia of success and happiness.
The myth of technological utopianism has to include survival and
health as part of the utopia, because it is a spatial myth. There is
no past nor future to this visual utopia, only an eternal present.
This results in an enormous ambiguity—we are already in the
utopia, but not everything is equally utopian. We are trapped in
a vicious circle: we strive for more consumption, but it is only
more of what we already possess. The myth of technological utopianism, dominated by visual images, translates all political and
moral issues into technical and aesthetical ones. The individual's
moral decisions are reduced to consumer choices, approving or
disapproving of what technical and bureaucratic organizations
do.[98] Television programs as much as advertisements share this
bias and thus reinforce each other. They attempt to convince us
that the meaning of life resides in consumption by enshrining it
in myth and ritual.

Magic in the Media

The central magical ritual of a technological civilization occurs
in the mass media—the festival. The festival celebrates the renewal of the milieu, the movement from negative to positive pole.
Here the negative aspect of the festival is the dramatization of
violence and sex, the positive dimension is technological creation—success as continued growth and happiness as total consumption. How does this magic work? Magic, as we have seen,
involves a belief that a set of practices produces a desired outcome. The practices are believed to embody the principle of transformation according to milieu: creative persuasion, retribution, or
causality. Here we believe that technological products and services solve (causality) all our problems and make (causality) us
permanently happy. Because we believe that the practices influence the desired outcome, the practices become more or less op-

erational indicators of the desired outcome. Magic works, then, as placebo or self-filling prophecy. As placebo, magic produces an emotional change (no matter how short-lived) in us; as self-fulfilling prophecy, magic continues to be practiced because by definition it produces the desired outcome. Psychological magic—the media and therapy—works as placebo to produce happiness and health, whereas administrative magic acts as self-fulfilling prophecy to produce success and survival. Although advertising and television programs cover the full range of mythological values from the symbols of collective success and survival to the symbols of individual happiness and health, the media's impact is psychological. As such it is our paramount placebo, a compensation for the ever more stressful reality that the technological system actually creates.

Magic, moreover, may refer to the means or the ends of an action. Technology objectively produces certain results; it is not magical in respect to means. But because we expect utopian results from it, technology is magical in respect to the ends. Psychological and administrative magic are magical in respect to both means and ends. They do not work objectively, but subjectively as placebo and self-fulfilling prophecy, and are magical in respect to their utopian ends. The psychological magic of the media is crucial to every other magical practice and utopian end. As a surrogate language and culture, the visual images of the mass media give "meaning" to everything that is done in a technological civilization; they provide utopian ends for technology and transform its imitations into technology. In this way, and this way only, does everything in a technological civilization become "an imitation of technology or a compensation for its impact." The magical rituals of the media express the deepest religious beliefs of this civilization—in the sacred power of technology.

Why then are we so cynical at times about advertising, and why do so many ads and programs adopt an attitude of self-mockery? The happiness a technological object brings us is fleeting; the placebo effect is transitory. Before we even have it home, Debord observes, it has begun to lose its luster.[99] But there is always the next object advertising proffers. Although intellectually most of us see through advertising as a form of manipulation, emotionally it captures us. The impact of the sacred in myth and ritual is irrational. We are schizophrenics—split between intellect and emotion—unable to unify our disparate selves. Advertising adopts a tone of self-derision, e.g., an ad for Weight Watchers states that the company desires for you to lose weight so that it can use you as a living ad for its program, to appeal to our intellectual cynicism.[100] "Smart" advertising lets us in on the con; it is a subtle attempt to win us over: buy our product, but retain your dignity as one who can't be duped.

More important, however, in accounting for our cynicism is the shallowness of technological utopianism. It stands exclusively for power, at the expense of symbolic meaning. As we saw in Chapter 2, symbolism in the milieu of technology becomes sterilized and meaning, because it is operationalized in visual images, turns materialistic. Moral meaning emerged in the milieus of nature and society from the need to symbolize an external power and control our own actions in relation to it. Because technology is our own creation and our milieu as well, we sense no need to symbolize our relationship to it. We have turned power into a value. Uncontrolled power, however, produces cynicism, for trust rests upon shared moral meaning that places some limitations on the exercise of power.

Because technological utopianism is untranscendent, it permits no sense of a future that provides a respite from the sufferings and death of this life. As Gabriel Vahanian once observed, when one ceases to believe in a soul or its equivalent, one turns to the perfection of the human body as a substitute. [101] Happiness and health have supplanted salvation. Our utopia is here and now, but, if anything, suffering has increased and death abounds. Meaning is reduced to the transitory "values" of pleasure, health, and survival. We anxiously live for the moment.

Finally, technological utopianism does not provide symbolic and moral unity; technology can only organize a society at the level of logic and power. Nor can it provide a normative guide for diversity. Technology renders a common morality obsolete; consequently, the various social groups, whether based on age, sex, race, ethnicity, or class are engaged in a relentless struggle for power and possessions. Diversity borders on anarchy because of cultural meaninglessness, and unity approaches totalitarianism because the technological system destroys language and with it individuality and freedom. Despite our cynicism and hopelessness we continue to believe in technology and its imitations because we perceive no alternative. Truly, technology is our fate and with it a world of magic to make it tolerable.

In the next chapter we will examine the prevalent forms of psychological magic that are practiced outside the media, but are still dependent on it. These include therapy, self-help and positive thinking. If the dominant mythological value in advertising is happiness (as consumption), the paramount one in therapy is health (as adjustment).

· 5 ·

Therapy, Self-Help, and Positive Thinking as Magic

The therapy of all therapies is not to attach oneself exclusively to any particular therapy, so that no illusion may survive of some end beyond an intensely private sense of well-being to be generated in the living of life itself. That a sense of well-being has become the end, rather than a by-product of striving after some superior communal end, announces a fundamental change of focus in the entire cast of our culture—toward a human condition about which there will be nothing further to say in terms of the old style of despair and hope.

Philip Rieff
The Triumph of the Therapeutic

Two strands of therapy, professional psychotherapy practiced by psychiatrists, clinical psychologists, and psychiatric social workers, on the one hand, and self-help groups and positive thinking based on principles of popular psychology and often practiced by nonprofessionals, on the other hand, have become less distinguishable in recent years because of their common theme—self-esteem.[1] I maintain that both strands are largely if not exclusively magical practices whose chief purpose is to bring about a quasi-mystical transformation of the self. In a technological civilization, as we have already seen, such practices will be represented as a form of applied science or technology. The twentieth century has witnessed an enormous increase in the number of people seeking both kinds of therapy for less serious psychological problems, for what are sometimes called psychoneuroses,

or what others might term the problems of living.[2] We are supposed to be happy in a technological utopia; consequently, suffering is perceived as abnormal.[3] The vicissitudes of life, no matter
how small, are grist for the mill of therapy.

Psychiatry, Clinical Psychology, and Clinical Social Work

Although physicians have long considered the emotional state
of their patients as a help or hindrance to their recovery, psychiatry did not become a discipline and medical specialty until the
eighteenth century. The early psychiatrists were known as "alienists" because they treated "mental alienation." The alienists of the
late eighteenth century perceived that the patient's problems were
a result of nervous overstimulation. Self-control was often pre-
scribed not as a moral remedy but because it would relax the
nerves. Patients with serious emotional problems who were members of the working class were often treated in "therapeutic asy-
lums," whereas the wealthy were assisted by private physicians
or later in private hospitals.[4]

In this period doctors made a distinction between serious psychological problems, to be treated by alienists (psychiatrists), and
minor problems (later to be termed neuroses) to be handled by
"spa doctors" and "society nerve doctors." The less serious dis-
turbances were thought to be the result of frayed nerves; water,
it was felt, had a therapeutic effect upon the nervous system. The
spas obviously did not cure all the wealthy neurotics and could
provide only the occasional treatment for those who were busy
and at a distance from the spa. As a result society doctors attended
to the well-heeled in their everyday environment. Hysteria, mel-
ancholy, and hypochondria were common diagnoses. The French
alienist Pierre Pomme coined the phrase "vapours" to refer to a
host of maladies that today we would term depression. His remedy: chicken soup and cold baths. Surprisingly, the spa doctors
and society nerve doctors were quite successful in curing patients,
often with the use of placebos. Beginning in the nineteenth century, psychiatrists handled the serious cases; other medical specialists treated the rest.[5]

The concept of mental illness arose coterminous with a scientific view of emotional problems: psychological anomalies were a consequence of a biological defect or disorder. In this view mental illness was more than a metaphor; it was a reality. From the beginning of modern psychiatry, most practitioners were biological psychiatrists rather than psychosocial psychiatrists. The latter located the causes of mental disorders in social and psychological processes and conflicts. The two perspectives could both be correct depending on the specific problem, but in any period one of the two approaches was dominant.[6]

The psychosocial psychiatrists in the early nineteenth century came to be known as Romantic psychiatrists. Following the lead of the Romantic Movement in literature and art, this relatively small group of psychiatrists, centered especially in Germany, stressed imagination and passion over against reason. German Romantic psychiatrists maintained that the cause of mental disorders was the failure to regulate morally one's passions, to which one would subsequently become subject. Others stressed the impact of social status and social relationships on mental life. For the Romantic psychiatrists therapy involved listening to patients, not merely about their symptoms and complaints, but as well about the social context of their emotional distress. Throughout the nineteenth century the psychosocial approach to psychiatry remained a minority viewpoint.[7]

Sigmund Freud and psychoanalysis were undoubtedly the paramount reasons that the psychosocial viewpoint became dominant in the twentieth century. Freud benefitted from a number of earlier discoveries, however. Somnambulism, hypnotic suggestion, the Doppelganger (the experience of having a double self), and dreams suggested that reason was at best captain of a ship buffeted by the sea and under attack from a mutinous crew. These discoveries, many of which were found in literature[8] (Freud often used Shakespeare for examples), pointed to the phenomenon most associated with Freud's thought—the unconscious. Freud's predecessors included Anton Mesmer, who discovered that hypnotic suggestion could cure, if only temporarily, neuroses such as hysteria; Jean-Martin Charcot, a practicing hypnotist whom Freud studied with; and Josef Breuer, from whom he learned the "talking-out method,"[9] whereby the patient's talking about a problem sometimes made it disappear temporarily. Later Freud discovered that if he permitted patients to say anything they wished, unconscious feelings would sometimes surface; hence, the concept of free association.

Although Freud thought that eventually we would discover the biological basis of psychological processes, he helped to establish the importance of the patient's views, including and even especially his fantasies. In one sense it made little difference where the therapist saw the source of the patient's disorder, whether in biological, psychological, or social forces, as long as the patient's emotional problems were seen to be amenable to discussion and advice from the therapist.[10] Analytical psychotherapy, then, stresses the primacy of the oral relationship between therapist and patient: The patient talks about past and present experiences, and the therapist interprets these experiences and make suggestions about how to live in a different way.

Psychoanalysis dominated psychotherapy for much of the twentieth century. Joel Kovel argues that "Freud with his methods and central insight remains the progenitor of modern therapy."[11] Psychoanalysis was not restricted to doctors; as both a theory and practice it was open to anyone who received training and accepted its insights. Even therapies that are not analytical (emphasis on a rational analysis of the patient's mental life) have been influenced by Freud's intellectual legacy that transformed Western attitudes toward the personality. Psychoanalysis, however, has been on the wane in recent decades as effective drugs for treating the symptoms of serious emotional distress became available.[12]

Other forms of psychotherapy include behavioral therapy, phenomenological psychotherapy, and humanistic therapy. Behavioral approaches draw heavily upon academic psychology for a learning theory. Sometimes based on principles of behavior modification, behavioral therapy stresses the observable part of a patient's emotional distress, isolates it form the larger context of his life, and helps the patient learn to avoid or overcome the destructive behavior.[13]

Phenomenological psychopathology takes just the opposite approach. It attempts to place the patient's problems into the context of her entire life as she relates to the world. This view maintains that one's inner life is best revealed in relating to one's environment and to others in everyday life. The patient becomes an ally in the attempt to describe her perceptions as completely as possible. How one confronts the questions of the meaning of existence is always a central concern.[14]

Humanistic therapy is almost a miscellaneous category. The various therapies that fall under this rubric—non-directive (Rogerian) therapy, primal therapy, encounter groups, transactional analysis, family therapy, group therapy, gestalt therapy, and countless others—share three things in common: they are eclectic in theory and practice; they de-emphasize a deep analysis of the patient's unconscious and conscious life; and they believe that within each patient lies a potentially decent person.[15] Behavioral and humanistic approaches picked up the slack that a decline in the popularity of psychoanalysis created; phenomenological psychopathology never took hold in the United States.

Clinical and counseling psychologists and clinical (earlier called psychiatric) social workers outnumber psychiatrists in the practice of psychotherapy. After 1950 there was a precipitous increase in the number of American therapists with a specialty in clinical or counseling psychology. In 1959 within the American Psychological Association, 2,500 psychologists checked off clinical or counseling psychology as their specialty; by 1988 that number had increased to 40,000. By 1995 there were approximately 90,000 professional licensed psychologists whether they belonged to the APA or not.[16] In 1945 there were about 2,000 clinical social workers in the United States, while in 1990 that number had increased to 80,000.[17] The number of psychiatrists, by contrast, has been declining in recent years. Between 1984 and 1994 the number of medical school graduates who planned to enter a residency in psychiatry had declined over 40 percent. One analyst attributes this in part to the fact that most psychiatrists end up treating neuroses and minor complaints rather than full blown psychiatric illnesses that make use of their medical training.[18]

In 1985 Americans spent 2.8 billion dollars on therapy from licensed, clinical psychologists and 2.3 billion dollars on the services of psychiatrists.[19] Given the large number of clinical social workers in private practice, one can see that the amount of money spent on therapy each year greatly exceeds 5 billion dollars. Therapy has apparently become a way of life for many Americans. This is only part of the picture, for self-help groups and books, recovery groups, and courses and seminars in positive thinking are part of the overall therapeutic impulse.

Self-Help and Positive Thinking

Positive thinking and self-help are not recent creations; they stretch back into the nineteenth century. Donald Meyer maintains that the separation of religion from science and medicine was a fundamental cultural shift of the nineteenth century.[20] Religion was freed to offer the psychological medicine of peace of mind to those in need. In so doing it became vulnerable to the bromides of popular psychology. Books on achieving success are more numerous than those on any other subject in the nineteenth and early twentieth century.[21] The novels, how-to books, pamphlets, and articles are not solely about success, however; happiness and health are also frequent themes. These themes form the heart of American popular culture during this period. They reveal how Americans who first associated success with moral character later linked it to the power of mind to motivate the self to assume a successful attitude (self manipulation), and the power of personality to control others. Success was eventually seen to be a consequence of a psychological technique.

Even after success had been shorn of its peculiarly religious motivation, as with Benjamin Franklin, it still retained a strong aura of traditional morality well into the nineteenth century: success and failure were viewed as a result of the presence or absence of character. By the 1830s the idea of success had been translated into a moral program. To achieve success one must possess the following qualities: industry, frugality, perseverance, initiative, sobriety, punctuality, courage, self-reliance, and honesty.[22] Success readily follows in the train of moral character; moreover, moral character can be inferred from success. So close was the identification of economic success with moral virtue that the two became as one. Moral virtue had become less important as an end in itself and more important as a means to economic success.

American ambivalence about success was expressed in the distinction between material success and true success. The former was represented as money, whereas the latter was defined in terms of individual happiness, the love and respect of others, doing one's best whatever the outcome, and peace of mind.[23] Most interesting is the tendency to define true success as a psychological phenomenon even prior to the "mind-cure" movement. Somehow the pursuit of true success was less offensive than the single-minded devotion to material success. And yet the turning of happiness or peace of mind into an end in itself was just as antithetical to the spirit of Christianity.

The association of success with moral character is most exemplified in the myth of the self-made man, who through sheer force of will and strength of character manages to rise from poverty to become rich and famous.[24] This basic plot line dominated both Christian and secular novels throughout most of the nineteenth century. There are many variations of the theme of upward social mobility. Rarely was the mobile individual truly poor to begin with; often he was of rural origin, confronting a hostile urban environment for the first time. The stories, while extolling success, were nevertheless directed against the perceived excesses of an industrial civilization. Hence the protagonist is never devoted exclusively to the pursuit of wealth but rather is an upholder of rural virtue.

In the second half of the nineteenth century, a rival to the character success ethic emerged: psychological techniques of self-manipulation, which went by the names of "mind cure," "mind power," and "new thought." The mind power ethic of success seemed to hold sway from the 1880s through the 1920s (although it continued long after that).[25] It claimed that the key to success was not one's character but one's state of mind.

From mind cure came religious movements such as Christian Science and New Thought. The quasi-mystical religious philosophies directed their followers to put their minds in communication with the "Universal," "the Divine Mind," "All-Power," "All Supply," "the great Fountain Head," and "Mother-Father."[26] This modern day mysticism sought to tap the rich resources for healing and success that nature could provide.

From the same self-help movement sprang popular psychologies, often referred to as mind-power or positive thinking, which promised personal success in life. Some of these psychologies were thoroughly secular, some were an adjunct to New Thought, still others were articulated within a Christian context. Not all of these popular psychologies were directed toward the power of mind; a few stressed will power. Frank Haddock, for example, author of *Power for Success, Business Power*, and *Practical Psychology*, published *Power of Will* in 1907. Claiming that will is more important than mind, Haddock rejected those religious inspirational writers, Christian and New Thought alike, who wanted their readers to subordinate their minds to the mind of a higher power. Instead Haddock outlined a set of exercises for the will, a psychological discipline by which success could be achieved:

> Exercise No. 10. Stand erect. Summon a sense of resolution. Absorbed in self, think calmly but with power these words: "I am standing erect. All is well! I am conscious of nothing but good!" Attaining the Mood indicated, walk slowly and deliberately about the room. Do not strut. Be natural, yet encourage a sense of forcefulness. Rest in a chair. Repeat, with rests, fifteen minutes.[27]

Will power never supplanted mind power as a psychological tool. Not that it matters, for in the end both are minor variations of a single theme—psychological efficiency through self-manipulation.

Mind cure was not directed solely at success; health and happiness were its targets as well. Advocating the use of mind to help cure physical illness, mind cure enthusiasts were concerned about the nervous American, whose loss of energy and general anxiety had become debilitating. Mind cure advocates anticipated the theory of the placebo in their recognition that the patient's belief that she was going to get well was part of the cure, if not the cure itself.[28] Christian Science is only the most famous of the many attempts to cure the body with the mind.

By the 1930s the self-help movement, both religious[29] and secular,[30] had turned to happiness as its chief interest, but happiness defined as adjustment. (In Chapter 4 we discussed happiness-health as consumption and health-happiness as adjustment; this is the latter.) The devotees of mind power, as early as the late nineteenth century, had advocated ease, relaxation, and comfort over against the ascetic virtues associated with the character ethic.[31] By the twentieth century, beginning in the Progressive period, the criticism of the striving for success in business as the rat race signaled an emphasis on a different set of values—health, leisure, fun.[32] The advocates of positive thinking, such as Dale Carnegie and Norman Vincent Peale, seemed more intent on providing the means for achieving inner peace and serenity than for achieving material success.

Dale Carnegie's *How to Win Friends and Influence People* was published in 1936. It is still in print. Carnegie's best-selling self-help book spawned courses and seminars on being successful and being happy. His approach to management will be discussed in the next chapter; but because he believed that the manipulation of others required self-manipulation, his ideas are pertinent here. Carnegie stressed the importance of the smile in the business world. Businessman Charles Schwab, his prototype, had a wonderful smile that, Carnegie was convinced, made him successful. Carnegie argued that we think people smile because they are happy; yet the opposite is also true: we smile to make ourselves feel happy.[33] This is a variation of a common approach to positive thinking: the "outer" verbalization of a feeling can create the inner feeling.[34] Carnegie developed courses and seminars, still in existence, for those who didn't have the time to read his book. His was among the first modern self-help groups.

The only positive thinker to rival Dale Carnegie's popularity in the mid twentieth century was Protestant minister Norman Vincent Peale. His 1952 seller *The Power of Positive Thinking* was the number one best-selling nonfiction book for two years;[35] it was the epitome of a self-help book. Peale was a spiritual technician who loved to enumerate rules that were already cliches: "The happiness habit is developed simply by practicing happy thinking." "While dressing or shaving or getting breakfast say aloud a few remarks such as the following, 'I believe this is going to be a wonderful day.' " Peale referred to this as "affirmation therapy."[36]

In *Inspiring Messages for Daily Living*, Peale gave the reader forty "health-producing, life-changing, power-creating thought conditioners."[37] Later Peale and his collaborator Smily Blanton opened a clinic. Peale could not accept Freud's theory of the unconscious; instead he saw it as a kind of tabula rasa that could be programmed to direct the client toward happiness; this way the conscious verbalization of uplifting thoughts could be bypassed.[38] Positive thinking had become subterranean.

In the early twentieth century success was increasingly defined in organizational terms; for the individual it became satisfaction with work and coworkers. One study of the success theme concludes that success in the twentieth century had become individual self-fulfillment.[39] A survey of American businessmen by the American Management Association in 1972 found that the largest number of respondents defined success as the achievement of goals. Upon closer inspection, however, the achievement of goals meant something entirely subjective. Achievement was defined variously as: satisfaction with one's outward performance; satisfaction with one's life; and satisfaction with a goal achieved, a task accomplished, or a job well done. Note that success has become psychological satisfaction. When other definitions of success such as self- actualization, happiness, peace of mind, and enjoyment in doing or in being are added to that of satisfaction, it becomes evident that close to 70 percent of the respondents defined success in predominantly psychological terms.[40]

John Cawelti[41] has described the positive thinkers' verbal sleight of hand about success and happiness:

> On the whole, positive thinking is less a new expression of the traditional ideal of rising in the world than a revelation of the failure of the dream. Without the social and religious sanctions of the eighteenth and nineteenth centuries, the dream of success is no longer a magical idea for Americans. Once success had been the road to religious salvation and middle class respectability. When these goals lost their force, success, too, lost much of its savor. There is no particular satisfaction in being able to purchase more of the same goods which an ever-more-efficient technology produces in ever-increasing amounts, and it is not easy to see what else success, without its social and religious sanctions, can offer. Sensing this vacuum, the exponents of positive

thinking try to fill it by establishing a relation between material success and an inner serenity, showing that happiness is the true way to success. Where its nineteenth-century proponents had proclaimed that the quest for success would lead to those moral and religious ends which alone create true happiness, the positive thinkers seem to be affirming the contrary, that success itself is contingent upon the individual achieving a happy and serene mental outlook. But such a reversal suggests that mid-twentieth-century prophets of success are no longer sure of the value of what they preach. If, in order to become successful, one must first become confident, serene, and happy, what then is the point of going on to become successful?

Positive thinking could make you successful, help you deal with failure, or allow you to be happy as compensation for the failure of success. Positive thinking was a quasi-mystical technique for self-transformation. If one's mind, will, or unconscious has the correct thoughts and intentions, one will achieve peace of mind (happiness). Increasingly positive thinking was a form of "adjustment therapy" that helped citizens accept the stress and conflicts of a technological civilization with a minimum of self-awareness.[42] It is no wonder that the primary criterion of mental health was adjustment; almost equally prominent was the idea of happiness. Indeed, research on definitions of mental health and mental illness in mid-twentieth century Europe and North America indicates that happiness was equated with or at least viewed as dependent upon adjustment.[43] If happiness was defined by advertising as consumption, it was conceptualized by therapists and positive thinkers as adjustment.

Self-help and positive thinking are as strong as ever, but are less tied to organized religion than they were earlier in the twentieth century. To a great extent they have merged with New Age thought and practices and humanistic therapy. Another important difference is the proliferation of courses, seminars, and self-help and recovery groups. Earlier in the century most self-help and positive thinking took the form of books, pamphlets and novels; Dale Carnegie with his courses and seminars on success was the exception to the rule. Today the omnipresent courses, seminars, and self-help groups share in common an emphasis on group process. The coming together of self-help (positive thinking) and group process represents the merger of two important historical trends.

"Democratic social engineering" is the term historian William Graebner has given to the group movement in America that began in the late nineteenth century and peaked before World War II. Because I will be discussing this in the context of management theory and practice in the next chapter, I will be brief here. Democratic social engineering was an ideology that believed that democracy could be made efficient; it possessed five key ideas: group, process, inquiry, democratic participation, and leadership. Its proponents stressed that its methodology was both efficient and democratic; that is, the group's investigation into and discussion of issues would invariably lead to the most practical and efficient outcome. It was touted as a scientific process.[44] This group process technique seemed to place unlimited confidence in the wisdom of the group, as Tocqueville argued, but only insofar as the group was willing to discover the best expert (scientific) advice. In a sense, the view that group process could be a scientific methodology was a screen for the real issue—both group leaders and followers were subordinate to expert advice. Democratic social engineers, however, had a tacit contempt for the judgment of ordinary people; consequently, the group leader was expected to be the one most able to discover the best knowledge to resolve the issues at hand.

Drawing upon pragmatism and a fascination with technology, democratic social engineering was applicable, its proponents thought, both to society as a whole and to groups and organizations within it.[45] Group process was formally applied in settlement houses; in schools as group discussion; in religious education; in recreation in the form of clubs; in public relations, e.g., Edward Bernay's theory that public relations was democratic engineering; in child rearing, e.g., Benjamin Spock's best-selling book; and in business as success seminars, e.g., Dale Carnegie. Democratic social engineering was doubly technological—in its reliance on group technique and upon technical advice outside the group. What went on in the group, as we will see later, was not really technical but magical. If group participants believed the bromide, "good things happen in groups," they might end feeling happy about themselves. But success is another matter. Just being in a democratic group does not guarantee an efficacious outcome.

Democratic social engineering as a theory began to decline even before World War II, but the larger belief in groups and democracy hung on. The 1960s witnessed an efflorescence of therapeutic groups and theories about groups. Professional psychiatry, psychology, and social work increased their use of group therapy, and T-groups and encounter groups became fashionable.[46] The greatest growth, however, occurred in the self-help and recovery group industry. Self-help includes courses, seminars, and workshops on success, health (alternative or holistic), and happiness. Recovery and support groups attempt to cure the emotional problem of "co-dependency." At first glance, the latter (recovery groups) appears to be serving the needs of those whose problems are more serious, but in fact there is considerable overlap in problem and membership. Some of these seminars, workshops, and groups are run by "professional" psychologists and counselors with varying academic degrees, others by lay people (those who have *experienced* the disability).

Almost all of the seminars, workshops, and support groups are based on a self-help book or genre of book, e.g., "inner child." As I walked through the local Barnes and Noble bookstore recently, I noticed the following sections: Self Improvement, Addiction/ Recovery, Alternative Medicine, and Relationships. There is considerable overlap in the content of books from section to section. Here are a few titles selected at random: *Betrayal Trauma; Broken Toys Broken Dreams: Understanding and Healing Boundaries, Codependence, Compulsion and Family Relationships; Getting the Love You Want; The Inner Child Workbook: What to do with your past when it just won't go away; Getting Through the Day*. Writing about recovery books, Wendy Kaminer says that "sales can fairly be called phenomenal."[47] Americans appear to have an insatiable desire for self-help books. We will examine the seminars on success in the next chapter; consequently we will briefly look at those that emphasize happiness and health.

Two of the leading kinds of self-help group experience are recovery groups, which are often based on the theory of codependency, and support groups, which sometimes follow a twelve-step program. Because of the expansion of the concept of co-dependency, however, the difference is rendered meaningless. Prior to the 1980s there was a distinction between an addict and his family, who in protecting him and themselves from the truth were co-dependents. No so today. The term "co-dependency" is now applied "to any problem associated with any addiction, real or imagined suffered by you or someone close to you."[48] Evidently co-dependency refers to every kind of emotional problem and is therefore a vacuous concept. Moreover, addiction is not just to alcohol or drugs; now it applies to sex, relationships, rage, shopping, and even negativity. Anything that causes us stress and from which we are unable to abstain is an addiction, or perhaps a co-dependency, or both.

Twelve-step programs, based on the model of Alcoholics Anonymous, are widespread; they merge science and religion in the form of psychological technique. Unlike many of the insipid popular therapies, they are muscular. Twelve-step programs can be reduced to three actions: (1) admit your problem; (2) tell it to others and to a "higher power"; and (3) reach out to others like yourself. The third action is both a cause and effect of recovery. Helping others is a way of helping oneself, for it reinforces one's commitment.[49]

Those who are "recovering" from emotional problems not normally defined as addictive and who are victims of others' problems sometimes attend workshops on child abuse, spouse abuse, relationship abuse, and the like. Child abuse is another term that is so broadly defined and applied as to be almost meaningless. Child abuse has almost become tantamount to child discipline. As Kaminer observes, "most people are mad at their parents."[50]

Workshops on the inner child are quite popular. Cathryn Taylor has written *The Inner Child Workbook* and conducts workshops on the same topic. She writes that "This book helps you rebuild your faulty foundation. It offers you a step-by-step formula for returning to your childhood and repairing the wounds that left you weak and vulnerable." And again: "Who are the children within? They are the voices inside you that carry the feelings you were unable to express as child."[51] Ms. Taylor describes the six steps of healing:

> Step one introduces you to the tasks that needed to be mastered at each developmental stage and helps you identify the pain that resulted if you were unable to complete these tasks.

Step two helps you research childhood events and attitudes that
influenced your development at each stage.

Step three helps you re-experience the feelings and sensations of
that time.

Step four helps you objectify those feelings and see them as separate you from your adult self.

Step five helps your inner self grieve.

Step six completes the healing process with a ceremony to emotionally, physically, and spiritually heal each of your children
within.[52]

Step six is roughly the same for all stages of childhood including that of young adult. The basic ritual (as it is self-consciously
called) involves a large number of props: pen, journal, drawings
of your inner self, sacred plants, e.g., juniper, bath salts, body oils,
and crystals. After cleansing the room with a sage stick, burning
incense if you feel the urge, burn a picture of your inner self. After
purifying the room with a sage stick, you and your revitalized
inner self bury the ashes outside. After a ritual bath and related
activities to release the pain of the inner child, you engage in a
series of spiritual activities in which you imagine that your higher
power embraces you and your inner child, heals the inner child,
and permits you to absorb the inner child into your total self.[53]
The instructions unfortunately read like the inner child is still pun-
ishing the author's common sense.

If inner child theory sounds like New Age thought, there is a
good reason—professional psychotherapy, popular self-help psychologies and New Age thought share certain cultural assumptions. Keep in mind that Americans were in therapy before there
was therapy. By that I mean that positive thinking and self-help
were well established long before psychotherapy became popular.
It is unlikely, then, that professional psychotherapy would have
provided a radical alternative to the culture that produced positive thinking and self-help. Therapy, both professional and self-
help, is an expression of the American belief that technology can
solve all natural and human problems.

Psychotherapy, self-help, and New Age thought converge about
several themes: self-esteem, happiness, and mental health. Psychologist Robyn Dawes has demonstrated that self-esteem is the
central theme of contemporary professional psychotherapy; he

terms the clinical and counseling psychology that promotes self-esteem "New Age."[54] Psychologist Paul Vitz concurs and maintains that self-esteem is valued because it is thought to be the foundation of personal happiness.[55] And happiness as adjustment is a key dimension of mental health. All three vague, reified terms—self-esteem, happiness, and mental health—refer to an individual's inner state. Therapy in the broadest sense of the term is preoccupied with the mystical self-transformation of the individual. No matter what the condition of the physical and social environment, one can always feel happy inside. The reasons for this turn toward mysticism will be explored later in the chapter.

The Effectiveness of Therapy

To get at the magical character of modern therapy (in the general sense of the term), perhaps it is best to start with its effectiveness. Therapy works: a majority of people who undergo psychotherapy report that their lives have been improved.[56] There are numerous qualifications and reasons why therapy works, however. Some of those who have studied why therapy works have already ascertained its magical character; their work will be discussed in this section. The research indicates that in general the effectiveness of therapy is unrelated to the experience and education of the therapist, the type of therapy employed, and the length of therapy.[57] Moreover, psychological experts are no better than ordinary people in predicting psychological problems.[58] Therapy works but evidently not as applied science (technology).

Those with little or no professional education and with little or no experience do as well in helping clients as those with more education and experience. In one study college professors did as well as experienced professional psychotherapists in the treatment of clients;[59] in another, high school students performed as well as psychiatrists and psychologists in predicting future violent behavior of patients based on a checklist of patient characteristics.[60]

In a review of forty-one studies comparing professionals and paraprofessionals, it was discovered that in twenty-eight studies there was no difference in effectiveness between the two groups, that in twelve studies the paraprofessionals were more effective, but that in only one study were the professionals more effective.[61] One qualification in the studies of the proficiency of therapists was that therapy with a professional therapist worked somewhat better for those "highly motivated for therapy" and eager to make changes in their lives. Often such patients are themselves college educated and expect their therapist to have advanced degrees.[62]

No single type of therapy has proved to be more effective than the others. Here and there a particular therapy may work better for a specific problem, e.g. behavioral therapy sometimes works better with phobias.[63] Multiple treatments, e.g., psychotherapy and medicine, are sometimes more effective than any single treatment. One study compared behavioral therapy, psychoanalysis, and being placed on a waiting list (after an initial psychological screening), and found no difference in the outcomes.[64] One psychiatrist even suggests that most "emotional nonpsychotic complaints . . . improve without treatment," what in medicine is sometimes called spontaneous remission.[65]

Length of treatment is unrelated to the relief of discomfort, but in one study it was related positively to the patient's ability to relate to others. The longer the treatment the less isolated, dependent, cautious, and inhibited the client became. This was most pronounced in group therapy.[66] One research psychologist summarizes the over 300 studies of the effectiveness of therapy, "studies supporting the unique efficacy of high-status mental health professionals in psychotherapy, or their unique ability to predict human outcome, or their unique ability to learn from experience in some ineffable and intuitive manner, simply don't exist."[67] This is even more reason to treat professional and popular psychology and therapy as one.

Given the preoccupation with self-esteem in psychotherapy and the larger culture, we should briefly summarize the research on the topic. Studies indicate low self-esteem does not lead to poor academic achievement, alcoholism, violence, teen pregnancy, or child abuse.[68] Instead, self-destructive and seriously immoral actions may lead to a lower self-esteem or personal unhappiness. There is scant evidence that self-esteem as an inner state is related to anything external to itself.[69] Suffering and unhappiness are an important part of life; indeed they can help us change our actions and attempt to alter our social environment. Hopelessness and a sense of meaninglessness, on the other hand, leave us unable to make the effort to address suffering, give it meaning, and begin to transcend it. Improved self-esteem, which is merely compensation for suffering and stress, may actually coexist with a deeper sense of hopelessness.

If therapy is by and large effective, should we not find a decrease in the number of people in seminars, workshops, and therapy? The opposite is occurring, however. There are a significant number of people who seem "addicted" to therapy; indeed this has pointed out as one of the pitfalls of our unrealistic expectations for therapy—that it will increase our self-esteem and personal happiness.[70] Clearly, in American culture no one can have high enough self-esteem or enough personal happiness.

Because therapy does not work as a form of technology but is still effective, psychiatric and psychological researchers have attempted to identify what makes it work. Some analysts discovered that the quality of the therapist-client relationship was important in explaining the efficacy of treatment. This was sometimes referred to as a "nonspecific effect" in contrast to the specific effect that one expected from the scientific knowledge and professional training of the therapist. Researchers broadened their search for factors explaining the outcome of treatment and are largely in agreement on the nature of psychotherapy and why it works.[71] I will be following Jerome Frank's *Persuasion and Healing* for the most part because it is the most comprehensive treatment of the subject and the basis for the others.

Frank identifies four common features of successful psychotherapy and five consequences. The first feature pertains to the quality of the therapist-client relationship. The patient must trust the therapist: he must perceive the therapist to be an expert and must believe that he genuinely cares about him.[72] Martin Gross maintains in addition that the client must be suggestible, beyond the basic trust in the therapist and his technique.[73] The second feature is that the locale, office, clinic, or hospital, is officially defined as a "place of healing." Both Frank[74] and Gross[75] understand this transforms the therapist's space into a sacred space. The third feature is an explanation or myth that both makes the client's problem intelligible to him and fits with his worldview, e.g., the psychoanalytical view that what happens to the individual in early childhood is responsible for subsequent problems.[76] The fourth feature is that therapy is perceived as a technique based upon some scientific theory that allows the patient both to see his mistakes and to be excused by the "causes" of his problem. Moreover, insofar as therapy requires the effort of the patient it is self-reinforcing and indirectly communicates the concern of the therapist.[77]

The consequences of these four features are not for the most part anticipated by the therapist. Therapy provides a medium by which the client can learn new attitudes and actions with the therapist as her model. Furthermore it can intensify the patient's expectation of a remedy which is based, as we saw earlier, on a faith in the therapist and his technique. Therapy is also a vehicle by which the client can experience some success through active participation in the therapeutic process. As the therapist praises and gives credit to the client, the latter's confidence begins to grow. Only the most seriously disturbed patient fails at everything the therapist recommends. Therapy can help overcome the patient's estrangement from others, if only in her dealings with the therapist. The client discovers that others have problems similar to hers. The final consequence is the emotional arousal of the client. All significant changes in one's life involve emotional, intellectual and normative aspects. Therapy, then, provides the client with belief (in the therapist and his technique), hope (that one will get better), a sense of self-mastery, and community (if only with the therapist).[78]

Therapy as Magic

Psychiatrists and anthropologists have studied the similarities between modern psychotherapy and ritual healing in traditional societies.[79] Ritual healing can be either secular or religious, and directed toward the individual or the group, or sometimes both. The sacred rituals for the expulsion of evil or rituals of scapegoating, for example, are a type of healing by which the entire community is purified. As we saw in Chapter 1, not all forms of magic are equally sacred. Those that are integral to the main seasonal rituals are most sacred, whereas those that attempt to heal individuals, even if performed in the context of the seasonal rituals, are less so. Let us examine two kinds of magical healing, one that uses the community as a backdrop, the other that involves the community in healing the patient and in so doing heals the community.

Claude Lévi-Strauss interpreted the autobiography of a Kwakuitl Indian from Vancouver, which Franz Boas had obtained in the 1920s. The sorcerer Quesalid began as a skeptic about magical healing, but later made use of it. Quesalid's technique of healing involved sucking on the patient in an attempt to extract the foreign body believed to be the cause of the illness. At the right moment the sorcerer throws up the small piece of down he has hidden in his mouth and shows to patient and onlookers alike the down covered with blood, which the sorcerer has obtained by biting his own tongue or pricking his gums. Sorcerers in other villages regarded illness as spiritual and not physical, so that they had nothing convincing to show the patient and community. Lévi-Strauss notes that many if not most illnesses cured are of the psychosomatic type so that Quesalid's cures were first psychological and then physiological. Quesalid was apparently the most successful sorcerer around; he had won the confidence of the entire community.

At this point Lévi-Strauss's analysis of the dynamics of healing begins. He demonstrates linguistically that the sorcerer's spiritual crisis and resulting healing powers are thought to be a divine gift. This cultural definition precedes the sorcerer's success at healing. Now the healing process involves a triad relationship of healer, patient, and community. As it turns out, the first and third terms—healer and community—are the most important. When the community accepts the healer's story about his calling to be a healer, it believes in him, and this belief is the source of the healing. As Lévi-Strauss notes, "Quesalid did not become a great shaman because he cured his patients; he cured his patients because he had become a great shaman."[80] After Quesalid had cured patients other sorcerers could not, his rivals were disconsolate because they realized at this point that the community had lost faith in them. And with that their already-limited healing power would be diminished if not lost altogether.

But it should not be thought that the healer's role in the drama of healing is completely subordinate to that of the community. On the contrary. In order to lend credence to his claim to be a healer, the sorcerer must be skilled at *abreaction*, in this case, the ability to recreate vividly the occasion of his calling. He must convince his audience that he truly has had a calling, whereupon their trust is bestowed upon him.

What role does the patient play in all this? By believing that he is cured if and when the sorcerer is convincing, he can aid the community in believing in both the patient's cure and the sorcerer's power to heal. Lévi-Strauss hypothesizes that it is not just the convincing performance of the healer in extracting the source of the disease but also the healer's ability to bring about a similar ecstatic experience in his patient, a sense of a calling and being divinely guided, that convinces the community. Hence there exists a close affinity between patient and sorcerer. Both are abnormal in the sense that they have psychological experiences foreign to the rest of the community. It is no wonder that so many former patients became sorcerers, for both roles are on the fringes of society. Yet the community must view and accept the abreactions or ecstatic states so that what cannot be fully understood because it has not been experienced can at least be integrated into a structure—healing—that the community sanctions.

Victor Turner provides an example of ritual healing that makes the community an integral part of healing and is more directly related to the main rituals for the expulsion of evil. The Ndembu of Zambia believe that a longstanding or acute illness is caused by ancestral shades, male sorcerers, or female witches. Rituals performed to exorcise such ancestors or evil spirits tacitly assume that social conflict in the community is behind the illness. Certain persistent illnesses are believed to be a result of an upper incisor tooth of a hunter who died. The tooth symbolizes the "biting" nature of gossip, jealousy, malice, and the like. Upon the hunter's death, relatives who are members of the Ihamba Cult, are supposed to carry the incisors in a pouch. If the hunter's teeth were not recovered before burial or if the relative loses a tooth, it may become embedded in someone else's body, thereby causing an illness. Everyone in the community shares the same cultural assumptions about the causes of persistent illness and the same beliefs about the efficacy of rituals to expel the ancestral shade whose tooth is embedded in the patient. Like Lévi-Strauss's sorcerer, Turner's doctor ("ritual specialist") performs a variety of rites and involves the community in the cure. But there are important differences between the two healers. In Turner's example the doctor defines his professional role as a mediator of community conflicts. The patient's disease is interpreted as evidence of dissension in the community. Public confession of the patient's conflicts with others and their antagonism toward him is used to bring the disease to a dramatic denouement. Thus the doctor's job is to restore good will among neighbors. Confession not only reunited the patient with the community, but symbolically integrated the community and the spirit world.[81]

Jerome Frank summarizes the effects of traditional ritual healings, which "raise the patient's expectancy of cure, help him harmonize his inner conflicts, reintegrate him with his group and the spirit world, supply a conceptual framework to aid this, and stir him emotionally."[82] Traditional healing like modern therapy provides the patient with something to believe in, hope for the future, self-mastery (involvement in the ritual), and community. Both traditional ritual healing and modern psychotherapy involve magical practices and are successful as placebos. Magic only works on humans, and when it is successful it works either as placebo or as self-fulfilling prophecy (placebo is a kind of emotional self-fulfilling prophecy). People are cured emotionally because they expect to get better, and because they expect to get better, they begin to change their lives, which in turn reinforces their sense of being cured. Like traditional ritualistic healing, therapeutic failures do not lead therapists to doubt the power of their magic.[83] Traditional magic and modern magic, however, operate according to markedly different principles: persuasion and retribution in the case of the former, and causality in the instance of the latter. Therapy, it is tacitly believed, embodies the sacred power of one's life-milieu. The modern therapist is a technical expert.

Let us examine, then, how therapy fits into the larger set of mythological beliefs and magical practices in a technological civilization. Modern therapy is based on a medical model, which, as Frank notes, possesses three characteristics: it is centered on the patient; it makes the therapist a technical expert; and it reflects a scientific worldview.[84] Traditional therapy is based on a religious worldview. This distinction, however, is based on a misleading distinction between science and religion. For technology, as we have seen, is perceived as sacred and justifies itself in the myth of technological utopianism; moreover, magic today imitates technology, and one of its paramount forms is therapy.

In the preceding chapter I noted that technological utopianism contains four mythological symbols, two of which, happiness-health as consumption and health-happiness as adjustment, make their fundamental appeal to the individual. Traditional myth had the community both as its subject and its audience. Traditional therapy cures the community or the individual by the community; modern therapy cures the inner state of the individual, providing happiness as adjustment.

In traditional societies, symbols, which were organized in a myth, were a way of giving meaning to a world believed to have an organic unity. Language in a technological civilization has lost its ability to express meaning. Key words that refer to human qualities have been rendered fully abstract as jargon and plastic words. The symbolic function of language has become sterilized. With the ascendance of visual images in the media, the "meaning" of words now resides in visual images. All of discourse, except for technical terms, has become "symbolic," but in a materialistic way. If my argument has merit, then the language of therapy should reflect these larger changes in verbal and visual representation.

L. J. Davis recently reviewed the fourth edition of the *Diagnostic and Statistical Manual of Mental Disorders*, a collaborative effort of the American Psychiatric Association. The manual is replete with jargon, vaguely defined terms, and faulty thinking. Admitting that the psychiatric designation *Bipolar* may not even exist, the manual proceeds to use it extensively. Davis describes the use of the terms *Bipolar* and *Antisocial Personality* in the manual:

> Welcome to the broad pathological world of the ingenious, versatile Bipolars and their catchall allies, the Antisocial Personali-

ties. In the vernacular, the Bipolars et al. come under the heading of *gotcha!*—the ever-popular rhetorical device of the ideologue or the man in the checkered suit with a briefcase full of shares in a pholgiston mine. For example, a telltale symptom of Antisocial Personality Disorder is the tendency of the victim to steal things. The layman, the hard scientist, and the policeman might take issue with the diagnosis, but vigorous dissent (and what, pray tell, is the definition of "vigorous"?) is a sure sign that the dissenter suffers from a Bipolar disorder and is therefore nuts. In other words, not only is anyone who pursues a goal with dedication, verve, and discipline a prime candidate for the therapist's couch but so is the psychiatrist who rises at a hospital staff meeting to protest the fact that their colleagues are ripping off everybody in sight with bogus diagnoses. One begins to understand what exceedingly handy tools these definitions be.[85]

Davis goes on to describe the confusion of cause and effect in the description of Reactive Attachment Disorder in Infancy or Early Childhood. The symptoms of the mental illness are "hypervigilance, ambivalence, and inhibition," whereas the conditions associated with it include "grossly pathological care" that involves the neglect of the child's "emotional needs for comfort, stimulation, and affection." As Davis observes, there is no mental illness here, but simply a normal reaction to an extremely abnormal environment.[86]

Internet Mental Health describes a new mental illness, "oppositional defiant disorder," found in children and early adolescents. Its symptoms include:

(1) often loses temper
(2) often argues with adults
(3) often actively defies or refuses to comply with adults' requests or rules
(4) often deliberately annoys people
(5) often blames others for his or her mistakes or misbehavior
(6) is often touchy or easily annoyed by others
(7) is often angry and resentful
(8) is often spiteful or vindictive.

Note: Consider a criterion met only if the behavior occurs more frequently than is typically observed in individuals of comparable age and developmental level.[87]

In definitions like this, mental illness simply becomes a short-hand term for frequent, disapproved attitudes and behaviors. If mental illness is only deviant attitudes and behavior, then why invoke the term at all?

The second edition of the *Diagnostic and Statistical Manual of Mental Disorder*, which was published in 1968, did not demand that every mental disorder be explained as the reaction to some set of determinations, whether biological, psychological, or sociological. From this moment on, mental illnesses were placed in a free-floating state; moreover, it became much easier to label something as a type of mental illness.[88] The manual taken as a whole suggests both that *everyone* is mentally ill or in danger of becoming so and that *everyone* can benefit from treatment.[89] Virtually any reaction to the vicissitudes of life can be viewed as a symptom of mental illness; consequently, for some, therapy has become a permanent way of life.

In 1977 R. D. Rosen gave the name "psychobabble" to the discourse of humanistic and pop psychology; the term is still with us, as is the vague and inflated prose he described. Psychobabble is more a "style of speech" than a hodgepodge of professional jargon; it is where psychiatric and psychological jargon enters public consciousness. Terms like "self-actualization," "whole person," "uptight," "hung-up," "co-dependency," "inner child," and "self-esteem," are part of the vernacular. Psychobabble, Rosen argues, is a shallow compensation for the ability to understand and face up to one's problems honestly. It is talk about "well-being."[90]

Mental illness, it would appear, is a symbol of maladjustment to a technological civilization. Mental health is a symbol of happiness as adjustment. Earlier in the chapter I noted that self-esteem was a vague concept that in turn was perceived to be the cause of or equivalent to personal happiness (adjustment), both of which are dimensions of or equivalent to mental health. Clearly we are in the realm of symbolism. Mental health, self-esteem, and adjustment refer to the inner state of the individual; the concepts are so abstract and vague that they have become reified and meaningless. The "meaning" of therapy and mental health has to be found in the visual images of the mass media.

Confession is the primary mode of televised discourse.[91] This idea refers not merely to talk shows and televised therapy (with call-in questions) but also to soap operas and parts of news programs. Even the dramas and comedies involve characters who talk about their lives in intimate detail to someone in the program but as well to us the spectators. We vicariously consume the lives of countless actors and celebrities.[92] We feel close to them because they have revealed themselves to us.

The sheer number of people we meet in the media is enormous. In traditional societies human relationships involved those one knew personally or those one knew through tradition and myth, e.g., ancestors. Today most of us know more people in the media than in real life, and know them more intimately.[93] Most of our relationships except for family and close friendships are impersonal, despite the veneer of cheerfulness with which we greet others. The visual images of the media make a fundamental appeal to our emotions, and dramatized relationships involving the revelation of the intimate details of one's life is the stuff of numerous programs. The media provide us with a fictive community of people who confess their lives to us.

The other side of this issue is that television is the medium that gives us the most therapeutic advice. In the 1980s *TV Guide* ran a series of articles touting television as a dispenser of therapeutic advice about family life, romance, and friendship.[94] This advice can be direct in the form of experts on talk shows who tell us how to lead our lives or indirect as a model for us to follow. Both television advertising and programs provide us with visual exemplars that are appealing because they are on television, one of our two sources of "reality" today. Television is both patient (the one who confesses) and therapist (the one who offers advice). Ironically the viewer is always passive. I receive the confession of others, but never offer advice, for television does that for me. Television is a closed system of problems and advice.

In the preceding chapter I argued that the mythological values of technological utopianism are expressed in advertising as central themes, and in programs as their elaboration in a story. Soap operas, talk shows, situation comedies, and dramas to varying degrees portray the mythological symbol of happiness-health as adjustment. They dramatize the problematic nature of life and the need to adjust to it. Yet at the same time technological utopianism is set in the present not the future. Hence life- adjustment problems cannot be all that bad. We are in the utopia, especially while we live in the media. But therapy outside the media is utopian because it has become a consumer service and a technique, part of the technological cornucopia. Hence the problems we face in everyday life are our problems and only ours. Adjustment requires a change in the inner state of the individual. Therapy has had no effect on the social sources of emotional distress and cannot; so it treats only what is treatable, the inner life of the individual.[95]

Why the Individual and Society Need Therapy

The individual needs therapy today for three main reasons: the interiorization of life, fear of others and loneliness, and the stress induced by a technological civilization. J. H. van den Berg attributes the interiorization of life, the development of an expansive inner self, to a decline of a moral community in Western Civilization beginning in the nineteenth century. The triumph of a scientific worldview, a view that only facts could be known objectively, eventually led to the subjectivization of ethical and aesthetical meaning. Common meaning becomes personal meaning: each individual has to discover meaning for herself. In a moral community, there is less a difference between the inner and outer self; common meaning obviates the need for constant experimentation in regard to meaning. There are fewer serious external differences among people, less need for a fully developed inner self to come to grips emotionally with the conflict that a proliferation of external differences (in function, status, and power) in the absence of a common morality engenders. At the levels of meaning and emotion, then, the loss of common moral purpose leads to a completely interiorized, subjective reality. More and more in modern life the individual has to spend time coming to grips with her emotions, her meaning, her relationships. What van den Berg calls the "factualization of understanding" creates a subjective world of emotion to which we are enslaved, because it is here that the meaning of life now resides.[96] No wonder we turn to therapeutic technique for assistance.

External differences between individuals, morally unmediated, create a more problematic existence. Not only does the loss of meaning make vague my relationship to others, but it makes them more dangerous. I do not know what to expect of the other, especially as he becomes more externally different. Søren Kierkegaard understood this very well when he talked about the basis of association in modern civilization being fear and envy.[97] Karen Horney's still timely *The Neurotic Personality of Our Time* allows us to understand how competitive human relationships have become. She attributes this in part to capitalism, but competition is inevitable to the extent the moral basis for cooperation begins to decline. The basic anxiety, shared to different degrees by both the neurotic and the normal person, is the "all-pervading feeling of being lonely and helpless in a hostile world."[98] Van den Berg calls loneliness the "central core" of mental illness.[99] We should not be misled by the preponderance of the extroverted, forced cheerful personality. It is a mask for fear and loneliness and a superficial way of making friends.

A technological civilization creates enormous stress for people. First, it increases the tempo of life: we have more to do in less time; consequently we often find ourselves doing several things at the same time.[100] One is cleaning the house, cooking, and listening to the news at the same time. The amount of information, images, and noise with which we are bombarded creates a kind of sensory overload. Second, technology objectifies human needs in advertising and human ability in the techniques we use in work and in leisure. The increased use of technology in every aspect of life creates a blizzard of technical and bureaucratic rules. The proliferation of technical rationality, the overorganization of human existence, creates a need for humans to escape this stress in various ecstatic experiences—television, computer games, alcohol, and the like.[101] Third, the meaninglessness that a technological civilization engenders is itself a cause of anxiety. It leaves one without hope to confront the sufferings and stress of everyday life.

The individual needs therapy but gets magic. Why? Because a technological civilization needs adjusted people. It needs us to accept reality as it is, without questioning it or attempting to radically change it. The technological system produces an endless series of technologies that act as compensation for the enormous human problems that it creates.[102] Therapy is such a compensation, an imitation technology and consumer service that acts as magic. Therapy involves the magical self-manipulation of the individual's inner state so that one can feel happy no matter what the condition of one's physical and social environments.

Recall the Ndembu doctor who cured his patient by getting him and his detractors to confess what they had done to each other and even to admit the evil thoughts they had harbored against one another. This medicine man cured the individual, who was lonely and fearful, by curing the community. This isn't even conceivable in a technological civilization, for there is no moral community. At most we can provide an ersatz community of celebrities in the media. Consequently therapy cannot get at this major source of discontent. Nor can it get at the other major source, technology, which is more than a means of doing something efficiently but the basis of a civilization.

Are there any modern psychological theories that have seen the seriousness of modern anxiety? Yes, a few. J. H. van den Berg, Karen Horney, and Harry Stack Sullivan, among others, have grasped the situation quite well. Therapy based on insights like these can at least avoid offering the client false hopes and momentary relief from acute distress. It may in effect help the individual struggle against the technological milieu rather than merely adjust to it.

Therapy (in the most general sense of the term) is usually effective. It is a psychological technique, a form of magic that operates as a kind of placebo. For the most part it is initiated by the individual and involves a mystical transformation of the self. Psychological techniques can also be used to manipulate others. Perhaps the most important of these manipulative techniques are certain management or administrative techniques. Some management techniques, however, are less psychological and more statistical in nature. In the next chapter we will examine techniques of management that rely upon either dramatized information or statistical information.

· 6 ·

Management as Magic

The magician is, above all else, the one who is able to disclose the future and eventually to change it. Nowadays we no longer have haruspices. Our century, which to be sure still uses tarot cards and coffee grounds, would no longer be happy, on the whole, with what is openly called superstition. To all appearances it has become scientific, and it brags about being rational. Fortune-telling is practiced only in secrecy and shame. Even today's fortune-tellers have taken a rational turn. Never has the future been so scrutinized, but now we do it in the scientific manner. Forecasts, projections, possibilities, prospects—these enterprises abound, and of course they bear the stamp of a certain rigor and rationality. Statistics and samplings are multiplied.

Jacques Ellul
Hope in Time of Abandonment

There are at least three major types of psychological technique or magic. The first, sales, has been discussed in the chapter on the mass media insofar as advertising is the primary means of sales today. The second, therapy, involves the transformation of the emotional state of an individual perceived to have a "life-adjustment" problem; group therapy and recovery groups provide the individual with the semblance of community. The third, management, sometimes entails the integration of the individual into the work group as a member of a "team" or "family" and the acceptance of the ideology of the organization. There are other management techniques, however, that involve the coordination of rational, especially statistical, information, rather than the dramatized information psychological techniques make use of.

Both kinds of management techniques are magical, and both are used in modern organizations.

A Brief History of Management

Bureaucracy is both a concept and a reality; the latter existed well before the former. Alfred Weber maintains that every great civilization rests upon a bureaucratic foundation.[1] In Western civilization there has been a more or less uninterrupted growth of power in the political state, much of which is the power of administration.[2] The centralized state, moreover, made possible the establishment of national markets for its own political and military purposes.[3] By the late nineteenth century bureaucracy had invaded the business world with the growth of corporations. The entrepreneur, who not only owned his company but also knew all the operations and all his employees, was giving way to the corporation, in which ownership and management were separated.[4] Stockholders knew little about the day-to-day operations of the company. The relative autonomy of management became absolute with technological specialization. The owner as a generalist had to defer to a plethora of experts, whose services required coordination. Moreover, the specialization of work in the factory required bureaucratic control. At this moment management took on a life of its own and acquired a greater degree of self-consciousness.

In the late nineteenth and early twentieth centuries, theories and techniques of management emerged in Europe and the United States. The various approaches to management tended to emphasize either the formal structure or the informal structure (interpersonal relations between employees). Among the earliest and easily the most influential of the formal approaches was Frederick Taylor's "scientific management." Taylor applied his training and experience as an engineer to virtually every aspect of work. In addition to making tools and machines more effective, he improved the flow of work by the rearrangement of equipment and personnel, invented better techniques of record-keeping, and conducted a series of time-motion studies on the act of labor. He believed his greatest contribution to production lay in planning the entire process so that at every step the necessary tools, materials, and laborers would be present exactly when needed. Taylor thought of organizations as machines that could be designed and modified to run more efficiently; not surprisingly, he regarded the employees at all levels as "component parts of a mechanism."[5]

In allocating all of the creative dimensions of work to management, he further reduced workers to cogs in a machine. He sought to "minimize the characteristics of workers that most significantly differentiate them from machines."[6] Although Taylor advocated that workers be permitted to advance to the highest level their abilities made feasible, this was only in the interest of greater productivity.[7] For Taylor regarded workers as children who were supposed to take orders—this was his idea of cooperation between labor and management.[8]

Taylor's system of scientific management did not merely destroy laborers' participation in and responsibility for their work, it also adversely affected the work of mangers. Management was part of the organizational machine; hence, it could be reduced to a series of specialized functions. Each manager was to be responsible for as few functions as possible, ideally one, and supervise workers in relation to that function. In practice this proved untenable. The worker had too many supervisors—one for each job or for each aspect of the job he performed.[9] For example, in the section of the factory where automobiles are painted, each task from preparation of the surface, to priming and painting it, to checking it for defects, and so forth, would require a specialized supervisor. Those companies that embraced "Taylorism" discovered that they had to make a number of modifications.[10] Eventually the concept of "line and staff" emerged so that direct supervision of a number of related functions belonged to the foremen or line supervisors, who, in turn, took orders from specialized managers.

Scientific management, at least Taylor's version, required departmental specialization on the basis of "technical similarity" rather than purpose. James Worthy describes this concept in practice: "factories which had previously been organized on the basis of products were reorganized in such a way as to bring together in one department all lathes, in another department all drill presses, in another department all milling machines, etc. (the 'process shop' vs. the 'product shop')."[11] All labor, manual and intellectual, was required to be categorized according to its function and placed in an appropriate administrative unit.

Taylor conceived of the coordination or integration of parts as an exclusively mechanical process. In segregating "thinking" from "doing," in making management even more specialized (and thus inadvertently reducing its intellectual function), and in combining activities solely on the basis of function, Taylor made it more difficult to coordinate the activities of an organization. Each functional unit has its own logic of operation, requirements, and interests because mechanical unity requires only external relations between more or less autonomous parts. In an open system, such as an ecological system, the relations between the parts are internal, that is, each part exists only in relation to the other parts and something new emerges from the relations between parts. Taylor tacitly desired organic unity but could only think of it as a mechanical engineer. Consequently, Taylor's mechanical conception of efficiency required more managers than would have otherwise been the case.[12] For each functional unit was relatively autonomous and potentially a special-interest group. Taylor inadvertently politicized the organization. Taylor's version of scientific management was more influential in regard to the coordination and supervision of machines and factory workers and less so in respect to how management should be organized. Managers resisted the mechanization of their own work.[13]

The "principles of management" theory originated in France but became available in Great Britain and the United States in the 1930s. Like scientific management it examined the formal structure of the organization. The principles of management school devoted itself to formal authority within the organization. Specifically it analyzed the line of authority or hierarchy of authority from the top of the organization to the bottom, the number of subordinates a manager should have, and how many managers an employee should answer to (the recommendation was one manager in sharp contrast to Taylor).[14] German sociologist Max Weber made the hierarchy of authority one of the characteristics of bureaucracy. But Weber's theory of bureaucracy had limited influence on the social sciences until the 1940s and little if any on management theory in business.[15]

The other major approach to management stresses the informal structure of an organization. The informal structure refers to the interpersonal relations and motivation of employees. If the emphasis on formal structure assumes employees to be rational, rule-directed automatons, this approach treats them as emotional and moral beings, whose motivation goes well beyond fear and money. The study of the informal structure as a key to management is known as the human relations approach.

Industrial psychology and sociology got a boost from the famous Hawthorne experiments conducted between 1924 and 1932 at a Western Electric plant near Chicago. The researchers wanted to discover under what working conditions was employee productivity maximized. To research director Elton Mayo's surprise, productivity rose no matter what the working conditions as long as they were changed as part of the experiment. From this finding Mayo concluded that concern shown to employees, e.g., being placed in an experimental group, increased their productivity.[16] In addition to the "Hawthorne effect," Mayo discovered that work groups exercised a strong influence on individual performance; groups sometimes established informal productivity norms, initially lower than those set by the company. Finally, Mayo realized that permitting the group to make decisions about their work environment and conditions of employment increased their motivation and productivity.[17] The Hawthorne experiments inspired a raft of studies that did not always demonstrate the Hawthorne effect. Regardless of the qualifications of Mayo's original findings, researchers and theorists realized that group dynamics had a substantial influence on worker productivity.

The human relations approach contains two denominations: the leadership branch and the group relations branch. Charles Perrow maintains that the difference between the two is slight, only a matter of emphasis.[18] The leadership model emphasizes the personal qualities of the manager. To be a leader one should be a person of character, be capable of inspiring others, and be democratic in one's relationships. The good manager-leader will improve worker morale, which will increase productivity.[19] This approach is part of the "democratic social engineering" movement of the early twentieth century.

The group relations branch of the human relations approach to management does not deny the importance of democratic leadership, but emphasizes changes in the organization of the company that would permit the work group to participate in decisions about its environment and conditions of employment as well as the work process itself. Some argue that if employees are allowed to participate more actively in the running of the company, they will accept its goals and ideology. Believing in the company, the argument goes, they will then work harder.[20]

The most influential management theorist for much of the twentieth century was Chester Bernard, whose 1930s *Functions of the Executive* became an instant success. What is important for our purposes is his ability to combine the formal and informal approaches to the study of organizations. His understanding of organization was less mechanical than that of Frederick Taylor: organizational efficiency arose not from the combined rationality of individual managers and workers but from the logic of their various interactions. Reason lay less in individuals than in the logic of organizational process. His theory anticipated open systems theory. Bernard, however, demonstrated some allegiance to the human relations school, for he argued that workers could supply the motivation and insight in ways that the formal organization could never do. The work group existed to reinforce and supplement the formal structure; this could only be done if workers shared in the "personality" of the organization.[21]

Both scientific management and human relations were concerned with increased productivity. In the first half of the twentieth century the invention of standard costing and budgeting created an ally in the quest for greater efficiency—accounting. Scientific management had a profound effect on accounting in the early twentieth century; only later did human relations have a more limited impact on it. Standard costing was a technique that applied scientific management principles to accounting. Rather than merely keeping track of the *actual* costs of labor and material as they were accumulated, standard costing involved predicting the "standard" rates at which labor and materials would be used in various manufacturing procedures. The time-and-motion studies of engineers (scientific managers) were a boon to this effort. The idea of predetermined statistical standards was important to engineers and accountants in three distinct ways before World War I: as a way of gauging the efficiency of labor or the use of materials, as a way of determining the variance between standard and actual costs, and as a way of measuring the value of inventory for purposes of financial accounting.[22] By 1925 management accounting—the measurement of the costs of transactions within an organization—was fully in place: "cost accounts for labor, material, and overhead; budgets for cash, income, and capital; flexible budgets, sales forecasts, standard costs, variance analysis, transfer prices and divisional performance measures."[23]

Scientific management and standard costs and budgets were part of a national efficiency movement that took root in both Great Britain and the United States in the early twentieth century. This movement, of which democratic engineering was a part, fostered health, eugenics, and efficiency in the work place. Standard costs enabled managers to provide each worker in the company with standards of efficiency translated into money terms. Efficiency was conceived of as a goal for both the individual and society. All of the institutions of society, including government and education, could benefit from the advice of efficiency experts.[24] Fundamentally, the concept of the efficient society was a nationalistic dream. Efficient societies would defeat their inefficient adversaries whether on the military or economic battlefield. Labor and management, socialist and liberal, religious believer and secularist saw better organization as the key to economic and political order.[25] The success manuals, too, reflected this change.

Success writers, many of whom did not fully understand Taylor's ideas, popularized scientific management as personal efficiency. They told their readers to imagine themselves as machines living according to ratios between "input and output, effort and results, expenditure and income."[26] By 1914 the new definition of success in popular magazine was "results" (efficacy), especially efficiency.[27] Self-help entrepreneur Dale Carnegie offered administrator Charles Schwab as a hero to his readers because Schwab was a man who knew how to organize and relate to his inferiors in an efficient way. The new hero was a high-salaried manager rather than an entrepreneur; he was someone who had a "positive" effect upon his subordinates and who knew how to adjust his own ambitions to the needs of the organization. In short, his success and that of the organization were one and the same.[28] The decline of the individual as hero did not go unrecognized. John Rockefeller wistfully noted: "The day of combination is here to stay. Individualism has gone, never to return."[29]

The human relations model of management was interested in increasing worker productivity and organizational efficiency; this approach would appear, however, to have no direct bearing upon accounting as did scientific management. But it did. The Hawthorne experiments had demonstrated that the work group greatly influenced how individuals worked and what formal rules they followed. Workers established their own norms, of production and of interpersonal relations, which sometimes ran counter to those of the organization. The work of Chris Argyris in the early 1950s called attention to the extent to which workers accepted the standards and goals of the organization. Cost accounting could not afford to be a purely hypothetical exercise, for it must incorporate findings about the way employees *respond* to budgets into the budget itself. Therefore, to be realistic, budgets had to be negotiated and ultimately accepted by all parties.[30] Scientific management and human relations both influenced cost accounting in the drive toward ever greater efficiency. Management had a greater array of techniques at its disposal at mid-century than ever before. Perhaps management had explored all its possibilities. Let us summarize, then, the various means of coordination that managers had at their disposal in the 1950s.

One student of management identified three main ways that internal activity is coordinated: mutual adjustment, supervision, and standardization. Mutual adjustment refers to the informal discussion between employees about a work-related problem and the practical knowledge that emerges from their interaction. As we will see later, total quality management attempts to exploit the ability of workers to solve problems in ways that have not been formalized. Supervision entails someone assuming responsibility for the work of others. Usually this takes the form of a hierarchy of authority, a basic characteristic of bureaucracy. Standardization can refer to work process, productivity, or skills. Standardization of work process refers to formal, technical rules according to which the work is to be performed; standardization of output involves the specification of norms of productivity or goals to be achieved; standardization of skills refers to the education or training the worker is required to possess.[31]

Bureaucracy (rational management) has emphasized supervision and standardization at the expense of mutual adjustment. The human relations models stresses mutual adjustment by emphasizing the motivation of workers that leadership and the informal work group can influence. The human relations approach is not perceived to be sufficient as the sole approach to management, except, of course, by certain management theorists of this ilk. More often managers perceive it as an adjunct to rational management. Management theory oscillates between the human relations pole and the rational management pole.[32] In the real world, however, management became ever more rational. Leading business management analyst Henry Mintzberg maintains that machine organization (bureaucracy) is still the dominant form of organization.[33] But the meaning of rational changed after World War II; it became even more statistical than Frederick Taylor imagined.

In the 1950s, just when innovation in rational management appeared to be stalled, along came the computer to provide managers with an enormous amount of statistical information and systems to process it. The computer did not dominate the collection and processing of statistical information immediately, for computers were too large and too slow and not available to enough employees at first. Systems analysis, which later came to be identified with the computer, derived from operations research in the military. Engineers had moved well beyond Frederick Taylor's mechanical approach to organization during World War II in the effort to integrate personnel and military technology into a single system of information. Taylor's view of organization was a collection of individual performances, all of which could be measured and standardized.

Operations research addressed the problems of uncertainty and alternatives that the response of others outside one's organization creates. There was a growing recognition that systems were not *closed* systems. The obvious fact that the enemy could continuously affect one's operation and plans led to this insight. Out of operations research came systems analysis, which, like so many social realities, defies precise definition. In general terms, systems analysis involves the quantitative assessment of objectives; the costs, benefits and risks of achieving them; and the formulation of alternatives, given the uncertainty of risk and the behavior of those outside of one's organization.

Military use of systems analysis spawned a number of techniques for the analysis of what was often hypothetical data: mathematical models of conflict, e.g., Monte Carlo; logistic simulations, e.g., Support-Availability Multi-System Operations Model; probability, risk, and uncertainty theory; tactical war gaming, and countless others.[34]

Cost-benefit analysis, which is nothing more than a financial calculation of the viability of a choice, benefitted from its association with systems analysis; the former became an indispensable ingredient of the latter. This harkens back to the nexus between scientific management and standard costs and budgets.[35] Rational management in business and government converged around systems analysis and cost-benefit analysis by the 1960s. As Ida Hoos ironically observes:

> The systems way was the way to run the business of government and the logic was clear: big government is big business. Big business owes its success to efficient operation through scientific management. Ergo, the government has only to apply the principles of scientific management as practiced in the military and its problems will be solved.[36]

This new style of scientific management is most tragically illustrated by William Gibson's account of how the American government used cost-benefit analysis to prosecute the Vietnam War. Secretary of Defense Robert McNamara attempted to run the war as an exercise in statistical management, specifically cost-benefit analysis. Every weapon, every machine and object, every person and behavior had to be quantified so that the ratio of cost-to-benefit could be calculated. Henry Kissinger's view of American foreign policy underlay McNamara's deadly management game. Kissinger maintained that *"technology plus managerial skills"* allowed the United States to make other countries conform to its reality. Kissinger appeared to understand that technology was creating reality by first simulating it. In short, the United States believed that it could impose its technical version of reality anywhere.[37]

Gibson describes a nightmare in which managers in the Defense Department imposed a set of productivity norms upon soldiers in the field that were out of touch with a reality that could not be bent to fit their mathematical models. The war managers, then, believed the Vietnam War could be conducted according to cost-benefit analysis. Body count was among the most important forms of production. Using the ratio of American and Republic of Vietnam dead to Viet Cong dead, or sometimes merely the number of enemy dead, war managers "measured" the skill level of combat units. Because a high body count was necessary for promotion, high-ranking officers often established productivity norms for the underlings.[38] As the pressure on the United States to win the war as quickly as possible mounted, the war managers greedily demanded higher body counts. Consequently, "systematic falsification of battle reports, routine violation of the rules of engagement and regulations covering treatment of prisoners, and systematic slaughter of Vietnamese noncombatants" ensued.[39] With hindsight it is clear that the concept of efficiency, hypothetical as it was, contradicted efficacy in the real world.

Like the Defense Department, the CIA eventually began to employ rational management techniques in the 1960s. The Directorate of Operations (clandestine service that recruits and manages foreign agents) employed the management by objectives technique. Case officers were evaluated by the number of foreign agents they recruited, apart from the quality of information and experience such agents possessed. This placed enormous pressure on case officers to recruit almost anyone and to pretend the information they had obtained was valid; it also left them vulnerable to double agents. Former officer Edward Shirley has demonstrated that rational management along with a lack of knowledge of a country's language and culture made the CIA both corrupt and ineffective.[40]

One need only recall how the CIA grossly overestimated the strength of the Soviet Union's economy during the Cold War.

Contemporary Management Theories and Practices

We will selectively examine theories and techniques of management—both rational and human relations—over the past thirty years. Over against the consulting literature, workshops, and seminars stands the way management is actually practiced. Two of the leading management gurus are Peter Drucker and Tom Peters; both have a primary allegiance to the human relations approach to management. Drucker had a brief flirtation with rational management in creating his popular technique "management by objectives." Apparently Drucker was reacting to what he thought was too strong a negative reaction to rational management. He wished to restore the proper balance between the two.[41] Paradoxically, even though many companies have embraced human relations seminars and workshops by allowing employees to attend them, the actual practices of most firms have moved in the opposite direction.

Let us look at rational management approaches first. Management by objectives (Drucker's creation) enjoyed great popularity in the 1960s and 1970s but began to lose ground to other techniques in the 1980s when criticism became more widespread. Typically there were three dimensions to it: mission statements (the articulation of objectives in quite general terms), contracts between management and employees that specify what the employees are required to do, and measures of performance. This "command-and-control" style of management attempted to turn long-term objectives into short-term goals, something only management had the training to do.[42] Human relations techniques could always be used to reinforce management by objectives. For example, employees might be allowed to participate in writing mission statements, which would always be vaguely stated because their "meaning" resides in the contracts and measures of performance that managers control.

Strategic planning grew out of what was called "long-term

planning" in the 1960s. Strategic planning is also related to management by objectives. In one sense it is only a fuller version of the latter; sometimes management by objectives is used as part of the overall strategic plan.[43] Strategic planning was quite popular in the 1970s and 1980s, but dramatically declined in the 1990s under a barrage of criticism.

Strategic planning, as defined by one of its leading proponents, has four characteristics. Strategic planning is concerned with the consequences of present decisions; it maps out probable outcomes and thus tries to anticipate the future. Second, it is a process that "begins with the setting of organizational aims, defines strategies and policies to achieve them, and develops detailed plans to make sure that the strategies are implemented so as to achieve the ends sought." Third, strategic planning is an "attitude, a way of life." Participants must *believe* in the technique. (One can readily perceive a magical attitude here.) Fourth, formal strategic planning brings together in one comprehensive plan "strategic plans, medium-range programs, and short-range budgets and operating plans."[44]

Most strategic planning guides provide the client with a set of planning stages. The first stage is often the objectives-setting stage. This entails establishing goals, which when measured, become objectives. For example, if a goal is to increase productivity, the objective may be to increase productivity by 10 percent. When the goals relate to values and other qualitative phenomena, the procedure becomes obtuse. As Henry Mintzberg observes, "much so-called strategic planning activity reduces to not much more than the quantification of goals as a means of control."[45]

The next stages, external audit and internal audit, represent an attempt to control the company's environments. To be able to plan, one must make predictions. Predicting the future is tantamount to controlling it. The external environment includes the larger society, which involves economic, political, technological, and social factors, and one's leading competitors. One strategic planning expert has a "strategy" for assessing the strength and weaknesses of competitors. One must ascertain the competitors' assumptions about themselves and the economy, their future goals, their capabilities, and their current strategy. Then one is in a position to plan ways to exploit their weaknesses. In short, one must come up with a strategic plan about a strategic plan. The internal audit stage involves the assessment of one's own strengths and weaknesses: facilities and equipment, personnel skills, organizational capabilities, and management capabilities. There appears to be a considerable overlap between organizational and management capability. The former seems to be more concerned with an organization's overall structure, technology, and resources; the latter more with issues of centralized and decentralized management, management of investments, and the like.

The strategy evaluation stage involves the precise calculation of each possible strategy's probability of success. Most of this involves financial analysis, for this more readily lends itself to quantification. Risk analysis and computer simulations play a large part in this stage.

Next comes the strategy operationalization stage. At this point most manuals on strategic planning become painstakingly detailed. All strategies must be broken down into substrategies, some of which must be broken down further. These hierarchies of strategies are differentiated by length of time—short-, medium-, or long-term—and purpose. Many strategists talk about three major types of operationalized strategy: corporate, business, and function. Corporate strategy is concerned with the "overall business portfolio of the diversified firm"; business strategy with "product-market positions" of each individual business; and functional strategy with specific activities such as marketing, manufacturing, and research. All the strategies and substrategies, arranged in various hierarchies, must give rise to "action programs," e.g., introduce new products, undertake an advertising campaign, expand geographically, downsize management, and the like. What holds this complex web of strategies and actions together is a "master plan." Finally the master plan has to have a timetable for its implementation.[46]

Strategic planning has proved to be a failure. Because we will examine the relationship between management technique and success later in the chapter, I will be brief in discussing the various criticisms of strategic planning. Mintzberg has identified the fallacious assumptions of strategic planning. The first assumption is that strategies can be formalized into an information system so that decisions and judgments become automatic. The second assumption is that thought can be divorced from action. Without practical knowledge that derives from action, planning becomes an abstract and ultimately vague exercise at the level of concepts. The third assumption is that strategy creation depends exclusively on quantified data so that everything qualitative is left out or distorted. The final assumption is that the future can be predicted. Because our planning process is logical, the outcomes we predict are inevitable. Reality, which itself is logical and mathematical, must conform to human logic.[47]

When strategic planning gets beyond its vague concepts, it is almost exclusively concerned with using statistical information about the present to predict the future. Quantitative data as the basis for management decisions are often unreliable because the data is superficial to begin with or the statistical categories invalid. Most importantly, statistical data simplifies and distorts complex, qualitative issues.[48] Sometimes the collection and use of statistical information in the company is highly politicized in the competition between administrative units or between executives. Statistics here are used to protect one's turf.[49]

Strategic planning failed because it was so complex and time-consuming to implement. No one knew what all the categories of strategic planning meant, e.g., where a goal left off and a strategy began, and just the creation of a master plan might take one beyond the expected time of its realization. It also failed because the future cannot be predicted, especially in a world made all the more uncertain by continuous technological innovation.

In the 1990s "reengineering" was the management technique that took the corporation by storm. This management theory is a hybrid, part human relations, part rational management, and as such is a good transition to the analysis of the human relations approach to management. Its initial appeal to managers was as a form of rational management that would make their jobs easier, but this interpretation was based on a misunderstanding of the technique.[50] Like scientific management, from which it attempts to distance itself, reengineering stresses process. In the typical firm with a specialized work force—both labor and management—and the hierarchy of authority, no one is in charge of an entire work process. Reengineering involves the use of individuals and sometimes work teams who become responsible for a process formerly divided among a number of specialists. For example, the processing of a credit form would normally require a number of managers to fill out a small portion of the form before sending it on the next specialist. Now a single secretary-clerk with the correct computer program can finish the work assignment that once took weeks in ninety minutes.[51]

The biggest threat reengineering posed to management in particular and to labor to a lesser extent was downsizing. The reengineering advocates were well aware that the use of information systems made middle management expendable. What began as a technique that gave workers more responsibility and thus made their jobs more interesting ended up being perceived as a threat to the job itself. The specter of downsizing appeared outside many managers' offices. This certainly had something to do with reengineering losing many of its devotees by the late 1990s. Just as important perhaps is the limited applicability: it appears to work best in "logistics and order fulfillment" allowing a firm to increase speed and service to customers and least in regard to intellectual labor.[52] But the fact remains that reengineering with its emphasis on the computer and work teams does pose a threat to middle management. Let us examine this in great detail, for it holds the key to future management.

Shoshana Zuboff's massive study of the use of information technology in several industrial plants and corporations clearly demonstrates that management information systems can either reinforce bureaucratic authority or subvert it. The logical conclusion of information technology is the creation of an "informated" workplace in which workers have equal access to information; incorrectly used, information technology produces an "automated" workplace that only reinforces the hierarchical control of information.

The computer allows for the establishment of an "electronic text" in which the organization's entire spectrum of work can be made visible and even quantified. The creation of a single electronic text means, of course, that the text is both a comprehensive logic and a system of specialized information. This leads to what Zuboff calls a "radical centralization" of power.[53] This power is not, however, one based on human experience and cultural tradition; rather it is the abstract and impersonal power of a technological system. If the electronic text invariably centralizes power, it can concurrently lead to a decentralization of power. If all employees have access to the computer system, then hierarchical authority (that which is based on the control of information and communication) is made superfluous. Computer or information systems used to their fullest potential contradict the hierarchical dimension of bureaucracy.

Zuboff's forecast about the workplace of the future includes a model of the informated organization.[54] Workers will have both the computer skills to master the entire program and make changes in it when necessary and have full access to the program. Instead of manager/employee relationships there will be collegial relations. She envisages the workers organized (symbolically if not spatially) in a series of concentric circles around the center: the electronic text, the database. One's distance from the center is a direct reflection of the "range and comprehensiveness" of responsibility and the extent of one's accountability to the organization. All in all the informated workplace will blur the distinction between blue-collar and white-collar workers as everyone becomes a computer programmer to a greater or lesser extent. The workers' skills based on practical knowledge decline, while their computer-based skills increase. The opportunity for mutual participation in the system's operations and for common learning will produce a shared sense of responsibility. Zuboff claims that this will produce an "anticipatory conformity" to avoid being shamed by one's peers.[55] This is human relations with a vengeance.

The informated workplace is already being experimented with. As one might expect, the resistance of middle managers is enormous.[56] They much prefer to have an automated workplace. This is one in which humans are turned into machines; that is, they are given a minimum of information (only what is necessary for the specific task), little if any flexibility in the performance of the job, and no chance to alter the system. Such an inflexible system is called an expert system; it contains a set of decision-rules or effective procedures that represents the experience of successful practitioners reduced to calculative rationality. Barbara Garson has documented the use of expert systems that in effect automate the workplace (without the replacement of personnel by machines). From employees at McDonalds to airline reservationists to stock brokers and estate planners, expert systems have rendered trivial their contribution to work.[57]

Whether modern organizations turn in the direction of an automated or informated workplace, the use of information systems allows information to assume a normative cast. The rules of the bureaucracy come to rest in the information system in one of two ways. The first is the expert system, which contains decision rules (effective procedures) and makes decisions when fed the proper information. The second case is a database with decision rules subject to modification. And yet even here (Zuboff's informated workplace) the tendency will be for the informated workplace to approximate an automated (expert system) workplace. How can any individual have complete abstract knowledge about the work of a complex organization in relation to the *world beyond the computer?* This is the crux of the matter: each individual worker is supposed to master the electronic text, but no individual can have sufficient knowledge about the work of an entire complex organization to prevent the information system from becoming largely automated. Partial knowledge is dangerous, for it may change in the context of the knowledge of the whole. Therefore, the tendency will be to defer to the extant information system and to alter it only in minor ways. Zuboff's informated workplace only makes sense in regard to organizations that are relatively small and produce a material product. Reengineering desires the informated workplace, a place where rational management (the information system) meets human relations (the work team).

Human relations management theories have been gaining ground on their rational management rivals since the 1960s.[58] The human relations model has two branches: leadership and group relations. There have been a raft of leadership books, seminars, and workshops appear in recent years. Margaret Wheatley's

Leadership and the New Science, published in 1992, is a popular tract on leadership as the basis of sound management. Like other management gurus she has her own institute. The title of the last chapter of the book, "The New Scientific Management," is the key to her human relations approach. Frederick Taylor's version of scientific management was based upon a mechanistic view of science; hers is founded upon chaos theory and quantum physics. She uses the concepts of self-organizing systems and relational holism to describe how organizations can function as open systems, that is, systems that exist only in relation to other systems and change through this interaction. Because information is the creative energy of the universe, as Wheatley's "new science" proclaims, and because the organization is an open system within the universe, good managers must look to employees as a source of information and creativity. Good organizations permit a high degree of employee participation in the decision-making process. At the same time good employees are those who make a moral and emotional commitment to the organization. Effective managers are democratic leaders who act as brokers between the organization and the individual employee. Respect your employees, and they will work harder and more efficiently.[59]

Stephen Covey's immensely popular *Seven Habits of Highly Successful People* is another example of the leadership branch of the human relations school of management. It is, of course, more than that; it is a cliche-studded self-help book, a moral cookbook, and a complete guide to life. Covey defines a habit as the "intersection of *knowledge*, and *skill*, and *desire*."[60] Covey's book is a motivation or self-help book that is long on instilling desire and short on knowledge and skills. This is not to say that nothing he says is helpful, but in most instances it appears to be warmed-over common sense. This is a manual on building character or wanting to build character.

The seven habits are interdependent. The first is "be proactive," or discharge positive energy and be a doer; not someone who merely reacts to others. This is a variation of the positive thinking of Dale Carnegie and Norman Vincent Peale. The second habit is "begin with the end in mind." This is a phrase for personal leadership, which means that one establishes principles to live by and goals to be achieved; he even advises writing a personal mission statement.

Habit three is "put first things first." It is the result of habits one and two; and involves an act of will to put into practice one's beliefs and to realize one's goals. Habit four is "think win/win." This is an attitude that the other party in any interaction should benefit as much as you do. One might simply call it cooperation. The fifth habit is "seek first to understand, then to be understood." This is the principle of empathy that allows us to understand someone whom we can then enlist in a cooperative and mutually beneficial venture.

Habit six is "synergize," which refers to "creative cooperation." When I cooperate with someone, we create something neither of us was capable of accomplishing alone. Habit seven is "sharpen the saw." This refers to the periodic need for "self-renewal," which has physical, mental, emotional, and spiritual dimensions. In self-renewal we restore balance to our lives and become more empathetic and more creative.

Covey's *Seven Habits of Highly Successful People* is a rehash of the earlier twentieth-century positive thinking tracts. There is really nothing new in it except for the cliches. It represents an attempt to turn every employee into a leader, that is, one who is cooperative and works diligently on behalf of the firm. Apparently every leader is a cheerful and docile employee.

Quality circles represent the groups relations branch of the human relations school. Quality circle can be defined as "a small group of workers, usually led by the foreman, who 'shares with management the responsibility for locating and solving problems of coordination and productivity.' "[61] Quality circles were popularized in Japan with the use of Edward Deming's theory of management, total quality management. Quality circles were only one part of an overall management technique that was highly statistical. Eventually quality circles became autonomous, and devotees trained managers and employees in the use of this technique without reference to a larger theory.[62]

Quality circles refer both to the actual performance of the work group and to their group discussions afterwards. The latter is necessary to work out the details of proposed innovations and to keep motivation high. The philosophy is that by making workers more creative in and responsible for their labor, they will work more efficiently and loyally. The expectation is that each employee will come to accept the company's ideology, with the work groups becoming and ally of management in enforcing and sustaining work commitment to organizational goals.

Human-relations style management uses the "sympathetic" leadership of managers or the work group to motivate workers and even at times to solve problems. Like scientific and other forms of rational management, its primary interest is the efficiency of the organization. Management theories come and go; obviously none of them lives up to its claims. How is management practiced, both apart from and including management theory?

Companies actively promote and pay for employees to attend seminars and workshops on leadership, like Covey's and Wheatley's previously described; but these seminars have little effect upon the daily activities of managers. Group relations approaches like quality circles are more time- consuming and difficult to implement. Guillermo Grenier's study of quality circles at Ethicon-Albuquerque, a suture-making subsidiary of Johnson and Johnson demonstrates humanized management in practice. Although Ethicon-Albuquerque used the quality circle technique in part to prevent the plant from becoming unionized, it also thought it could improve worker morale and increase productivity. Facilitators (who worked for management) dominated the meetings that had become mandatory for member of each production team; they controlled the agenda but still needed to appear open to worker suggestions.[63] Team decisions never affected the distribution of power in the plant, nor were they ever important to either management or labor.

According to Grenier, the humanized management that creates the trappings of participatory democracy as a way of manipulating workers is a "method of de-bureaucratizing control" that possesses "greater sophistication, efficiency, and subtlety" than typical bureaucratic control. And yet this technique of psychological control is set within a larger bureaucratic structure. Grenier describes the seven characteristics of de-bureaucratizing control:

(1) personalized authority of a manager who is "one of us"; (2) a manager's right to make rules for the work group if he perceives his control is waning; (3) managerial latitude to chastise workers for deviant acts unrelated to work efficiency; (4) mandatory participation; (5) preventing team decisions from being effective; (6) the attitude that peers are responsible for one another's performance; and (7) the fiction that the difference in power between workers and managers is offset by their common commitment to corporate culture.[64]

Manager-inspired rules thrived in this climate:

> It was a rule that team members interview potential employees and evaluate their capabilities and ability to fit into the team concept. It was a rule that team members evaluate each other on a wide range of issues, not all clearly related to production. It was a rule that team members discuss personal difficulties at meetings to help the facilitator decide whether and what intervention was required. It was a rule for peers to control and regulate each other. It was even a rule that workers had to belong to a team and attend team meetings.[65]

These rules were necessary because without them participation in the quality circle program would have vanished. The workers knew to a greater or lesser extent that they were being manipulated, but the ideology of quality control made it difficult for them to articulate their grievances. How can one effectively oppose participatory democracy for the worker without appearing to be antilabor and even anti-American?

The ideology of human relations and the promotion of the computer as a technology that gives employees more power have created the illusion of decentralization; yet bureaucracy thrives and the computer has only reinforced hierarchical control ("automated" workplace). Zuboff's research into those companies that have used the computer to construct an "electronic text" of the entire spectrum of work and productivity indicates that those who use it to create an "informated" workplace are in a distinct minority.[66]

If the use of the computer to supplant middle management were taking hold, one would expect to find a decrease in the number of business managers. The myth of downsizing notwithstanding, *"The weight of the bureaucratic burden has actually been growing, not contracting, through the mid-1990s,"* argues economist David Gordon.[67] The bureaucratic burden is the massive size and cost of managers and supervisors in private corporations; the size is measured by the ratio of managers and supervisors to workers. Gordon admits that corporations fired some managers in the 1980s, but the number of workers fired greatly exceeded the number of managers and supervisors, keeping the ratio of managers to workers about the same. Moreover, corporations began to hire back managers in the 1990s at a rate that permitted the ratio of managers to workers to grow slightly. The United States has the largest bureaucratic burden of any modern society.[68]

The growth of bureaucracy in government is legendary. Administrative centralization has been growing unabatedly since World War II. More troublesome than sheer growth, however, has been the hardening of bureaucratic rules. Philip Howard has documented the triumph of procedural rules that have become "final rules," where "every decision is a binary choice." Legal absolutism prevails in administrative law. Howard notes that "government approaches its new tasks every year in the same absolutist way: problems must be solved once and for all. With enough procedures, no bureaucrat will ever again put his hand in the till; and so, as uncovered in 1994, the Defense Department spends more on procedures for travel reimbursement ($2.2 billion) than on travel (2 billion)."[69] Such procedural rules try to account for every eventuality and eliminate all ambiguity. But this vain attempt actually obliterates responsibility, judgement, and trust. When law is based on a set of related principles, however, it permits those who apply it to make judgements and use common sense.[70] We are fast approaching the world of Kafka's *The Castle*. Can we not see the influence of a technology in the widespread use of final rules in organizations?

The Relation between Managerial Technique and Success

Does management theory and technique make an organization successful? Undoubtedly some companies make large profits and some governmental agencies operate more or less efficiently. But is the success due to a specific management theory and technique, or to other factors? Management technique is as unsuccessful as therapy is successful. The measure of success for the former, however, is *external*, whereas for the latter it is *internal* (within the individual). Let us examine, then, what works and doesn't work in management and why.

Management decisions include the following: strategy formulation, planning and budgeting, performance measurement, resource allocation, "human resource" management, physical plant operations, and communications with the board.[71] Some of these processes, e.g., physical plant operations, can be validly measured, but most cannot be. Organizational success is in general not due to formal knowledge—statistical information, procedural rules, and decision rules.

In an analysis of the literature on the subject, Ida Hoos concludes that "there is no proof that computers are helping managers make better decisions" nor are they increasing profits.[72] Economist Lester Thurow argues that more information does not improve the decision-making of accountants and other white-collar employees. Thurow observes that "computers made accounting faster, but that speed was used not to reduce the employment of accountants but to increase the frequency and types of accounting."[73] Much of the new information being gathered and processed was irrelevant. An empirical study of the relationship between strategic planning and financial performance in twenty-one companies in Great Britain found little if any support for the "basic assumptions on which corporate planning is established."[74] Mintzberg's exhaustive study of strategic planning likewise found it to be a failure;[75] moreover, his analysis of how effective managers perform their work discovered that formal information was of little consequence for the most important decisions.[76] Martha Feldman and James March have studied the relationship between information and decision making in organizations. They conclude that much of the information has little relevance for making decisions, that much of it is used to justify a decision made before the data were collected, and that requested information is often not used to help make the decision for which it was requested.[77]

As the basis for decision making, formal information suffers from the following deficiencies: (1) it is too abstract, that is, it leaves out that which is qualitative and depends on context for its meaning; (2) it is too general if it is in the form of aggregate data; (3) it is sometimes unreliable, especially if it is only based on a guess; (4) it is sometimes politicized if the department, division, or agency of origin senses the need to protect itself by inflating or deflating the data;[78] (5) it is only convenient, that is, information and managerial techniques are often chosen because they are accessible to a time-strapped manager.[79] Bureaucratic rules, which most often are final rules, eliminate the judgment and common sense of the manager. Expert systems, which combine formal information and decision rules, take formalization to an even higher level. If formal information and rational management techniques are not effective, what is?

Successful managers make extensive use of their own informal knowledge, that is, practical knowledge based on experience and that of others both inside and outside the company. Consequently, their decisions are judgments, not calculations or logical conclusions.[80] They make use of formal knowledge where appropriate, for some things can be measured and some decisions are simple and logical. But to know when to calculate and when to make a qualitative judgment is based on experience and requires a judgement. Formal decision-making models imply an "anticipatory, consequential logic." They employ hypothetical data and trace out alternative *future* outcomes depending on which choices one makes. Decisions based on experiential learning are grounded in past and present experiences with the understanding that experience is only a *rough* guide to making a decision, for the experience has to be applied to different and ever-changing contexts, and that the future will contain many surprises.[81] Formal decision-making models, information systems, and formal planning assume that all reality is logical, if not mathematical.

Much of life, however, including that in the business world, is highly ambiguous, even contradictory; moreover, it may change unexpectedly and decisively. James March identifies a number of ambiguities that characterize decision-making in business. First, managers may have ambiguous or conflicting preferences in terms

of goals, e.g., short-term profits versus long-term profits and survival. Second, decisions are sometimes ambiguous in respect to
the actions required to carry them out. This is especially true when
the manager making the decision has limited understanding of
the work processes involved. Third, reality is not fully logical, and
information about it is less than complete; consequently, managers
have to rely upon experience and judgment as well as formal
knowledge and procedures. Hence intelligence is ambiguous.
Fourth, meaning is ambiguous. No matter how the supporters of
informational systems may try, they cannot prevent the goals of
an organization and the means of realizing them from acquiring
an indirect (symbolic) meaning apart from the organization's pro-
fessed values. For example, statistical information symbolizes
technology.[82]

Rational management systems attempt to create a closed system
of formal information and final rules. Such formal knowledge
would only fit an unambiguous and static reality. All social realities are ambiguous. What sets a technological civilization apart
from others is the amount of and unpredictability of change. Random occurrences can interfere with any rational attempt to realize
an organization's goals; sometimes success in the business world
is due to luck. Sometimes managers perceive that any individual's
success and that of the company is a result of "being in the right
place at the right time."[83]

A technological civilization has made reality increasingly more
unpredictable.[84] Technology introduces new chemicals into the environment at an alarming rate, and their overall impact is impossible to gauge, for every new factor introduced into the
environment interacts with those already there. Biological species
are rapidly disappearing with serious consequences for the biosphere. Technology has made possible the global economy, which
in addition to its deleterious impact on the environment (especially in developing countries), is inherently unstable left to itself.
George Soros has demonstrated the fallacy of classical economic
theory with its assumption of equilibrium. Financial markets do
not automatically move toward equilibrium because the expectations of buyers and sellers, which act as self-fulfilling prophecies,
interact with supply and demand.[85] Financial markets are

therefore inherently unstable, and the global economy only exacerbates this instability.

Lester Thurow identifies four factors in addition to the global economy that have created enormous change and uncertainty: (1) the collapse of Communism; (2) a shift to information technology as the main economic driving force; (3) populations that are growing larger, getting older, and becoming geographically mobile at a startling rate; (4) no dominant economic, political, or military power.[86] One would be tempted to add the growth and proliferation of religious fundamentalism all over the world. Technological growth has created intense competition for resources, capital, and information; consequently, political and religious tensions have become magnified.

The business organization is a microcosm of the international community. Robert Jackall[87] and Henry Mintzberg[88] have demonstrated how the emphasis on formal knowledge and final rules in the quest for efficiency creates an amoral, politicized work environment. Because formal knowledge does not guarantee success, and because one cannot control the market and one's competitors, managers become suspicious of each other and band together for protection. The politicizing of relations in the organization makes efficacious management ever more uncertain. With all this change and uncertainty we suffer form a glut of formal information that becomes disinformation because we cannot integrate it and make sense of it; as a result, not only can we not predict the future, we cannot judge the severity of some of the risks we are taking.[89]

Management as Magic

The human relations approach to management operates according to the placebo effect, whereas the rational management approach functions according to the principle of the self-fulfilling prophecy. The placebo effect is a kind of self-fulfilling prophecy (expectations our actions make come true); its influence is largely emotional, however. The self-fulfilling prophecy may be either unconscious and unintended: e.g., the false belief that a bank is insolvent creates a run on the bank making the bank eventually become insolvent, or intended, e.g., a magical practice designed to influence one's environment. In the instance of the intended self-fulfilling prophecy, the magical practice is believed to account for successful outcomes, for it is always used. When the magic fails, no one doubts its efficacy because it "obviously" worked at other times.

The magic of human relations management is similar to that of therapy. Both function as placebos. Recall that the aim of human relations is to integrate the worker more completely into the company by getting her to accept the prevailing ideology with or without participating in a work team. In other words, the employee must become adjusted. A happy employee will have better morale and be more productive. The goal of therapy is a happy or well-adjusted client. No wonder no one knows exactly where human relations business seminars end and recovery and self-help seminars begin. They share a common origin in the positive thinking movement. Psychological magic, it is believed, embodies the sacred power of the life-milieu—technical causality.

Management technique promotes itself as instrumental in achieving organizational success. We saw previously that early in the twentieth century individual success was redefined as happiness (adjustment). Adjusted employees may temporarily become more productive as a result of a management seminar, but this will have little impact on the overall success of the company. Just as therapy does not usually confront the social sources of the patient's stress, so human relations management techniques ask for adjustment in the face of an impersonal, bureaucratic organization that reduces the employees to cogs in a machine. The only lasting employee satisfaction with work would be the result of a reduction in bureaucratic structure, worker democracy, and a drastic reduction in economic inequality. Even this could not guarantee success.

Rational management techniques do not guarantee organizational success, which is largely due to informal knowledge. Consistent as they are with the larger bureaucratic structure of most organizations, rational management techniques are almost a constant feature of government and business. Especially prominent are information systems that collect and process an enormous amount of statistical data. Hence, there is a correlation between the use of rational management procedures and an organization's success. Rational management techniques act as self-fulfilling prophecies; they do not produce their intended outcome, but because they are always used to some extent, they *appear* to be efficacious. The statistical information of rational management symbolizes technology; consequently, rational management magic is believed to incorporate the sacred power of the life-milieu.

The magical nature of management technique can be ascertained from its use of symbolic words, images, and statistics. In Chapter 2, I argued that words and images symbolized technology as information, means, and object. Plastic words, such as "information," "communication," "progress," "management," "model," "solution," "planning," and "strategy," symbolize technology as an abstract system of information. Poerksen maintains that administrators are among the heaviest users of plastic words.[90] Plastic words are for the most part the province of rational management theorists.[91]

Other words and phrases, jargon, cliches, and commonplace expressions "symbolize" technology in one way or another in their association with other words and images. Human relations management shares with therapy a penchant for vague words that refer to the individual's inner state. Stephen Covey, as we have already seen, has a talent for the buzz word and cliche: "upward spiral of growth," "synergy," "proactive," "emotional bank accounts," and "deposits of unconditional love."[92] The jargon of the human relations managers has less international appeal than the plastic words of rational managers. Yet there are terms both share in common, such as "paradigm" and "quality."

Of special note are the sports and military metaphors that abound in the management literature. Military metaphors, such as "reconnaissance," "good intelligence," and "battle plan" compare the business leader to a military officer, even Attila the Hun; military metaphors characterize the rational management theorists, who want management to be muscular or coldly rational.[93]

More widespread than the military metaphor is the sports metaphor, which is used by both types of management theorists. The human relations theorists stress the "team" and "teamwork," "commitment to the team," and "team-effort." There will also be references to winning, as with Covey's "win/win." The rational management theorists stress metaphors like "slam-dunk," "game-plan," "touchdown," "prevent defense," "all-out rush," "home run," and so forth. These sports metaphors are all about success or winning. There is a preponderance of football metaphors among the sports metaphors. Football as the most technical sport in terms of equipment, organization, and strategy appeals to the technological imagination. Sports metaphors are used extensively by politicians as well.[94] Earlier in the twentieth century sports enthusiasts used business metaphors, suggesting that business was the model for emulation. Business metaphors were widely used in biology, as with Darwin's "struggle for existence."[95] The great reversal began in the 1940s when business leaders were supplanted by sports and other entertainers as heroes in the mass media.[96] Eventually business and politics are compared to sports.

Statistics plays a dominant role in rational management technique. Statistical information is the key to good management. Feldman and March indicate our irrational relationship to formal or statistical information. Formal information is requested no matter how much managers already have and even while ignoring what they do have. Information is sometimes requested after a decision has already been made. In short, managers request more formal information, whether useful or not, at any time, and then ignore much of it. It is evident, then, that formal information has symbolic value in the modern organization. Feldman and March point out that people have a tendency to attribute success in an organization to "factors they control."[97] This is the practice of magic as a self-fulfilling prophecy. They suggest that this practice is a result of information being a symbol of reason and rational decision making.[98] Or is statistical information a symbol of technology, specifically the computer? The computer stores and processes the formal information that allows an organization to succeed. Reality and the ability to manipulate it are in the computer.

The mass media provide a dramatization of the mythological

universe of technological utopianism. As such the visual images of the media are the central symbols of the technology. We saw previously that advertising's primary mythological symbol is happiness-health as consumption; therapy's is health-happiness as adjustment; management's is success (although human relations merges with therapy in an emphasis on adjustment). The television programs that most symbolize success are sports programs. We can now understand why sports metaphors are dominant in business and politics today. Sports has become extremely popular because of television coverage. The mass media present us with a technological utopia against which everything else must be compared. Sports success is ritualistically enacted in the media, thereby providing a model for business and political organizations to emulate. Sports programs unite, as it were, the two approaches to management, for it is often the "teamwork" of well-adjusted athletes and the game plan that together produce the victory.

Management technique involves magical practices, either the psychological magic of human relations that depends upon dramatized information, or the administrative magic of rational management that depends upon statistical information. The mass media, therapy, and management are the main types of technological magic. Each represents one of the mythological symbols of technological utopianism. Advertising especially ritualizes happiness (as consumption); therapy ritualizes health (as adjustment); management, success/survival. Television advertising and programs encompass all the magical techniques under the unifying myth of technological utopianism.

Why Society and the Individual Need Management

Management theory (technique) is faddish; theories have a brief shelf life, and old theories are constantly being repackaged with new buzzwords and cliches. Obviously they don't work—they don't control uncertainty and predict the future. So why are we so susceptible to each new preposterous theory, each new preposterous technique? Management technique promotes itself as a kind of technology; it clothes itself in the aura of technology. So if this management technique does not work, the next one to come along will likely succeed.

Human relations techniques (like therapy) attempt to produce adjusted employees, who, no matter how bleak the circumstances of their employment, retain a cheerful disposition and a positive outlook. Rational management techniques, however, serve the paramount purpose of management—to predict and control the future. In creating a closed system of statistical information, procedures, and decision rules, rational management magically assures us that we can control economic markets and employees, despite the fact that a technological civilization is the most unpredictable of civilizations. In the grips of a technological vertigo, our minds crushed by technical rationality, we cannot perceive the obvious—that decentralized administration and practical knowledge, which does not attempt to predict and control the future, but only anticipate it, is the only way to live in the present. The obsession with rational control and prediction leads to an ever-increasing irrationality.[99]

· 7 ·

The Triumph of the Irrational

*Man, exposed to the horror of unrestrained reason, bidden to serve it
without comprehending it, caught in the toils of a process that develops
far over his head, caught in the toils of his own irrationality, man is
like the savage who is bewitched by black magic and cannot see the
connection between means and effect.*

Hermann Broch
The Sleepwalkers

Every advance in technical rationality today is surpassed by a
decline in common sense and a growing irrationality, the signs
of which are everywhere.

Female fashion models sometimes have a wan look, like someone dying of consumption or long on the run from the police.
Near anorexic, they appear to be depressed, hopeless, and hol-
lowed out. The clothes they model suggest, at times, poverty or a
rejection of society. The tattooing, piercing, and branding of the
human body have become vogue, for no reason other than to
shock, to call attention to oneself, and as a sign of group identity.
Then there is the cult of the celebrity and proliferation of fan clubs
for every movie, television, recording, and athletic star. We wear
shirts with their pictures and names on them with no apparent
embarrassment. New religious sects spring up like weeds, as do
ersatz religious groups that emphasize holistic and alternative
medicine. We consume herbs and vitamins in vast quantities
seemingly in a vain quest for immortality. We are vulnerable to
every new therapy and management technique that comes along;
our critical reason has been blunted. Our expectations for the com-

puter—that it will solve the problem of education, make us more intelligent, and give us total information about every aspect of life—are absurd.

Adults seem like children today, susceptible to every new toy, game, and amusement to come along. We have sentimentalized children; consequently, their spontaneity and impulsiveness have become a cultural ideal. Adults are slaves to work and schedules; children are free to play and have fun. How can we not attempt to become more childlike?

And yet we go to work every day and rationally do what we are told. The computer dominates work; procedural rules proliferate rapidly. Leisure too has been reduced to a rational technique. For example, travel is organized and packaged as tourism. The *form* of human activity is rational, but increasingly the *content* is irrational. There does not appear to be any purpose to much of what we do other than mere possibility: if it is possible, it must be done.[1] In a technological civilization the tension between what is and what ought to be (an ethical norm) is supplanted by that between what is and what is possible. But mere possibility gives rise to all the irrational attitudes and actions previously described. What I wish to discuss, then, is how technology attacks common sense and creates ever greater irrationality. Deprived of common sense and distracted by irrational pursuits, we do not realize that our desire to live as free persons has atrophied.

To exercise common sense, to learn by experience, to reflect on that experience, and to make moral judgments, the individual must be in immediate contact with reality. But technology causes us to lose contact with reality.[2] Technology makes our knowledge, opinions,[3] and even our emotions[4] secondhand, for it mediates reality. In other words, it makes reality abstract. Technology at the level of means and knowledge must reduce reality to logical if not mathematical categories. But reality is sensuous, symbolic, and utterly ambiguous. To interpret reality I must bypass technology with a personal knowledge of history, culture, and other people. To the extent that I rely upon technology, I reduce history, culture, and other people to logical categories and statistics. Public opinion, which depends upon the mass media for its formation and dissemination, provides us with ready-made opinions on every issue. Moreover, the media with their emphasis on visual images, manipulate our emotions about imaginary events and people. They provide us with vicarious experiences, thereby helping to release superficial and fleeting emotions. No one can remain rational in a subjective and normative sense if reality recedes into a series of random abstractions. If this happens, one will find reality in the irrational—instinct, emotion, and fantasy. The mass media, then, both mediate and compensate for an ever more abstract reality with knowledge, opinion, and emotion that is only secondarily ours. Television in particular ensconces us in a shell of irrationality. The decline of common sense results either in an irrational use of reason or a retreat into the world of sensation pursued for its own sake.[5]

Technology not only encourages us to lose touch with reality, it makes us attempt to escape it as well. Technology increases the tempo of life: information is processed more quickly and human activity is more tightly compressed. Never before have people been expected to assimilate so much information and stuff as many activities into the day.[6] This extends even into the realm of leisure, which is as technologically controlled as work. Humans often find themselves doing several things concurrently, e.g., fixing breakfast, listening to the news, and getting dressed. This is, of course, a source of stress. Life is subject to schedules and an endless list of regulations. Under the circumstance of extensive rational control and stress, humans feel the need to escape into fantasy, dreams, and ecstasy.[7]

In *Understanding Media* Marshall McLuhan compared technology's psychological impact upon the self to the physiological effect of injury or disease upon the central nervous system. When faced with stress or irritation, the organism has two principal means of restoring equilibrium to the central nervous system. The first is the elimination of the irritant by overcoming it or escaping it; the second is counterirritation in which the central nervous system "amputates" (that is, numbs) the affected limb or organ at the point of stress. Pleasure and therapy, McLuhan noted, are counterirritants, just as comfort is the elimination of stress or irritation. Physical shock and schizophrenia are extreme counterirritants: shock allows one to narcoticize physical stress, and schizophrenia "amputates" psychological stress. By way of analogy we can compare the self's handling of psychological stress to the central nervous system's control of physical stress. Pleasure is a chief form of counterirritation. McLuhan's examples include alcohol, sports, and entertainment.[8] Traditional societies had a psychological outlet for stress in the festival, a time for the ritualized consumption of food, drink, and sex. The modern counterpart lies in the mass media.

Technology indirectly contributes to the tendency to escape reality by destroying the common meaning that is the foundation of every culture. As we have previously seen, humans do not perceive a need to symbolize technology (our milieu), for it is our own creation. Consequently, we do not create common meaning, which, among other things, attempts to limit the power of one's milieu. Moreover, the growing power of technology over the past two centuries militates against any attempt to develop a common morality. For there is an inverse relationship between power and values: when power becomes too great it destroys morality, which to be effective has to place some limitations on the exercise of power.[9]

Most important perhaps are the issues of suffering and death. All traditional cultures had to face the question of the meaning of life in the face of daily suffering and imminent death. Compassion, friendship, and love were answers to the meaning of life, tragically conceived.[10] That is, life inevitably leads to death, and suffering rather than happiness is our daily fare; happiness is only an occasional respite from adversity. Technological utopianism contradicts the tragic view of life in substituting happiness as the permanent condition of human society. Inadvertently it makes compassion and love superfluous. For these acts only realize their potential in relation to human suffering. No wonder, then, that today we have "bereavement counselors" and can "rent" hospital visitors to offer encouragement to our loved ones.[11] It is best to ignore suffering and death as much as possible in our technological utopia; otherwise happiness may disappear.

The technological utopianism of the mass media provides us with false meaning, that is, meaning insufficient to provide us with hope. The meaning of life invariably provides us with a sense of transcendence—suffering can be transcended by love and a fear of death by a belief in immortality. Hope means nothing unless it goes against certainty and fate; it rejects the apparent hopelessness of the present projected into the future.[12] Hope is inexorably tied to meaning that is sufficient to contest daily suffering and the inevitability of death. The mass media define meaning as consumption. This banal meaning is insufficient for the individual, let alone as a basis for a moral community; furthermore, it provides no basis for hope. Of course, in a utopia there is no need for hope.

Hopelessness leads to despair and to escape, if it does not result in severe depression or suicide.[13] For most of us, our hopelessness lies buried deep within, because escapist activities, such as television, sports, shopping, alcohol, and other kinds of amusement, distract us from the questions of suffering and meaning. It is hopelessness, I think, that is behind the increasing unwillingness of individuals to be alone with themselves to reflect upon such issues. We much prefer to have the radio, television, or CD player going. Silence frightens us. Amusement and pleasure, pursued for their own sake (as an escape), however, lead to a constant experimentation with lifestyle and behavior. This pushes us in the direction of ever greater irrationality, for today's "narcotics" are insufficient for tomorrow.

Apart from promoting the need to escape, technology enlarges the power of human instincts by liberating them from moral control. Every conventional morality places limitations on aggression, sexuality, and the like. In the milieu of society, the locus of a common morality is gradually split between the individual and the community. In those societies that come to value the individual, reason, and freedom, self-control becomes a virtue.[14] The individual is expected to internalize a set of moral attitudes, not at times without some modicum of freedom in doing so, and to apply them even in the face of the opposition of others. When neither the community nor the individual controls the power of the instincts, they are given free reign; consequently, the impulse to satisfy one's irrational instincts grows more powerful.

There is a tendency as well for the individual today to equate the instinctual with the subjective. In a technological civilization reason is collectivized as technical reason; concurrently, subjective and normative reason, the ability to make judgements and to exercise critical reason, diminishes. The individual is rational largely in the context of technical and bureaucratic rationality, which in being centralized and collectivized requires little if any judgment on his part. Subjectivity comes tacitly to be identified with emotion. If much of my life has been colonized by technical and bureaucratic rules, at least my emotions are still mine. Recall that the "meaning" of the visual images of the media is instinctual power, for as material representations their primary impact is emotional.

The irrational finally becomes an ideal in that it represents the creative part of the self and an indirect resistance to the rational system that almost totally controls us. We tacitly sense that the more powerful the technological system becomes, the less powerful we are; that the more rational the system is, the less meaning and hope it can provide; and that our refuge is in the irrational. The sentimentalized[16] child is our idealized irrationality: the spontaneous, impulsive, emotional child who turns to reason only as a last resort. Children, we believe, perfectly embody the ultimate (for the individual) mythological symbol of technological utopianism—happiness. The child is symbolically far from suffering and death.

This helps to explain the puerilism of modern culture. In observing this over sixty years ago, J. H. Huizinga argued that the paramount characteristic of puerilism is the inversion of work (and everything serious) and play. We regard the serious activities of life as a game; at the same time we treat play, e.g., sports, amusement, and entertainment, with a deadly seriousness. Witness the growing fanaticism of sports spectators all over the world and the amount of television coverage that is given to it. Business and politics come to be regarded cynically as a kind of game whose sole purpose is personal advantage over others.[17] Huizinga lists among the examples of puerilism: "the need for banal entertainment, a need easily met but never satiated" and the "search for gross sensations." In the traditionally more serious aspects of life, "people react in exaggerated fashion to each other's words, impute to one another bad intentions or motives, show intolerance toward opinions other than theirs" and are easily flattered.[18] Sixty years after Huizinga puerilism is omnipresent. Simply consider the investigation of President Clinton by Kenneth Starr and its coverage in the media. All parties involved have behaved in the most childish ways imaginable. It is as if the entire country has been turned into a junior high school, where competing groups all point fingers at one another and then gloat over their opponents' misfortunes.

Magic, however, is the most dangerous form of irrationality today, for it masquerades as technical reason, as a form of technology. Moreover, its exclusive purpose is to help us adjust to the technological system by compensating for its lack of meaning and the excessive stress it produces. One form of irrationality—therapeutic magic—is used to combat other forms of irrationality—drug abuse, mental illness, violence. The mass media magically transform reality into a utopia and provide technology with its magical aura. We are entombed in a sea of irrationality. But how could it be otherwise? When reason is not under moral direction, it falls under the sway of instinctual power. Reason is irrationally driven by the desire to master and dominate nature and society.[19] But it can only do so by creating a closed rational system, statistical and technological, that cannot accomplish its "rational" goals. Our worship of technology and irrational belief in its omnipotence prevent us from seeing the obvious: the technological system can accomplish none of its mythological goals. It can guarantee us neither happiness and health, nor success and survival. Instead, the technological system is the greatest threat to their realization.

The Failure of Education

One response to the threat of widespread irrationality is to emphasize education; indeed, it is our last hope in the battle for reason. Schools, especially universities, appear to be a haven for reason. Unfortunately, technical reason and magic have crowded out the subjective (normative) reason that was embodied in the humanities. The struggle to retain this humanistic knowledge is feeble, for the liberal arts are dying. They no longer constitute a living tradition, ensuring some measure of continuity with the past. The wisdom and experiences contained in the humanities are irrelevant to life in a technological civilization. Does anyone really believe anymore in the promise of the liberal arts, in the ideal of a well-rounded human being who pursues truth and wisdom as much as power and technical knowledge?

Today, knowledge of art, literature, history, philosophy, and language can only function as nostalgia or as ideological compensation for the imperialism of technical knowledge. The humanities were at one time a preparation for reflective participation as a citizen and for intellectual labor. A facility with language and an ability to interpret texts were indispensable.[20] Not so today. The public, business, and parents demand technicians; and we give our customers what they want.

The modern university is almost completely technical and magical in orientation, in its administration, teaching, research, and student services. The growing technologization of the university is reflected in its bureaucratic structure, which means centralization of power and technical rationality, among other things. Our educational administrators are magicians par excellence as they recycle models and magical practices from the business world, including various assessment and accountability measures and planning exercises. What the university does administratively is reflected in the various departments that offer courses and degrees in administration. There is not a whit of difference, however, among the business administration, educational administration, hospital administration, airport administration, and hotel administration programs. The details vary from application to application, but the occult management techniques remain constant. Courses in statistics and the computer are omnipresent; almost every department in the university requires a knowledge of statistics and a facility in the use of the computer. The problem, of course, is that students get the distinct impression that all knowledge can either be quantified or reduced to a logic.

The applied human sciences likewise generate the dramatized information that forms the basis of psychological technique. Communication, business administration, educational psychology, sociology, social work, clinical and counseling psychology, and others provide the vague and ideological concepts that undergird psychological techniques. Nor does the modern university neglect the mass media, which house the most powerful psychological techniques. Even students outside of communications, marketing, and public relations are taught how essential it is to use the mass media to influence others.

The resurgence of interest in teaching in the university is not about the content of courses but about the style of the teacher. The search for the perfect technique that will both motivate students and make learning painless is as magical as the search for the Holy Grail. These teaching wizards advocate approaches like collaborative learning, smart classrooms, and long distance learning. Equally superstitious is the advocacy of critical-thinking courses, as if one could teach critical thinking as a technique. These magical approaches to teaching reflect, I'm afraid, an unconscious recognition that most students don't want to become reflective and don't want to learn anything that isn't vocationally relevant.

But can we blame the students? We have unintentionally created a technological and magical world in which there is no room for reflection, normative reason, and moral judgement. The university has abandoned its historical mission, always only imperfectly realized, to teach students to learn as much about themselves and their culture as they learn about the larger universe. We are training students to be unreflective technicians and magicians. Those of us in the social sciences and applied human sciences are most to blame for this tragedy. We are the magicians who provide the information and techniques, whose sole purpose is to adjust students as future technicians to the technological milieu while giving them the deadly impression that they are free individuals. We are responsible for enveloping technique within a magical cocoon.

Irrationality and Freedom

The images of the mass media promote emotion and instinct as the last refuge of individuality and freedom. Nothing could be farther from the truth. Reason is a prerequisite for freedom but does not guarantee it. Reason must be aligned to an internalized set of moral attitudes in order for one to make moral judgements. If moralism is destructive of freedom—the freedom of others— moral judgement is the highest expression of freedom.[21] Moralism involves rigidly applying abstract moral rules to others as a way of feeling superior to them, without any sense of one's own responsibility in the matter, and without acting upon one's judgement. That is, I express an opinion without changing my life in any way. Moral judgement, on the other hand, entails a sympathetic application of a moral attitude, with critical awareness of one's own complicity in the evil of this world, and with a decision to act as an individual to combat the evil.

We can lose our freedom to the tyranny of our instincts or the tyranny of others. Freedom necessarily involves conflict—with oneself and with others. If morality is a necessary ingredient in freedom, it can easily become tyrannical. For morality to be a source of freedom, the individual must have some say about its composition and application. The principle of civil disobedience is the highest expression of moral freedom: I am free to dissent from a moral standard of the community when I believe it to be unjust, but I am willing to suffer the consequences of punishment for my transgression.

A component of exercising moral judgement is critical reflection. This can only be done in and through language, however. Our ability and desire to symbolize our milieu is the origin of all human qualities and the basis for morality. Language can always be used for purposes of propaganda and totalitarian control, but every natural language contains the seeds of new meaning and liberating thought. With the sterilization of language and its subordination to the images of the media, we have abandoned freedom.[22]

This danger to the human race is as great as that presented by genetic engineering. Andrew Kimbrell and Jeremy Rifkin have written about the enormous dangers of genetic engineering when there is no way to foresee the consequences of what we do. The use of gene therapy to change the human germ line and the release of transgenic organisms into the biosphere, for example, will undoubtedly lead to a serious change in the biological and psychological constitution of the human being. The attempt to create a perfect human being may result in a more imperfect one.[23] The deconstruction of language, however, will result in a human being denied the essential ingredient for living as a free person—a living language. We will lack the ability to criticize those forces that enslave us and those, like genetic engineering, that threaten our future.

But does anyone really want to be free? Perhaps Tocqueville and others are right: we desire security more than freedom.[24] As the old folk song goes, "freedom is having nothing left to lose." Most of us only want to be free when our backs are up against the wall, when life is perceived to be intolerable, and when others lead the way to freedom. The mass media attempt to convince us daily to give up what crumbs of freedom that are left for the security and happiness of a technological utopia. We appear only too eager to do so. In *Autopsy of Revolution* Jacques Ellul mentions two conditions for a nonviolent cultural revolution to occur: first, the economy and political state must be unable to provide people's basic material needs; second, people must consciously perceive that life has become intolerable, that the meaninglessness and hopelessness that are endemic to a technological civilization make us profoundly unhappy.[25] Over twenty years ago Ellul maintained that neither condition had been met, but everything he wrote pointed to ever greater crises—demographic, economic, political, military, and environmental—for the technological system is out of control.

I have written this book to help clarify the experiences of those who sense that life has become intolerable without understanding why and who still value freedom. Those who have gotten this far in the book out of mere curiosity need go no further. Perhaps the book can be enjoyed as an interesting theory. In a technological civilization all ideas that are not technical are reduced to the level of play. Intellectual aesthetes entertain endless theories without having to act. But for those who are still morally engaged, who haven't given in totally to the plethora of pleasurable escapes, there is a need to resist the magnetic pull of the technological system. The task ahead is unprecedented, for the struggle is not against technology, which is a simplistic understanding of the problem, but against a technological system that is now our life-milieu. Technology as a system gives rise to a fatalism as strong as the fatalism that characterized the milieu of nature. Remember, however, that we overcame the fatalism of nature. Only those with a stomach for an apparently hopeless fight will join in the struggle initially. But as long as a few resist, there will be fissures in the system, even if they are almost imperceptible.

To become a radical today one must contest the power of the state, total administration, science in the service of technology, the mass media, and all forms of psychological technique. The global economy must be opposed, but behind it is the technological system. Ellul has discussed all of this before and at greater length. We must familiarize ourselves with his ideas, which provide the clearest, deepest, and most complete analysis of the technological system. My contribution has been to expose magic in its technological forms: the mass media, therapy, and management. Each form of magic is principally related to a specific mythological symbol: advertising to happiness (as consumption), therapy to health (as adjustment), and management to success/survival. The mass media organize the various magical forms under the unifying myth of technological utopianism. Without magic, technology would have no fatal sway over us. It is here that the struggle for freedom must begin.

Notes

Introduction

1. Marcel Mauss, *A General Theory of Magic*, trans. Robert Brain (London: Routledge and Kegan Paul, 1972), 127.

2. Margot Adler, *Drawing Down the Moon* (Boston: Beacon Press, 1979), 153–54.

3. Catherine Albanese, *Nature Religion in America* (Chicago: University of Chicago Press, 1990), 179.

4. Adler, *Drawing Down the Moon*, 153–54.

5. Ibid., 359.

6. Jacques Ellul, *The Technological Society*, trans. John Wilkinson (New York: Vintage, 1964), ch. 5.

7. Douglas Rushkoff, *Cyberia* (San Francisco: Harper Collins, 1995), 152.

8. Mark Dery, *Escape Velocity* (New York: Grove Press, 1996), 50.

9. Rushkoff, *Cyberia*, 152.

10. Ibid., 151–52.

11. Dery, *Escape Velocity*, 48–66.

12. Jennifer Cobb, *Cybergrace* (New York: Crown Publishers, 1998), 172.

13. Ibid., 168.

14. Jeremy Rifkin, *The Biotech Century* (New York: Putnam, 1998), ch. 6.

15. R. C. Lewontin, *Biology as Ideology* (New York: Harper Perennial, 1991), 59–83.

16. William Arney, *Medicine and the Management of Living* (Chicago: University of Chicago Press, 1984).

17. Jacques Ellul, *Perspectives on Our Age*, trans. Joachim Neugroschel (Toronto: CBC Enterprises, 1981), 48.

18. Theodore Roszak, *From Satoris to Silicon Valley* (San Francisco: Don't Call It Frisco Press, 1986), 32–41.

19. R. Laurence Moore, *Selling God* (New York: Oxford University Press, 1994), 257.

20. Michael Brown, *The Channeling Zone* (Cambridge: Harvard University Press, 1997), 7.

21. Ibid., 43.

22. Dr. Wayne Dyer, *Real Magic* (New York: Harper Paperbacks, 1992), 22.

23. Ibid., 24–29.

24. John Micklethwait and Adrian Wooldridge, *The Witchdoctors*, (New York: Times Books, 1996), 65–67.

25. Cited in *The Servant Leader* (Spring, 1997), 2.

26. Ibid., 3.

27. Micklethwait and Wooldridge, *The Witch Doctor*, 71.

28. Henry Mintzberg, *Mintzberg on Management* (New York: The Free Press, 1989), 73–78.

29. Robert Jackall, *Moral Mazes* (New York: Oxford University Press, 1988), 70–73.

30. Martha Feldman and James March, "Information in Organizations as Signal and Symbol," *Administrative Science Quarterly* 26 (1981), 171–86.

31. Sal Randazzo, *Mythmaking on Madison Avenue* (Chicago: Probus, 1993), 51.

32. Neil Postman, "The Parable of the Ring Around the Collar," in *Conscientious Objections* (New York: Knopf, 1988), 66–71.

Chapter 1. Both Technology and Magic

1. Fernand Braudel, *On History*, trans. Sarah Matthews (Chicago: University of Chicago Press, 1980).

2. Norbert Elias, *The Court Society*, trans. Edmund Jephcott (New York: Pantheon, 1983), ch. 1.

3. Jacques Ellul, *What I Believe*, trans. Geoffrey Bromiley (Grand Rapids: Eerdmans, 1989), chs. 8–11.

4. Ibid., chs. 9–11.

5. Hans Kelsen, *Society and Nature* (New York: Arno Press, 1974).

6. Colin Renfrew, *Archaeology and Language* (New York: Cambridge University Press, 1987), 274–75.

7. Ellul, *What I Believe*, 105.

8. Conrad Kattak, *Cultural Anthropology* (New York: McGraw-Hill, 1991), 103.

9. Colin Turnbull, *The Forest People* (New York: Simon and Schuster, 1961), 109–25.

10. Victor Barnow, *Cultural Anthropology* (New York: McGraw-Hill, 1991), 256–67.

11. Marshall Sahlins, *Stone Age Economics* (Chicago: Aldine-Atherton, 1972), ch. 5; Nurit Bird-David, "Beyond 'The Original Affluent Society': a Culturalist Reformulation," *Current Anthropology* 33 (1992): 25–34.

12. Ellul, *What I Believe*, 114.

13. C. Scott Littleton, *The New Comparative Mythology* (Berkeley: University of California Press, 1973), 3–6.

14. Ellul, *What I Believe*, 106; Alexander Marshack, *The Roots of Civilization* (New York: McGraw-Hill, 1972), 272.

15. Turnbull, *The Forest People*.

16. Mircea Eliade, *The Quest* (Chicago: University of Chicago Press, 1969), 174.

17. Turnbull, *The Forest People*, 93.

18. Walter Ong, *Orality and Literacy* (New York: Metheun, 1982).

19. Louis Dumont, *Homo Hierarchicus*, trans. Mark Sainsbury, Louis Dumont, and Basia Gulati (Chicago: University of Chicago Press, 1980).

20. Ellul, *What I Believe*, 199.

21. Mircea Eliade, *The Myth of the Eternal Return*, trans. Williard Trask (Princeton: Princeton University Press, 1954).

22. Kelsen, *Society and Nature*.

23. Jacques Ellul, *The Technological Society*, trans John Wilkinson (New York: Vintage, 1964), xxv.

24. Ivan Illich, "Disabling Professions," in *Disabling Professions*, ed. Ivan Illich et al. (Boston: Marion Boyars, 19–78), 11–39.

25. Søren Kierkegaard, *The Present Age*, trans. Alexander Dru (New York: Harper and Row, 1962); Alexis de Tocqueville, *Democracy in America*, trans. T. J. Mayer (Garden City: Anchor Books, 1969).

26. Jacques Ellul, *The Political Illusion*, trans. Konrad Kellen (New York: Vintage, 1967).

27. Bertrand de Jouvenel, *On Power*, trans. J. F. Huntington (Boston: Beacon Press, 1962).

28. Philip Howard, *The Death of Common Sense* (New York: Random House, 1994).

29. Jacques Ellul, *The Humiliation of the Word*, trans. Joyce Hanks (Grand Rapids: Eerdmans, 1985).

30. Richard Stivers, *The Culture of Cynicism: American Morality in Decline* (Cambridge: Blackwell, 1994).

31. Richard Stivers, *Evil in Modern Myth and Ritual* (Athens: University of Georgia Press, 1982), ch. 3.

32. Mircea Eliade, *The Sacred and the Profane*, trans. Willard Trask (New York: Harper and Row, 1961).

33. Richard Stivers, "The Festival in Light of the Theory of the Three

Milieus," *Journal of the American Academy of Religion* 61 (Fall 1993): 505–38.

34. Stivers, *Evil in Modern Myth and Ritual*, 2–3.

35. Stanley Tambiah, "Form and Meaning of Magical Acts: a Point of View," in *Modes of Thought*, ed. Robin Horton and Ruth Finnegan (London: Faber and Faber, 1973), 218–27.

36. Stanley Tambiah, *Magic Science, Religion, and the Scope of Rationality* (New York: Cambridge University Press, 1990), ch. 3.

37. Tambiah, "Form and Meaning of Magical Acts," 218–27.

38. Michelle Rosaldo, "It's All Uphill: The Creative Metaphors of Ilongot Magical Spells," in *Sociocultural Dimensions of Language Use*, eds. Mary Sanches and Ben Blount (New York: Academic Press, 1975), 200–202.

39. Tambiah, "Form and Meaning of Magical Acts," 222–23.

40. Rosaldo, "It's All Uphill," 200–202.

41. Owen Barfield, *Saving the Appearances* (New York: Harcourt Brace Jovanovich, 1957).

42. Turnbull, *The Forest People*.

43. Stivers, "The Festival," 520–26.

44. Turnbull, *The Forest People*, 144–45.

45. Tambiah, "Form and Meaning," 223.

46. Roger Caillois, *Man and the Sacred*, trans. Meyer Barash (Glencoe: Free Press, 1959), 185.

47. Anthony Wallace, *The Death and Rebirth of the Seneca* (New York: Vingage, 1969).

48. René Girard, *The Scapegoat*, trans. Yvonne Freccero (Baltimore: Johns Hopkins University Press, 1986).

49. Wallace, *The Death and Rebirth of the Seneca*, chs. 3–4.

50. Girard, *The Scapegoat*, ch. 4.

51. Turnbull, *The Forest People*, 93.

52. Mauss, *A General Theory of Magic*.

53. Eliade, *The Myth of the Eternal Return*, ch. 4.

54. Wallace, *Death and Rebirth*, 59–75.

55. Jacques Ellul, *The New Demons*, trans. C. Edward Hopkin (New York: Seabury, 1975), 200–202.

56. Mauss, *A General Theory of Magic*, 142.

57. Kelsen, *Society and Nature*.

58. Ellul, *The Technological Society*, 45.

59. Mauss, *A General Theory of Magic*, 86ff.

60. Eliade, *The Myth of the Eternal Return*, ch. 3.

61. Ellul, *The New Demons*, 209–228.

62. Paul Ricoeur, "Listening to the Parables of Jesus," in *The Philosophy of Paul Ricoeur*, ed. Charles Reagan and David Stewart (Boston: Beacon Press, 1978), 239–45.

63. Will Herberg, *Protestant Catholic Jew* (Chicago: University of Chicago Press, 1973).

64. Ellul, *The New Demons*, 70–80.

65. Jacques Ellul, *The Betrayal of the West*, trans. Matthew O'Connell (New York: Seabury, 1978), 165–68.

66. Ellul, *The Technological Society*, 387–427.

67. Caillois, *Man and the Sacred*, 98.

68. Ellul, *The New Demons*, 80–87.

69. Jouvenel, *On Power*; see also Jacques Ellul, *Autopsy of Revolution*, trans. Patricia Wolf (New York: Knopf, 1971.)

Chapter 2. Dramatized Information

1. Kenneth Hudson, *The Language of the Teenage Revolution* (London: Macmillan, 1983), 22.

2. Thomas Schachtman, *The Inarticulate Society* (New York: Free Press, 1995), 100–101.

3. Ibid., 28.

4. Jane Healy, *Endangered Minds* (New York: Simon and Schuster, 1990), 92–93.

5. Shachtman, *The Inarticulate Society*, 107.

6. Ibid., 119–34.

7. Ibid., 134.

8. Neil Postman, *Amusing Ourselves to Death*, chs. 3–4.

9. Healy, *Endangered Minds*, 37–38.

10. Hudson, *Teenage Revolution*, 23.

11. M. P. Baumgartner, *The Moral Order of the Suburb* (New York: Oxford University Press, 1988), ch. 3.

12. Peter Burke, *The Art of Conversation* (Ithaca: Cornell University Press, 1993), ch. 4.

13. Jacques Ellul, *The Technological Society*, trans. John Wilkinson (New York: Knopf, 1964), ch. 5.

14. Steffan Linder, *The Harried Leisure Class* (New York: Columbia University Press).

15. R. Murray Schaefer, *The Tuning of the World* (New York: Knopf, 1977), 185–89.

16. Robert Pattison, *The Triumph of Vulgarity* (New York: Oxford University Press, 1987), 6.

17. Schachtman, *The Inarticulate Society*, 211.

18. Ibid., 33; Tannis Williams, *The Impact of Television* (Orlando: Academic Press, 1986), 395f.

19. Schachtman, *The Inarticulate Society*, 67.

20. Healy, *Endangered Minds*, 26–36.

21. Ibid., 132.

22. John Holloway, *The Slumber of Apollo* (Cambridge: Cambridge University Press, 1983), 66.

23. Ibid., 65.

24. Healy, *Endangered Minds*, ch. 8.

25. Hudson, *Teenage Revolution*.

26. Owen Barfield, *Poetic Diction: A Study in Meaning* (New York: McGraw-Hill, 1964).

27. Tzvetan Todorov, *Mikhail Bakhtin: The Dialogical Principle*, trans. Wlad Godziek (Minneapolis: University of Minnesota Press, 1984), ch. 4.

28. Barfield, *Poetic Diction*; Owen Barfield, *Saving the Appearances* (New York: Harcourt, Brace & Jovanovich, 1957).

29. Henri Lefebvre, *Everyday Life in the Modern World*, trans. Sacha Rabinovitch (New Brunswick: Transaction, 1990), 110–27.

30. J. H. Van den Berg, *The Changing Nature of Man*, trans. H. T. Croes (New York: Norton, 1961).

31. Jacques Ellul, *Propaganda*, trans. Konrad Keller (New York: Knopf, 1965).

32. Paul Ricoeur, *Interpretation Theory: Discourse and the Surplus of Meaning* (Fort Worth: Texas Christian University Press, 1976), 19–22.

33. Barfield, *Poetic Diction*; Stephen Talbott, *The Future Does Not Compute* (Sebastopol: O'Reilly, 1995), ch. 23.

34. Stanley Gerr, "Language and Science," *Philosophy of Science* 9 (April 1942): 156.

35. Raymond Gozzi, *New Words and a Changing American Culture* (Columbia: University of South Carolina Press, 1990), 96–97.

36. Uwe Poerksen, *Plastic Words: The Tyranny of a Modular Language*, trans. Jutta Mason and David Cayley (University Park: Penn State Press, 1995), 4–5.

37. Ibid., 25–26.

38. Ibid., 45–47.

39. Ibid., ch. 3.

40. Ibid., 88

41. Ibid., 41.

42. Walter Nash, *Jargon* (Oxford: Blackwell, 1993), 5.

43. Kenneth Hudson, *The Jargon of the Professions* (London: Macmillan, 1978), ch. 5.

44. Nash, *Jargon*, Part II.

45. Ralph Hummel, *The Bureaucratic Experience* (New York: St. Martin's, 1982), 160.

46. *The Pantagraph*, 9 June 1998: C3.

47. Charles Weingartner, "Three Little Words," *Et cetera* 38 (Summer, 1981), 148.

48. Van den Berg, *Changing Nature of Man*, ch. 2.

49. Karen Horney, *The Neurotic Personality of Our Time* (New York: Norton, 1937).

50. Poerksen, *Plastic Words*, 44–45.

51. Daniel Boorstin, *Democracy and Its Discontents* (New York: Random House, 1974), 39–42.

52. Jacques Ellul, *A Critique of the New Commonplaces*, trans. by Helen Weaver (New York: Knopf, 1968), 3–27.

53. Ibid., 250–54.

54. Richard Stivers, *The Culture of Cynicism: American Morality in Decline* (Cambridge: Blackwell, 1994), 61–62.

55. Anton Zijderveld, *On Cliches* (London: Routledge and Kegan Paul, 1979), 15.

56. Ibid., 14, 65–70.

57. Ibid., 16.

58. The fundamental work on the subject is Jacques Ellul, *The Humiliation of the Word*, trans. Joyce Hanks (Grand Rapids: Eerdmans, 1985). See also Guy Debord, *The Society of the Spectacle* (Detroit: Black and Red, 1983).

59. E. H. Gombrich, "The Visual Image," *Scientific American* 227 (September 1972): 82–96.

60. Ellul, *The Humiliation of the Word*, ch. 1.

61. Gombrich, "The Visual Image."

62. Jerry Mander, *Four Arguments for the Elimination of Television* (New York: Quill, 1978), 252.

63. Cited in ibid., 255.

64. Edmund Carpenter, *Oh, What a Blow That Phantom Gave Me* (New York: Holt, Rinehart and Winston, 1973), 61–66.

65. Ellul, *The Humiliation of the Word*, 139–47.

66. Andrew Tutor, *Image and Influence* (New York: St. Martin's Press, 1975), 215.

67. Ellul, *The Humiliation of the Word*, 123–24.

68. Tzvetan Todorov, *Symbolism and Interpretation*, trans. by Catherine Porter (Ithaca: Cornell University Press, 1982), 9–23.

69. Barfield, *Saving the Appearances*, 119.

70. Paul Ricoeur, *Interpretation Theory* (Fort Worth: Texas Christian University Press, 1976), 57.

71. Barfield, *Saving the Appearances*.

72. Barfield, "The Nature of Meaning," *Seven* 2 (1981): 35.

73. Barfield, *Saving the Appearances*.

74. Ibid., 96–116.

75. Barfield, "The Nature of Meaning," p. 40.

76. Josephine Miles, "Values in Language; or, Where Have Goodness, Truth, and Beauty Gone?" *The State of the Language*, eds. Leonard Mi-

chaels and Christopher Ricks (Berkeley: University of California Press, 1980), 375.

77. Geoffrey Hughes, *Words in Time* (Oxford: Blackwell, 1988), 225–26.

78. Richard Stivers, *Evil in Modern Myth and Ritual* (Athens: University of Georgia Press, 1982), ch. 3.

79. Erich Auerbach, *Mimesis: The Representation of Literature in Western Civilization*, trans. Willard Trask (Princeton: Princeton University Press, 1953), 551–52).

80. John Aldridge, *The American Novel and the Way We Live Now*, (New York: Oxford University Press, 1983), chs. 10 and 11.

81. Jacques Ellul, *The Technological System*, trans. Joachim Neugroschel (New York: Continuum, 1980), 45–46.

82. Jacques Ellul, "Symbolic Function, Technology and Society," *Journal of Social and Biological Structures* 1 (1978): 207–18.

83. Gozzi, *New Words*, 86.

84. Ibid., 85.

85. Ibid., 86.

86. Ibid., 60.

87. Ellul, *The Humilation of the Word*, 148–54.

88. See Barfield, *Poetic Diction*; and Ricoeur, *Interpretation Theory*, on this point.

89. Ellul, *The Humiliation of the Word*, 31.

90. Barfield, *Saving the Appearances*, 53–57.

91. Barfield, *Poetic Diction*, 183–96.

92. Ellul, *The Humiliation of the Word*, 209.

93. Talbott, *The Future Does Not Compute*, 224.

Chapter 3. Statistical Information

1. Kenneth Hudson, *The Language of the Teenage Revolution* (London: Macmillan, 1978), 22.

2. Henri Bergson, *Time and Free Will*, trans. F. Pogson (London: George Allen and Unwin, 1910), 79–80.

3. Stanley Rosen, *The Ancients and the Moderns* (New Haven: Yale University Press, 1989), 137.

4. Georges Duby, *The Age of the Cathedrals*, trans. Eleanor Levieux and Barbara Thompson (Chicago: University of Chicago Press, 1981); see also Johan Huizinga, *The Waning of the Middle Ages* (Garden City: Doubleday Anchor, 1954), chs. 22 and 23.

5. Erich Auerbach, *Mimesis: The Representation of Reality in Western Literature*, trans. Willard Trask (Princeton: Princeton University Press, 1953), chs. 3, 7, 8.

6. Ibid., 202.

7. Duby, *The Age of the Cathedrals*, 117.

8. Alfred Crosby, *The Measure of Reality* (New York: Cambridge University Press, 1997), 17.

9. Ibid., ch. 1.

10. William Irvins, Jr., *On the Rationalization of Sight* (New York: Metropolitan Museum of Art, 1938; see also Crosby, *The Measure of Reality*, ch. 7.

11. Ibid., 228.

12. Daniel Boorstin, *The Americans: The Democratic Experience* (New York: Random House, 1973), 167.

13. David Landes, "Statistics as a Source for the History of Economic Development in Western Europe: the Protostatistical Era," *The Dimensions of the Past*, eds. Val Lorwin and Jacob Price (New Haven: Yale University Press, 1972), 53–54.

14. Ian Hacking, *The Taming of Chance* (New York: Cambridge University Press, 1990), 5.

15. Landes, "Statistics as a Source," 54.

16. Theodore Porter, *Trust in Numbers* (Princeton: Princeton University Press, 1995), 49–51.

17. James Beniger, *The Control Revolution* (Cambridge: Harvard University Press, 1986), 291–93.

18. Paul Starr, "The Sociology of Official Statistics," in *The Politics of Numbers*, eds. William Alonso and Paul Starr (New York: Russell Sage, 1987), 15.

19. Hacking, *The Taming of Chance*, 17.

20. Landes, "Statistics as a Source," 54.

21. Starr, "The Sociology of Official Statistics," 16.

22. Porter, *Trust in Numbers*, 35.

23. Landes, "Statistics as a Source," 61.

24. Starr, "The Sociology of Official Statistics," 18–20.

25. Ibid., 12.

26. Patricia Cohen, *A Calculating People* (Chicago: University of Chicago Press, 1982), 159–64.

27. Hacking, *The Taming of Chance*.

28. Ibid., 76.

29. Ibid., 29.

30. Beniger, *The Control Revolution*, 17.

31. Porter, *Trust in Numbers*, 91.

32. Ibid., 97.

33. Boorstin, *The Americans*, 200–205.

34. Beniger, *The Control Revolution*, 423.

35. Lorraine Daston, "The Domestication of Risk: Mathematical Prob-

ability and Insurance 1650–1830," in *The Probabilistic Revolution*, vol. 1: *Ideas in History*, ed., Lorenz Krüger, Lorraine Daston, and Michael Heidelberger (Cambridge: MIT Press, 1987), 244.

36. Ibid.

37. Ibid., 239–44.

38. Ibid., 248–55.

39. Hacking, *The Taming of Chance*, ch. 6.

40. Porter, *Trust in Numbers*, 39–40.

41. Hacking, *The Taming of Chance*, 52.

42. Porter, *Trust in Numbers*, 107–10.

43. Ibid., 102–6.

44. Boorstin, *The Americans*, 174.

45. Ibid., 186–87.

46. Daniel Boorstin, *Democracy and Its Discontents* (New York: Random House, 1974), 12–15.

47. Boorstin, *The Americans*, 148.

48. Ibid., 151–52.

49. Roland Marchand, *Advertising the American Dream* (Berkeley: University of California Press, 1985), 175.

50. Boorstin, *The Americans*, 154–55.

51. David Shenk, *Data Smog* (New York: Harper Edge, 1997), 114.

52. Arnold Mitchell, *The Nine American Life-Styles* (New York: Macmillan, 1983).

53. Dan Nimmo, *The Political Persuaders* (Englewood Cliffs: Prentice-Hall, 1970).

54. Alexis de Tocqueville, *Democracy in America*, trans. J. P. Mayer (Garden City: Anchor Books, 1969), 435.

55. F. Allan Hanson, *Testing Testing* (Berkeley: University of California Press, 1993).

56. Ibid., 191–93.

57. Ibid., 194.

58. Ibid., 231–34.

59. Boorstin, *The Americans*, 224–25.

60. Stephen Jay Gould, *The Mismeasure of Man* (New York: Norton, 1981), 148–58.

61. Hanson, *Testing, Testing*, 5.

62. Richard Stivers, *The Culture of Cynicism* (Cambridge: Blackwell, 1994), 37–38.

63. Lorraine Daston, "Rational Individuals versus Laws of Society: From Probability to Statistics," in *The Probabilistic Revolution*, vol. 1, 296.

64. Hacking, *The Taming of Chance*, 96.

65. Ibid., 107.

66. Ibid., 108.

67. Ian Hacking, "Statistical Language, Statistical Truth and Statistical Reason: the Self-Authentification of a Style of Scientific Reasoning" in *The Social Dimensions of Science*, ed. Ernan McMullin (Notre Dame: Notre Dame University Press, 1992), 148–49.

68. Hacking, *The Taming of Chance*, 127–32.

69. Richard Stivers, *Evil in Modern Myth and Ritual* (Athens: University of Georgia Press, 1982), 82–85.

70. Paul Ricoeur, "Creativity in Language" *Philosophy Today* 17 (Summer 1973): 97–111.

71. Hacking, *The Taming of Chance*, 182.

72. Ibid., 186.

73. Ibid., 187.

74. Ibid., 188.

75. C. Wright Mills, *The Sociological Imagination* (New York: Oxford University Press, 1959), ch. 3.

76. Hacking, *The Taming of Chance*, 188.

77. Carl Becker, *The Heavenly City of the 18th Century Philosophers* (New Haven: Yale University Press, 1932).

78. Ian Hacking, "Normal People," in *Modes of Thought*, ed. David Olson and Nancy Torrance (New York: Cambridge University Press, 1996), 62.

79. Ibid., 65–66.

80. Hacking, *The Taming of Chance*, 164–66.

81. Ibid., 165–69.

82. Ibid., 168.

83. Ibid., 144.

84. Ibid., 168–69.

85. Émile Durkheim, *Professional Ethics and Civic Morals*, trans. C. Brookfield (London: Routledge and Kegan Paul, 1957).

86. Hacking, *The Taming of Chance*, 178.

87. William Arney and Bernard Bergen, *Medicine and the Management of Living* (Chicago: University of Chicago Press, 1984), ch. 7.

88. Ibid., 9–10.

89. Hacking, "Normal People," 59–61.

90. Boorstin, *Democracy and Its Discontents*.

91. Max Weber, *Economy and Society*, vol. 2 (Berkeley: University of California Press, 1978), ch. 11.

92. Tocqueville, *Democracy in America*.

93. Søren Kierkegaard, *The Present Age*, trans. Alexander Dru (New Harper and Row, 1962), 47–67; see also Stivers, *The Culture of Cynicism*, 111–12.

94. J. H. Van den Berg, *Divided Existence and Complex Society* (Pittsburgh: Duquesne University Press, 1974).

95. Starr, "The Sociology Official Statistics," 45.

96. Porter, *Trust in Numbers*, 37.

97. Ian Hacking, "The Looping Effects of Human Kinds," in *Causal Cognition*, eds. Dan Sperber, David Premack, and Ann Premack (Oxford: Clarendon Press, 1995), 351–83.

98. Ian Hacking, "The Making and Molding of Child Abuse", *Critical Inquiry* 17 (Winter 1991): 264–74.

99. Gould, *The Mismeasure of Man*, 24.

100. John Frow, "The Last Things Before the Last: Notes on *White Noise*," *The South Atlantic Quarterly* 89 (Spring 1990): 414–29.

101. Don Delillo, *White Noise* (New York: Penguin Books, 1984), 38–39.

102. Mark Seltzer, *Bodies and Machines* (New York: Rutledge, 1992), 105–6.

103. Hacking, *Taming of Chance*, 133.

104. Auerbach, *Mimesis*, 473–81.

105. Delillo, *White Noise*, 141.

106. Ibid., 84.

107. Boorstin, *The Americans*, pts. 2 and 3.

108. Søren Kierkegaard, *Either/Or*, trans. by Howard Hong and Edna Hong (Princeton: Princeton University Press, 1987).

109. Nicholas Eberstadt, *The Tyranny of Numbers* (Washington, D.C.: AEI Press, 1995).

110. Cynthia Crossen, *Tainted Truth* (New York: Simon and Schuster, 1994).

111. Jacques Ellul, *The Technological System*, trans. Joachim Neugroschel (New York: Continuum, 1980), 117–21.

112. Nathan Keyfitz, "The Social and Political Context of Population Forecasting," in *The Politics of Numbers*, 235.

Chapter 4. The Mass Media as Magic

1. Daniel Boorstin, *The Americans: The Democratic Experience* (New York: Random House, 1973), 142–43.

2. William Leiss, Stephen Kline, and Sut Jhally, *Social Communication in Advertising* (New York: Metheun, 1986), 74–75.

3. Ibid., 76.

4. Frank Presbrey, *The History and Development of Advertising* (New York: Greenwood Press, 1968), 455–56.

5. Ibid., 479–81.

6. Ibid., 482.

7. Christopher Wilson, "The Rhetoric of Consumption," in *The Culture of Consumption*, eds. Richard Fox and T. J. Jackson Lears (New York: Pantheon, 1983), 49–53.

8. Leiss et al., *Social Communication*, 83–84.

9. Ibid., 113.

10. Ibid., 89.

11. Pat Aufderheide, "Music Videos: the Look of the Sound," *Journal of Communication* 36 (1986): 57–78.

12. Leiss et al., *Social Communication*, 93.

13. Ibid., 98.

14. Michael Schudson, *Advertising, the Uneasy Persuasion* (New York: Basic Books, 1984), 171.

15. Leiss et al., *Social Communication*, 101.

16. Ibid., 180.

17. Roland Marchand, *Advertising the American Dream* (Berkeley: University of California Press, 1985), 234.

18. John Stauber and Sheldon Rampton, *Toxic Sludge is Good for You* (Monroe: Common Courage Press, 1995), 13.

19. Cited in ibid., 18.

20. Ibid., 19.

21. Ibid., 22–23.

22. Ibid., 1.

23. Leslie Savan, *The Sponsored Life* (Philadelphia: Temple University Press, 1994), 1.

24. Irving Rein, Philip Kotler, and Martin Stoller, *High Visibility* (New York: Dodd, Mead, 1987), 278.

25. Stauber and Rampton, *Toxic Sludge*, 2, 13, 183.

26. Ibid., 3.

27. Stan Sauerhaft and Chris Atkins, *Image Wars* (New York: Wiley, 1989), 14.

28. Stauber and Rampton, *Toxic Sludge*, 3.

29. Ibid.

30. Daniel Boorstin, *The Image* (New York: Harper and Row, 1961), 185.

31. Leiss et al., *Social Communication*, 189–90.

32. Ibid., 231–32.

33. Ibid., 190–215.

34. Chuck Pettis, *Technobrands* (New York: American Management Association, 1995), xi.

35. Clive Chajet and Tom Shachtman, *Image by Design* (Reading: Addison- Wesley, 1991), 100–101.

36. Rein et al., *High Visibility*, 34.

37. Ibid., 68–69.

38. Ibid., 194–95.

39. Tom Shachtman, *The Inarticulate Society* (New York: The Free Press, 1995), 119–34; see also Jacques Ellul, *The Political Illusion*, trans. Konrad Kellen (New York: Vintage, 1967), ch. 3.

40. Kiku Adatto, *Picture Perfect* (New York: Basic Books, 1993), 172–73.

41. Boorstin, *The Americans*, 137.

42. Daniel Boorstin, "The Rhetoric of Democracy," in *Democracy and Its Discontents* (New York: Random House, 1974), 26–42.

43. Will Herberg, *Protestant Catholic Jew* (Chicago: University of Chicago Press, 1983), ch. 5.

44. Jacques Ellul, *Propaganda*, trans. Konrad Kellen and Jean Lerner (New York: Knopf, 1965), 95–102.

45. Boorstin, *Democracy and Its Discontents*, 20.

46. Ibid., 19.

47. Neil Postman, "The News" in *Conscientious Objections* (New York: Knopf, 1988), 72–81; see also Mark Crispin Miller, *Boxed In: The Culture of TV* (Evanston: Northwestern University Press, 1988), 3–27.

48. Ellul, *Propaganda*, 205–6.

49. Henry Jacoby, *The Bureaucratization of the World*, trans. Eveline Kanes (Berkeley: University of California Press, 1976), ch. 6.

50. Jacques Ellul, *The Technological System*, trans. Joachim Neugroschel (New York: Continuum, 1980), 37.

51. Ellul, *The Political Illusion*, 49–67.

52. Guy Debord, *Society of the Spectacle* (Detroit: Black and Red, 1977).

53. Ibid., paragraph 65.

54. Ibid., paragraph 60.

55. Max Horkheimer and Theodor Adorno, "The Culture Industry as Mass Deception," in *Dialectic of Enlightenment*, trans. John Cumming (New York: Herder and Herder, 1972), 154–56.

56. Ibid., 145.

57. Debord, *Society of the Spectacle*, paragraph 57.

58. George Trow, *Within the Context of No Context* (New York: Atlantic Monthly Press, 1997), 48.

59. J. H. Van den Berg, *The Changing Nature of Man*, trans. H. F. Croes (New York: Norton, 1961), ch. 3.

60. J. H. Van den Berg, *A Different Existence* (Pittsburgh: Duquesne University Press, 1972).

61. Trow, *Within the Context*, 54–57.

62. Ibid, 43–49, 72–74.

63. Søren Kierkegaard, *The Present Age*, trans. Alexander Dru (New York: Harper and Row, 1962), 64.

64. Ibid, 47.

65. Ibid., 52.

66. Ellul, *Propaganda*, 62–70.

67. Willem Vanderburg, *The Growth of Minds and Cultures* (Toronto: University of Toronto Press, 1985).

68. See Richard Stivers, *The Culture of Cynicism: American Morality in Decline* (Cambridge: Blackwell, 1994), chs. 2 and 3 for a fuller discussion of technological utopianism.

69. Leiss et al., *Social Communication*, 233.

70. Ibid., 246.

71. Gunnar Andren et al., *Rhetoric and Ideology in Advertising* (Stockholm: Liber Foilag, 1978), 137, 151.

72. Ibid., 140.

73. Jonathan Price, *The Best Thing on TV* (New York: Viking, 1978), 44, 53.

74. Marchand, *Advertising the American Dream*, 363.

75. Andren et al., *Rhetoric and Ideology*, 137.

76. Stuart Ewen, *Captains of Consciousness* (New York: McGraw-Hill, 1976), 143.

77. Andren et al., *Rhetoric and Ideology*, 121.

78. Ewen, *Captains of Consciousness*, 47.

79. Leiss et al., *Social Communication*, 210–15.

80. Andren et al., *Rhetoric and Ideology*, 139.

81. Leiss et al., *Social Communication*, 221–22.

82. Jerry Mander, *Four Arguments for the Elimination of Television* (New York: Quill, 1978), 323–28.

83. Ewen, *Captains of Consciousness*, 191, 213.

84. Neil Postman, "The Parable of the Ring Around the Collar," in *Conscientious Objections*, 66–71.

85. Barbara Wootton, *Social Science and Social Pathology* (London: Allen and Unwin, 1959), 218.

86. Robert Cialdini et al., "Basking in Reflected Glory," *Journal of Personality and Social Psychology* 34 (1976): 366–75.

87. Wilbert Leonard II, *A Sociological Perspective of Sport* (New York: Macmillan, 1988), 67.

88. Gary Gumpert, "The Telltale Tape, or the Video Replay and Sportsmanship," in *Talking Tombstones* (New York: Oxford University Press, 1987), 54–75.

89. Allen Guttmann, *From Ritual to Record* (New York: Columbia University Press, 1978).

90. Tom Engelhardt, "The Shortcake Strategy," in *Watching Television*, ed. Todd Gitlin (New York: Pantheon, 1986), 104.

91. Ellen Seiter, *Sold Separately* (New Brunswick: Rutgers University Press, 1993), chs. 5 and 6.

92. Engelhardt, "The Shortcake Strategy," 74.

93. Elias Canetti, *Crowds and Power*, trans. Carol Stewart (New York: Seabury, 1978), 227.

94. Ruth Rosen, "Search for Yesterday," in *Watching Television*, 62.

95. Mary Cassata, Thomas Skill, and Samuel Boadu, "Life and Death in the Daytime Television Serial: A Content Analysis," in *Life on Daytime Television*, ed. Mary Cassata and Thomas Skill (Norwood: Ablex, 1983), 52.

96. Todd Gitlin, "We Build Excitement," in *Watching Television*, 136–61.

97. Aufderheide, "Music Videos: the Look of the Sound," 69–71.

98. Stivers, *The Culture of Cynicism*.

99. Debord, *Society of the Spectacle*, paragraph 65.

100. See especially Miller, *Boxed In*, 3–27.

101. Gabriel Vahanian, *The Death of God* (New York: George Braziller, 1961).

Chapter 5. Therapy, Self-Help, and Positive Thinking as Magic

1. See among others Robyn Dawes, *House of Cards* (New York: Free Press, 1994), ch. 8; and Wendy Kaminer, *I'm Dysfunctional, You're Dysfunctional* (Reading: Addison-Wesley, 1992).

2. Edward Shorter, *A History of Psychiatry* (New York: John Wiley, 1997), 293–95.

3. Marin Gross, *The Psychological Society* (New York: Simon and Schuster, 1978), 6.

4. Shorter, *A History of Psychiatry*, 1, 17–18.

5. Ibid., 23–26.

6. Ibid., 26–29.

7. Ibid., 29–32.

8. J. H. van den Berg, *Divided Existence and Complex Society* (Pittsburgh: Duquesne University Press, 1974).

9. Thomas Szasz, *The Myth of Psychotherapy* (Garden City: Doubleday, 1978), 102–3.

10. Joel Kovel, *A Complete Guide to Therapy* (New York: Pantheon, 1976), 66–70.

11. Ibid., 63.

12. Shorter, *A History of Psychiatry*, ch. 5.

13. Kovel, *A Complete Guide to Therapy*, 199–200.

14. J. H. van den Berg, *A Different Existence* (Pittsburgh: Duquesne University Press, 1972), 125–39.

15. Kovel, *A Complete Guide to Therapy*, 108–98.

16. Dawes, *House of Cards*, 12.

17. Shorter, *A History of Psychiatry*, 293.

18. Ibid., 325–27.

19. Dawes, *House of Cards*, 11.

20. Donald Meyer, *The Positive Thinkers* (New York: Pantheon Books, 1980), ch. 1.

21. Kenneth Lynn, *The Dream of Success* (Boston: Little, Brown, 1955), 3.

22. Richard Huber, *The American Idea of Success* (New York: McGraw-Hill, 1971), 95.

23. Ibid., 97.

24. See Irvin Wyllie, *The Self-Made Man in America* (New Brunswick: Rutgers University Press, 1954); John Cawelti, *Apostles of the Self-Made Man* (Chicago: University of Chicago Press, 1965).

25. Huber, *The American Idea of Success*, 124–85.

26. Ibid., 155–56.

27. Quoted in Meyer, *The Positive Thinkers*, 165.

28. Ibid., ch. 2.

29. Louis Schneider and Sanford Dornbusch, *Popular Religion* (Chicago: University of Chicago Press, 1958), 112.

30. Cawelti, *Apostles of the Self-Made Man*, 209–18.

31. Richard Weiss, *The American Myth of Success* (New York: Basic Books, 1969), 15.

32. Cawelti, *Apostles of the Self-Made Man*, 202.

33. Meyer, *The Positive Thinkers*, 184–86.

34. Schneider and Dornbusch, *Popular Religion*, 115–16.

35. Meyer, *The Positve Thinkers*, 262.

36. Quoted in Kaminer, *I'm Dysfunctional, You're Dysfunctional*, 46– 47.

37. Quoted in Meyer, *The Positive Thinkers*, 263.

38. Ibid., 267–68.

39. Lawrence Chenoweth, *The American Dream of Success* (North Scituate, Mass.: Duxbury Press, 1974).

40. Dale Tarnowieski, *The Changing Success Ethic* (New York: American Management Associations, 1972), 43.

41. Cawelti, *Apostles of the Self-Made Man*, 217–18.

42. Schneider and Dornbusch, *Popular Religion*, 123–24.

43. Barbara Wootton, *Social Science and Social Pathology* (London: George Allen & Urnwin, 1959), 214–18.

44. William Graebner, *The Engineering of Consent* (Madison: University of Wisconsin Press, 1987), ch. 1.

45. Ibid., 10.

46. Andrew Malcolm, *The Tyranny of the Group* (Ottowa: Littlefield, Adams, 1975).

47. Kaminer, *I'm Dysfunctional, You're Dysfunctional*, 11.

48. Ibid., 9.

49. Richard Stivers, *The Culture of Cynicism* (Cambridge: Blackwell, 1994), 99.

50. Kaminer, *I'm Dysfunctional, You're Dysfunctional*, 28. See also, Ian Hacking, "The Making and Molding of Child Abuse," *Critical Inquiry* 17 (Winter 1991): 253–88.

51. Cathryn Taylor, *The Inner Child Workbook* (New York: Putnam, 1991), 1.

52. Ibid., 17.

53. Ibid., 65–69.

54. Dawes, *House of Cards*, 9–10, 33–34, ch. 8.

55. Paul Vitz, *Psychology as Religion* (Grand Rapids: Eerdmans, 1994), 19.

56. There is a vast literature on the subject. Among the best books, which include a discussion of the relevant research, are Dawes, *House of Cards*, 50–54; Jerome Frank, *Persuasion and Healing* (New York: Schocken Books, 1974), chs. VI and VII; Gross, *The Psychological Society*, ch. II; E. Fuller Torrey, *Witchdoctors and Psychiatrists* (New York: Harper and Row, 1986), ch. 12.

57. Dawes, *House of Cards*, 52.

58. Ibid., ch. 3.

59. Hans Strupp and Suzanne Hadley, "Specific vs. Nonspecific Factors in Psychotherapy," *Archives of General Psychiatry* 36 (September 1979): 1125–36.

60. Dawes, *House of Cards*, 205–6.

61. Torrey, *Witchdoctors and Psychiatrists*, 207.

62. Strupp and Hadley, "Specific vs. Nonspecific Factors in Psychotherapy," 1135.

63. Lester Luborsky, Barton Singer, and Lise Luborsky, "Comparative Studies of Psychotherapy," *Archives of General Psychiatry* 32 (August 1975): 1003.

64. Torrey, *Witchdoctors and Psychiatrists*, 199.

65. Gross, *The Psychological Society*, 25.

66. Frank, *Persuasion and Healing*, 152–56.

67. Dawes, *House of Cards*, 227–28.

68. Ibid., ch. 8.

69. Vitz, *Psychology as Religion*, 15–19.

70. Torrey, *Witchdoctors and Psychiatrists*, 204.

71. See Frank, *Persuasion and Healing*; Torrey, *Witchdoctors and Psychiatrists*; Gross, *The Psychological Society*; Dawes, *House of Cards*. The authors have summarized the results of the multitude of studies on why therapy works.

72. Frank, *Persuasion and Healing*, 325–26.

73. Gross, *The Psychological Society*, 48.

74. Frank, *Persuasion and Healing*, 326–27.

75. Gross, *The Psychological Society*, 36.

76. Frank, *Persuasion and Healing*, 327–28.

77. Ibid., 328–29.

78. Ibid., 329–30.

79. Frank, *Persuasion and Healing*; Ari Kiev (ed.), *Magic, Faith, and Healing* (New York: The Free Press, 1964); Torrey, *Witchdoctors and Psychiatrists*; and Shashi Pande, "The Mystique of 'Western' Psychotherapy: An Eastern Interpretation," *Journal of Nervous and Mental Disease* 146 (June, 1968): 425–32.

80. Claude Lévi-Strauss, "The Sorcerer and His Magic, "in *Structural Anthropology*, trans. Claire Jacobson and Brooke Schoepf (Garden City: Anchor Books, 1967), 174.

81. Victor Turner, "An Ndembu Doctor in Practice," in Kiev, *Magic, Faith, and Healing*, 230–63.

82. Frank, *Persuasion and Healing*, 66.

83. Ibid., 328.

84. Ibid., 324.

85. L. J. Davis, "The Encyclopedia of Insanity," *Harper's* 294 (February 1997): 64.

86. Ibid., 65.

87. Phillip Long, *Internet Mental Health* (http://www.mental health.com) (1995–97), chs. 5, 21.

88. Ibid., 64.

89. Ibid, 61.

90. R. D. Rosen, *Psychobabble* (New York: Atheneum, 1977), 3–14.

91. Frederic Raphael, "The Language of Television" in *The State of the Language*, eds. Leonard Michaels and Christopher Ricks (Berkeley: University of California Press, 1980), 309.

92. Mimi White, *Teleadvising* (Chapel Hill: University of North Carolina Press, 1992), 66–67.

93. Jay Martin, *Who Am I This Time?* (New York: Norton, 1988), 219–20; John Caughey, *Imaginary Social Worlds* (Lincoln: University of Nebraska Press, 1984), ch. 2.

94. White, *Teleadvising*, ch. 2.

95. Dawes, *House of Cards*, 292–93.

96. J. H. van den Berg, *The Changing Nature of Man*, trans. H. F. Croes (New York: Norton, 1961).

97. Søren Kierkegaard, *The Present Age*, trans. Alexander Dru (New York: Harper and Row, 1962).

98. Karen Horney, *The Neurotic Personality of Our Time*, (New York: Norton, 1937), 89.

99. J. H. van den Berg, *A Different Existence*, ch. 3.

100. Steffen Linder, *The Harried Leisure Class* (New York: Columbia University Press, 1970).

101. Jacques Ellul, *The Technological Society*, trans. John Wilkinson (New York: Knopf, 1964), 387–427.

102. Jacques Ellul, *The Technological System*, trans. Joachim Neugroschel (New York: Continuum, 1980), 111–17.

Chapter 6. Management as Magic

1. Cited in Henry Jacoby, *The Bureaucratization of the World*, trans. Eveline Kanes (Berkeley: University of California Press, 1973), 9.

2. Bertrand de Jouvenel, *On Power*, trans. J. F. Huntington (Boston: Beacon Press, 1962).

3. Karl Polanyi, *The Great Transformation* (Boston: Beacon Press, 1957), ch. 6.

4. Joseph Schumpeter, *Capitalism, Socialism, and Democracy* (New York: Harper and Row, 1950), ch. 12.

5. James Worthy, *Big Business and Free Men* (New York: Harper and Brothers, 1959), 65.

6. Ibid., 67.

7. Charles Perrow, *Complex Organizations* (New York: Random House, 1986), 57.

8. Worthy, *Big Business and Free Men*, 70–71.

9. Ibid., 68–69.

10. James Beniger, *The Control Revolution* (Cambridge: Harvard University Press, 1986), 297.

11. Worthy, *Big Business and Free Men*, 68–69.

12. Ibid., 71–73.

13. Perrow, *Complex Organizations*, 57.

14. Henry Mintzberg, *The Structuring of Organizations* (Englewood Cliffs: Prentice-Hall, 1979), 9.

15. Perrow, *Complex Organizations*, 52.

16. Beniger, *The Control Revolution*, 314.

17. William Graebner, *The Engineering of Consent* (Madison: University of Wisconsin Press, 1987), 73–74.

18. Perrow, *Complex Organizations*, 97.

19. Ibid., 85–96.

20. Ibid., 97–114.

21. Ibid., 62–76.

22. H. Thomas Johnson and Robert Kaplan, *Relevance Lost* (Boston: Harvard Business School Press, 1987), 49–51.

23. Ibid., 12.

24. Peter Miller and Ted O'Leary, "Accounting and the Construction of the Governable Person," *Accounting, Organizations and Society* 12 (1987): 243–54.

25. Richard Weiss, *The American Myth of Success* (New York: Basic Books, 1969), 184–85.

26. Richard Huber, *The American Idea of Success* (New York: McGraw-Hill, 1971), 219.

27. Theodore Greene, *America's Heroes* (New York: Oxford University Press, 1970), 319.

28. Ibid., ch. 8; C. Wright Mills, *White Collar* (New York: Oxford University Press, 1951), ch. 12.

29. Quoted in Weiss, *The American Myth of Success*, 9.

30. Miller and O'Leary, "Accounting and the Construction of the Governable Person," 256–59.

31. Mintzberg, *The Structuring of Organizations*, 3–9.

32. John Micklethwait and Adrian Wooldridge, *The Witchdoctors* (New York: Random House, 1996), 15–17.

33. Henry Mintzberg, *Mintzberg on Management* (New York: The Free Press, 1989).

34. Ida Hoos, *Systems Analysis in Public Policy* (Berkeley: University of California Press, 1983), 43–47.

35. Ibid., xviii.

36. Ibid., 47.

37. William Gibson, *The Perfect War* (Boston: Atlantic Monthly Press, 1986), 15–16.

38. Ibid., 112–13ff.

39. Ibid., 125.

40. Edward Shirley, "Can't Anybody Here Play This Game?" *The Atlantic Monthly* 281 (February 1998): 45–60.

41. Micklethwait and Woodridge, *The Witchdoctors*, ch. 3.

42. Ibid, 287, 71–72.

43. George Steiner, *Strategic Planning* (New York: The Free Press, 1979), 32.

44. Ibid., 13–15.

45. Henry Mintzberg, *The Rise and Fall of Strategic Planning* (New York: The Free Press, 1994), 54.

46. The preceding discussion of the stages of strategic planning was taken from Mintzberg, *The Rise and Fall of Strategic Planning*, 52–65.

47. Ibid., 221–25.

48. Ibid., 259–66.

49. Micklethwait and Wooldridge, *The Witchdoctors*, 146–48.

50. Ibid., ch. 1.

51. Ibid., 27.

52. Ibid., 37.

53. Shoshana Zuboff, *In the Age of the Smart Machine* (New York: Basic Books, 1988), 180f.

54. Ibid., 387–414.

55. Ibid., 346.

56. Ibid., ch. 7.

57. Barbara Garson, *The Electronic Sweatshop* (New York: Simon and Schuster, 1988).

58. Micklethwait and Woodridge, *The Witch Doctors*, 16.

59. Margaret Wheatley, *Leadership and the New Science* (San Francisco: Berrett-Koehler, 1992).

60. Stephen Covey, *Seven Habits of Highly Effective People* (New York: Simon and Schuster, 1989), 47.

61. Guillermo Grenier, *Inhuman Relations* (Philadelphia: Temple University Press, 1988), 4.

62. Ibid., ch. 1.

63. Ibid., 64-69.

64. Ibid., 131.

65. Ibid., p. 135.

66. Zuboff, *In the Age of the Smart Machine*.

67. David Gordon, *Fat and Mean* (New York: The Free Press, 1996), 35.

68. Ibid., 51-60.

69. Philip Howard, *The Death of Common Sense* (New York: Random House, 1994), 174.

70. Ibid., 175-77.

71. Thomas Davenport, *Process Innovation* (Boston: Harvard Business School Press, 1993), 285-96.

72. Hoos, *Systems Analysis in Public Policy*, 194.

73. Lester Thurow, *Head to Head* (New York: William Morrow, 1992), 172.

74. P. H. Grinyer and D. Norburn, "Planning for Existing Markets: Perceptions of Executives and Financial Performance" *Journal of the Royal Statistical Society* 138A, 1 (1975), 70-97.

75. Mintzberg, *Rise and Fall of Strategic Planning*.

76. Mintzberg, *Mintzberg on Management*.

77. Martha Feldman and James March, "Information in Organizations as Signal and Symbol," *Administrative Science Quarterly* 26 (1981): 174.

78. Mintzberg, *Mintzberg on Management*, 72-77.

79. Charles O'Reilly, III, "Variations in Decision Makers Use of Information Sources," *Academy of Management Journal* 25 (1982), 756-71.

80. Mintzberg, *Mintzberg on Management*, chs. 2-5.

81. James March and Guje Sevon, "Gossip, Information and Decision-Making," in *Decisions and Organizations*, ed. James March (Oxford: Blackwell, 1988), 433-34.

82. James March, "Ambiguity and Accounting" in *Decisions and Organizations*, 384-407.

83. Robert Jackall, *Moral Mazes* (New York: Oxford University Press, 1988), 72-73.

84. Jacques Ellul, *The Technological Bluff*, trans. Geoffrey Bromiley (Grand Rapids: Eerdmans, 1990), ch. 2.

85. George Soros, "The Capitalist Threat," *The Atlantic Monthly* 279 (February, 1997), 45-58.

86. Lester Thurow, *The Future of Capitalism* (New York: Penguin, 1996), ch. 1.

87. Jackall, *Moral Mazes*.

88. Mintzberg, *Mintzberg on Management*.

89. The more uncertain and unpredictable reality becomes, the more we face it with the closed system of rational management. This should not be surprising because we look to technology or its facsimile to solve all problems.

90. Uwe Poerksen, *Plastic Words*, trans. Jutta Mason and David Cayley (University Park: Penn State Press, 1995), 25–26.

91. Ibid., 76–78.

92. Micklethwait and Wooldridge, *The Witchdoctors*, 306–7.

93. Ibid., 142.

94. Ike Balbus, "Politics as Sports: the Political Ascendency of Sports Metaphor in America," in *Sport Sociology*, ed. Andrew Yiannakis et al. (Dubuque: Kendal/Hunt, 1976), 77.

95. Jeremy Rifkin, *The Biotech Century* (New York: Putnam, 1998), 202–7.

96. Leo Lowenthal, "The Triumph of Mass Idols" in *Literature and Mass Culture* (New Brunswick: Transaction Books, 1984), 203–35.

97. Feldman and March, "Information in Organizations as Signal and Symbol," 181.

98. Ibid., 184.

99. Jackall, *Moral Mazes*, 202; Mintzberg, *Mintzberg on Management*, ch. 17.

Chapter 7. The Triumph of the Irrational

1. Jacques Ellul, *The Technological Bluff*, trans. Geoffrey Bromiley (Grand Rapids: Eerdmans, 1990), 218–20.

2. Arnold Gehlen, *Man in the Age of Technology*, trans. Patricia Lipscomb (New York: Columbia University Press, 1980), 81.

3. Jacques Ellul, *The Technological Society*, trans. John Wilkinson (New York: Vintage, 1964).

4. Gehlen, *Man in the Age of Technology*, 78–80.

5. Herbert Hendin, *The Age of Sensation* (New York: Norton, 1975).

6. Ellul, *The Technological Society*, ch. 5.

7. Ibid., 420–26.

8. Marshall McLuhan, *Understanding Media* (New York: McGraw-Hill, 1964), 42–45.

9. Jacques Ellul, *The Ethics of Freedom*, trans. Geoffrey Bromiley (Grand Rapids: Eerdmans, 1976).

10. Miguel de Unamuno, *The Tragic Sense of Life in Men and Nations*, trans. J. E. Flitch (New York: Dover, 1954).

11. John McKnight, "John Deere and The Bereavement Counselor," in *The Careless Society* (New York: Basic Books, 1995), 3–15.

12. Jacques Ellul, *Hope in Time of Abandonment*, trans. C. Edward Hopkin (New York: Seabury, 1973).

13. Ibid., 70.

14. Jacques Ellul, *The Betrayal of the West*, trans. Matthew O'Connell (New York: Seabury, 1978), ch. 1.

15. Ellul, *Hope in Time of Abandonment*, 9–15.

16. Ann Douglas, *The Feminization of American Culture* (Garden City: Anchor Books, 1977), 12–13.

17. Johan Huizinga, *In the Shadow of Tomorrow* (New York: Norton, 1936), 170–82.

18. Cited in Gehlen, *Man in the Age of Technology*, 87.

19. Ellul, *The Betrayal of the West*, 148–69.

20. Richard Stivers, "The Deconstruction of the University," *The Centennial Review* 35 (Winter, 1991), 115–36.

21. Ellul, *The Ethics of Freedom*; Tzvetan Todorov, *Facing the Extreme: Moral Life in Concentration Camps* (New York: Metropolitan Books, 1996).

22. Jacques Ellul, *The Humiliation of the Word*, trans. Joyce Hanks (Grand Rapids: Eerdmans, 1985).

23. Andrew Kimbrell, *The Human Body Shop* (New York: Harper San Francisco, 1993); see also Jeremy Rifkin, *The Biotech Century* (New York: Putnam, 1998).

24. Alexis de Tocqueville, *Democracy in America*, trans. George Lawrence (Garden City: Anchor Books, 1969), vol. 2, part 4, ch. 6.

25. Jacques Ellul, *Autopsy of Revolution*, trans. Patricia Wolf (New York: Knopf, 1971), ch. 5.

Index